The All-Time
All-Star
Baseball Book

The All-Time All-Star Baseball Book

by
Donald Dewey
Nick Acocella

The Elysian Fields Press

Brown & Benchmark
A Division of Wm. C. Brown Communications, Inc.

Library of Congress Cataloging in Publication Data:

DEWEY, DONALD 1940

THE ALL-TIME ALL-STAR BASEBALL BOOK

Library of Congress Catalog Card Number: 91-73707
ISBN: 0-697-14594-8

Printed in the United States of America by The Elysian Fields Press, 2460 Kerper Boulevard, Dubuque, IA 52001.

10 9 8 7 6 5 4 3 2 1

Mission Statement of The Elysian Fields Press Imprint

The purpose and philosophy of The Elysian Fields Press is grounded in an appreciation of baseball as a central mythology of American culture. We wish to explore in print, via periodicals and books of essay, history, fiction, biography, poetry and anthology, the unifying romance of baseball as it connects us with our larger heritage and the natural cycles of generation.

Dedication

For Adam, Anthony, and Thea

Contents

Introduction

Baseball fans thrive on statistics, conjecture, and argument. A fan who doesn't know about Walt Dropo's 12 consecutive hits or Joe Adcock's 18 total bases is someone who goes to the refreshment stand for a hot dog when the home team has loaded the bases in the bottom of the ninth. A fan who doesn't wonder about what might have happened if the Red Sox had held on to Babe Ruth has no imagination. One who has no opinion about Roger Maris's home run record or Pete Rose's Cooperstown credentials is better off playing computer games. Baseball is numbers, fantasy, and creed, and the baseball fan is somebody who spends each season, Hot Stove League, and spring training trying to marshal these elements into an explanation for what actually occurs on the field. The uninformed call it a pastime; the true fan knows there is little leisure involved.

The All-Time All-Star Baseball Book is a compendium of statistics, conjecture, and argument. Its format—the lineup—is not only baseball's most basic organizational unit but also the scheme most commonly adopted by millions of fans when they muse about the best and the worst, the greatest and the most grating, the most overrated, underrated, and overrated underrated. Included, of course, are lineups that point up the achievements of the Cobbs and the Robinsons, but also included are those that point out the uniqueness of the Bloodworths and Southworths. On the following pages, the O'Briens become teammates of the Mizes, the Furillos of the McGraws, the Sparky Andersons of the Gair Allies—and all for usually overlooked reasons.

In general, there are three kinds of lineups in The All-Time All-Star Baseball Book. The first group consists of teams put together on the basis of cold numbers. Many players might have seemed great at this or that, but what exactly do the statistical facts say? Included in this group are such lineups as the best hitters in the history of the game (none of whom are in the Hall of Fame), the worst hitters of all time (none of whom ever got a hit), and one of the strangest collections of all, players who held down starting berths for one season, but otherwise never wore a big league uniform.

A second group of lineups concerns the identical, the coincidental, and the bizarre: pitchers who arrived on the scene to pitch no-hitters and then disappeared; catchers carried on rosters just to instigate fights; a team of players exchanged by the Mets to obtain third basemen. Yes, indeed. Not to mention other lineups centered around major league games played in Dayton, Ohio, and on Staten Island, New York; teams that existed for only one year; and players who managed to outshine their more famous brothers, however briefly. They're all here.

Last, but hardly least, are the lineups of the purest prejudice—those in which the authors reveal themselves as the fools that they are. Our only defense for the selections in this group is that of age: We never asked Cap Anson for his autograph, never saw Chuck Klein hit the ball into the bleachers. But it is also most of all in these lineups that *The All-Time All-Star Baseball Book* has its primary purpose—to start an argument.

Note: For the sake of clarity, we have referred throughout the book to existing National League (NL) franchises by their present nicknames, such as the Cubs, even if the teams in question had been known by other monikers in the past. Extinct NL teams, such as Washington, are referred to by their cities. We identified teams belonging to third major leagues—the Players League for instance—by city and league. Also note that all statistics, and the opinions based on them, run only through the 1990 season.

1 Most Influential

Because boardroom and courtroom wrangles have been as crucial to the history of baseball as on-the-field heroics, a line-up of the game's most influential players is necessarily a mixed bag. For every player who has made his impact with a bat or a glove, another left his mark with the assistance of an agent or an attorney. Some of those earning recognition were innovative or daring in their skills, others were caught up in situations over which they had little control. But whether it was because of what they did or what was done to them, all the members of the Most Influential Team hung up their spikes on a sport that was significantly different from the one they had known as rookies. In one way or another, then, every other lineup in this book stems from a starting nine of:

    1B—Charlie Waitt
    2B—Jackie Robinson
    3B—Joe Dugan
    SS—Dickey Pearce
    OF—Babe Ruth
    OF—Roy Thomas
    OF—Curt Flood
     C—King Kelly
     P—Al Spalding

Waitt wore the first glove in 1875 and thereby steered baseball toward most of the defensive elements with which we associate it today. Take away Waitt's glove, in fact, and you would have to take away everything from a Walter Johnson and Nolan Ryan to a mean batting average of .250.

Robinson, of course, had the task of unraveling the 60 years of racism that had blanketed the sport from the 1880s until his arrival in Montreal in 1946 and in Brooklyn the following year. His adventurous psychological tactics against the pitcher, brought along from the Negro leagues, also added a new element to baseball offense.

Dugan's trade to the Yankees in August 1922 enabled the New Yorkers to edge the St. Louis Browns for the American League (AL) pennant. When the Browns objected to such a late-season deal (and the Cardinals filed a similar protest over another swap involving the Giants and Braves), Commissioner Kenesaw Landis imposed the June 15 trading deadline that remained officially in effect until the 1980s. Admittedly, owners skirted the restriction on numerous occasions through gentlemen's agreements on waiver purchases, but considering the number of pennants decided by only a handful of games during the six decades when the rules were in effect, the consequences of the formal deadline were enormous.

Pearce, who only played 33 games for the St. Louis franchise in the National League's debut years of 1876 and 1877, had already influenced the game forever by being the first to move in from an originally mapped fourth outfield position to the infield spot between the second and third basemen. He is also credited with being the first player to bunt a ball.

Ruth's home runs so impressed major league owners with their ability to draw crowds that the lively ball was introduced in 1921 in the interests of increasing numbers in both team home run columns and at the turnstiles. Ruth has also been without peer as a symbol of the game.

It was Thomas's penchant for standing up at the plate and fouling off balls to his heart's content that prompted the National League in 1901 to introduce the regulation that the first two fouls be regarded as strikes. (The American League followed suit two years later.) Pitching strategy would never be the same again, nor would hitting .400 prove as easy.

Flood refused to accept his 1970 trade from the Cardinals to the Phillies and took the reserve clause to court. Although he himself lost, Flood's challenge turned out to be the opening salvo in the war that ultimately brought about the end of management's practically career-long control over a player and brought on free agency.

Kelly's claims to importance are several: For one thing, he was the foremost exponent of the hook slide during his playing days for the Chicago and Boston franchises in the 1880s. For another, he was the first catcher to use finger signals with pitchers. Finally, his antics as a "tenth man" off the bench (such as leaping up and announcing his presence in the lineup so he could catch a foul ball coming his way) led to precise rules about when and under what circumstances substitutes could take the field.

It is hard to imagine the business or mythology of baseball without Spalding. Aside from his association with the company that made sports goods a thriving industry, he was one of the founders of the National League, the official most responsible for the breaking of the rebellious Players League in 1890, and the sport's most active propagandist both nationally and internationally in the 19th century. Moreover, it was a commission that Spalding put together in 1905 that gave official-looking sanction to the myth that baseball was the absolute creation of Americans, and particularly of Abner Doubleday. On the field, he was also credited with being the first pitcher to use a changeup.

Numerous other players merit special mention for the Most Influential Team. Filling out the roster are

Infielders. While manager of the Chicago White Stockings, Cap Anson refused to play an exhibition game against a minor league team that included black players, prompting the ban that excluded blacks until the arrival of Jackie Robinson. On a more positive note, Brooks Robinson's exploits afield in the 1960s and 1970s for Baltimore focused attention on defense generally and, most specifically, on the need to station something more than a boulder at third base. Luis Aparicio and Maury Wills should also be acknowledged for inspiring a new emphasis on running and on stealing bases as an offensive weapon.

Outfielders. Ned Hanlon, as player-manager for Pittsburgh in the 1800s, introduced the strategy of using righties against lefties and lefties against righties, mainly because of his own difficulties as a left-handed hitter against southpaws. Tommy

McCarthy's habit in the 1890s of tapping fly balls between his bare and gloved hands while running toward the infield prompted the rule that says runners can advance as soon as a fly ball touches a fielder, not only when a clean catch or error is made. Dummy Hoy, a deaf mute in the 19th century, forced umpires to give hand signals as well as verbal calls for their decisions. It was also Hoy who, for reasons of self-defense, began the practice of holding out his arm to signal to teammates that the catch was going to be his.

Catchers. Moses Walker, a black who played with the American Association's Toledo, Ohio, franchise in 1884, was Jackie Robinson's unsuccessful forerunner; it was his defensive skills that embarrassed white players and made it easier for segregationist policies to be adopted. Fred Thayer, the author of "Casey at the Bat," also invented the first catcher's mask in 1875. A number of catchers have been linked with the development of the other tools of ignorance, but Red Dooin's case merits special mention. In apparent dread of being criticized for less than manly behavior, Dooin wore shinguards and a chest protector under his uniform for two years; he admitted to them only after Roger Bresnahan had begun wearing them openly.

Pitchers. Although definitive evidence will never be forthcoming, it has become generally accepted that Candy Cummings threw the first curve in competition in the early 1870s after several years of experiments. Charlie Sweeney is cited as having thrown the first screwball in 1880; Tricky Nichols the first sinker in 1875; and George Blaeholder the first slider many years later in the 1920s. The origins of the spitter are probably argued about more than those of the curve. One of the more popular stories is that Frank Corridon taught it to Elmer Stricklett while both were with a Newark, New Jersey, team at the turn of the century and that Stricklett taught it in turn to Ed Walsh, who popularized it with the 1904 White Sox.

Three pitchers who exerted a considerable influence on the game while away from the diamond were Andy Messersmith,

Dave McNally, and George Zoeterman. Messersmith and McNally were the first successful challengers to the reserve clause and paved the way to free agency in 1975 when they secured their freedom from the Los Angeles Dodgers and Montreal Expos, respectively. Although Zoeterman never appeared in a major league game, it was his drafting from a Chicago high school in 1947 by the White Sox that prompted more stringent regulations with regard to plucking undergraduates out of the classroom. (It is not widely remembered today, but the White Sox were actually thrown out of the American League for two weeks in the fall of 1947 when they refused to pay a fine over the Zoeterman affair. There is an argument to be made that Commissioner Happy Chandler's decisiveness in the case was a conclusive reason why team owners elected much less resolute figures to the commissioner's chair in subsequent years.)

The rest of baseball's most influential franchise would include:

Manager. Harry Wright, who introduced what is now referred to as "professionalism" into the sport. Before 1860, baseball had been theoretically amateur—meaning that players were often paid under the table. In 1869, Wright, then manager and center fielder for the Cincinnati Red Stockings, ended the hypocrisy by openly paying team members.

Owner. Arthur Soden, who introduced the reserve clause in 1879; it proved to be the chief bone of contention between players and management throughout the history of baseball.

General Manager. Branch Rickey, who introduced the concept of a farm system, forced the racial integration of the game with the signing of Jackie Robinson, and pioneered the use of batting helmets after seeing them used in the Negro leagues.

Business Manager. Luke Sewell, who as manager of the Reds in the late 1940s, came up with the idea of having groundskeepers drag the infield after the fifth inning so fans could go to the refreshment stands and contribute more to Cincinnati's coffers.

Groundskeeper. An anonymous gentleman who, in 1893, misunderstood an instruction to increase the distance from the pitcher's mound to home plate from 50 feet to "six-six" feet. He placed the rubber 60 feet and six inches away from all future batters.

Others:

Umpire. Alexander Cartwright, who drew up the first written regulations of the game. Among other things, he is responsible for establishing nine players a side and 90 feet between the bases. Tradition has it that the first game held under these rules took place at the Elysian Fields in Hoboken, New Jersey, on June 19, 1846, when the New York Nine beat Cartwright's Knickerbockers, 23–1. Cartwright umpired and fined one of the players for swearing.

Official. Harry Chadwick, who codified the rules of the national pastime and was its first official scorer.

Entrepreneur. William Cammcyer, who built the first enclosed stadium on Brooklyn's Union Grounds in 1862 and had a big role in the construction of other parks.

Inventor. George Cahill, who demonstrated the efficacy of a light tower that would make night baseball possible as early as 1909. Although another 30 years came to pass before Larry MacPhail aggressively promoted the first night game, it is worth noting that the Cincinnati Reds had the benefit of Cahill's demonstration and the same Reds hosted the first night contest.

Finally, let us not forget Oliver Wendell Holmes's Supreme Court Nine. In 1922, Holmes and his eight teammates decided unanimously for major league owners in a suit brought six years earlier by the Baltimore Terrapins of the disbanded Federal League. In its attempt to recover damages from the settlement reached between other Federal League owners and the National and American leagues, the Terrapins claimed that baseball was in violation of antitrust laws and that the reserve clause in particular abrogated constitutional guarantees. Holmes wrote the decision holding that professional baseball was a sport in which no commodity was produced, no "chattel slavery" was involved; therefore, antitrust provisions were not applicable.

2 National League Franchises

This chapter presents an all-time all-star team for every 20th-century franchise in the senior circuit. We include separate teams for the Boston, Milwaukee, and Atlanta versions of the Braves; for the Brooklyn and Los Angeles Dodgers; and for the New York and San Francisco Giants. The crucial factor here is what players did for particular teams, not what they did over their careers.

——BOSTON BRAVES——

Want to know about the Boston Braves? Try this: Of the 20 most important offensive records established by Boston–Milwaukee–Atlanta players, only 7 are held by players who starred in Massachusetts, and 4 of those 7 were the result of Tommy Holmes's 1945 season. When you consider that the Boston club existed for 53 years and the Milwaukee team (holder of most individual records) for only 13, it's easy to understand why the Red Sox were always Boston's first team.

    1B—Fred Tenney
    2B—Bill Sweeney
    3B—Bob Elliott
    SS—Rabbit Maranville
    OF—Tommy Holmes
    OF—Wally Berger
    OF—Hugh Duffy
     C—King Kelly
     P—Kid Nichols

Honorable mentions to Vic Willis, Warren Spahn, Johnny Sain, Tommy McCarthy, and Tommy Tucker. Manager: George Stallings.

——MILWAUKEE BRAVES——

With the exception of Rico Carty, this is the team that won pennants in 1957 and 1958 and lost a season-ending playoff to Los Angeles in 1959.

    1B—Joe Adcock
    2B—Red Schoendienst
    3B—Eddie Mathews
    SS—Johnny Logan
    OF—Hank Aaron
    OF—Wes Covington
    OF—Rico Carty
     C—Del Crandall
     P—Warren Spahn

Honorable mention to Lew Burdette. Manager: Fred Haney.

—— ATLANTA BRAVES ——

As evidenced by the necessary selection of Rafael Ramirez, the Georgia version of the Braves has been as infamous for its shortstops as the Mets once were for their third basemen.

    1B—Orlando Cepeda
    2B—Felix Millan
    3B—Bob Horner
    SS—Rafael Ramirez
    OF—Hank Aaron
    OF—Rico Carty
    OF—Dale Murphy
     C—Joe Torre
     P—Phil Niekro

Honorable mentions to Felipe Alou and Glenn Hubbard. Manager: Joe Torre.

—— BROOKLYN DODGERS ——

The boys of summer never really had a left fielder and had only Don Newcombe as a repeat 20-game winner. Otherwise, an Ebbets Field hall of fame would come from those teams that played in six World Series between 1947 and 1956.

    1B—Gil Hodges
    2B—Jackie Robinson
    3B—Billy Cox
    SS—Pee Wee Reese
    OF—Zack Wheat
    OF—Duke Snider
    OF—Carl Furillo
     C—Roy Campanella
     P—Dazzy Vance

Honorable mentions to Burleigh Grimes, Pete Reiser, Dixie Walker, Babe Herman, and Dolf Camilli. Manager: Charlie Dressen.

—— LOS ANGELES DODGERS ——

If there has been a constant in the California history of the Dodgers, it has been the erratic defense that has made its pitching more vulnerable than it should have been.

    1B—Steve Garvey
    2B—Davey Lopes
    3B—Ron Cey
    SS—Maury Wills
    OF—Tommy Davis
    OF—Dusty Baker
    OF—Pedro Guerrero
     C—John Roseboro
     P—Sandy Koufax

Honorable mentions to Don Drysdale, Don Sutton, Frank Howard, Steve Sax, and Mike Scioscia. Manager: Walter Alston.

—— CHICAGO CUBS ——

At .336 for 14 seasons, outfielder Stephenson holds the second highest career average for any player not in the Hall of Fame. (The highest is held by Shoeless Joe Jackson, who was excluded because of the Black Sox scandal.)

1B—Cap Anson
2B—Ryne Sandberg
3B—Stan Hack
SS—Ernie Banks
OF—Riggs Stephenson
OF—Hack Wilson
OF—Kiki Cuyler
C—King Kelly
P—Mordecai Brown

Honorable mentions to Gabby Hartnett, Billy Herman, Billy Williams, Ferguson Jenkins, and Ron Santo. Manager: Frank Chance.

—— CINCINNATI REDS ——

The greatest pitcher the Reds ever had was one they were in a hurry to get rid of at the turn of the century—Christy Mathewson. Otherwise, even the team's most successful pitchers were very much within striking distance of .500 careers. Now as for the hitting,

1B—Tony Perez
2B—Joe Morgan
3B—Pete Rose
SS—Dave Concepcion
OF—Frank Robinson
OF—Edd Roush
OF—George Foster
C—Johnny Bench
P—Eppa Rixey

Honorable mention to Ernie Lombardi. Manager: Sparky Anderson.

—— NEW YORK GIANTS ——

This is the only franchise that can boast a Hall of Famer at every position.

    1B—Bill Terry
    2B—Frankie Frisch
    3B—Freddy Lindstrom
    SS—Travis Jackson
    OF—Mel Ott
    OF—Willie Mays
    OF—Ross Youngs
      C—Roger Bresnahan
      P—Christy Mathewson

Among the Cooperstown residents not making the team are Tim Keefe, Mickey Welch, Monte Ward, Buck Ewing, Roger Connor, George Kelly, Amos Rusie, Carl Hubbell, Monte Irvin, Rube Marquard, and Dave Bancroft. Manager: John McGraw.

—— SAN FRANCISCO GIANTS ——

The West Coast Giants have always had slugging outfielders and rarely had catchers who lasted more than a couple of seasons.

    1B—Orlando Cepeda
    2B—Robby Thompson
    3B—Jim Davenport
    SS—Chris Speier
    OF—Willie McCovey
    OF—Willie Mays
    OF—Bobby Bonds
      C—Tom Haller
      P—Juan Marichal

Honorable mentions to Gaylord Perry, Will Clark, and Kevin Mitchell. Manager: Roger Craig.

—— PHILADELPHIA PHILLIES ——

Given the owners they had in the 1920s and 1930s, when Philadelphia players were considered only as good as the checks they could attract from other teams to buy them, it's a wonder the Phillies are still around at all.

    1B—Fred Luderus
    2B—Bill Hallman
    3B—Mike Schmidt
    SS—Larry Bowa
    OF—Chuck Klein
    OF—Richie Ashburn
    OF—Cy Williams
     C—Andy Seminick
     P—Grover Alexander

Honorable mentions to Nap Lajoie, Sam Thompson, Elmer Flick, and Robin Roberts. Manager: Danny Ozark.

—— PITTSBURGH PIRATES ——

The Pirates have had chronic weaknesses on the mound and behind the plate. The most reasonable alternatives to the following battery, for example, would be a pitcher (Bob Friend or Vernon Law) who won 20 games only once and a catcher (Smokey Burgess) more noted for pinch hitting than back-stopping.

    1B—Willie Stargell
    2B—Bill Mazeroski
    3B—Pie Traynor
    SS—Honus Wagner
    OF—Ralph Kiner
    OF—Paul Waner
    OF—Roberto Clemente
     C—Manny Sanguillen
     P—Ray Kremer

Honorable mentions to Max Carey, Fred Clarke, Lloyd Waner, Dick Groat, and Dave Parker. Manager: Danny Murtaugh.

—— ST. LOUIS CARDINALS ——

This team includes six Hall of Famers, seven Most Valuable Player titles, and 15 batting championships.

```
1B—Johnny Mize
2B—Rogers Hornsby
3B—Ken Boyer
SS—Ozzie Smith
OF—Stan Musial
OF—Joe Medwick
OF—Lou Brock
 C—Walker Cooper
 P—Bob Gibson
```

Honorable mentions to Frankie Frisch, Enos Slaughter, Dizzy Dean, Mort Cooper, Chick Hafey, Marty Marion, Terry Moore, Ted Simmons, Bill White, Orlando Cepeda, Joe Torre, and Keith Hernandez. Manager: Billy Southworth.

—— HOUSTON ASTROS ——

Yes, Mike Scott and Nolan Ryan were great, but no pitcher in an Astros uniform came so close to dominating the game for a few years as did our selection.

```
1B—Bob Watson
2B—Joe Morgan
3B—Doug Rader
SS—Roger Metzger
OF—Cesar Cedeno
OF—Jim Wynn
OF—Jose Cruz
 C—Alan Ashby
 P—J. R. Richard
```

Honorable mentions to Scott, Ryan, Larry Dierker, Terry Puhl, and Glenn Davis. Manager: Bill Virdon.

—— NEW YORK METS ——

While attention has remained focused on the Mets' legacy of strong pitching, some pretty good hitters have sneaked into the lineup over the last decade.

```
1B—Keith Hernandez
2B—Felix Millan
3B—Howard Johnson
SS—Bud Harrelson
OF—Cleon Jones
OF—Darryl Strawberry
OF—Rusty Staub
 C—Jerry Grote
 P—Tom Seaver
```

Honorable mentions to Ron Hunt, Jerry Koosman, Tommie Agee, Tug McGraw, Lee Mazzilli, Dwight Gooden, and Ron Darling. Manager: Davey Johnson.

—— MONTREAL EXPOS ——

The Expos seem to have to build their pitching staffs from scratch every season, making the franchise's mound efforts still synonymous with Steve Rogers.

```
1B—Andres Galarraga
2B—Ron Hunt
3B—Tim Wallach
SS—Tim Foli
OF—Andre Dawson
OF—Tim Raines
OF—Rusty Staub
 C—Gary Carter
 P—Steve Rogers
```

Honorable mentions to Bob Bailey, Ellis Valentine, and Jeff Reardon. Manager: Buck Rodgers.

—— SAN DIEGO PADRES ——

Wait another year before changing the catcher. Some of the others get named for showing up two seasons in a row.

        1B—Nate Colbert
        2B—Roberto Alomar
        3B—Graig Nettles
        SS—Ozzie Smith
        OF—Cito Gaston
        OF—Dave Winfield
        OF—Tony Gwynn
         C—Terry Kennedy
         P—Randy Jones

Honorable mentions to Rollie Fingers, Eric Show, Garry Templeton, Steve Garvey, and Benito Santiago. Manager: Dick Williams.

—— ODDS AND ODDS ——

A lineup of National League franchise trivia:

1B—Jim Bottomley (1922 Cardinals)
2B—Lou Bierbauer (1891 Pirates)
3B—Eddie Mathews (Career)
SS—Eddie Bressoud (1962 Astros)
OF—Gino Cimoli (1958 Dodgers)
OF—Ollie Brown (1969 Padres)
OF—Derrel Thomas (Career)
 C—Hobie Landrith (1962 Mets)
 P—Tim Keefe (1885 Giants)

Bottomley was the first regular developed through the innovative farm system of Branch Rickey. Because of its allegedly underhanded behavior in signing Bierbauer, Pittsburgh's franchise became known as the Pirates. Mathews was the only Brave to play for the Boston, Milwaukee, and Atlanta versions of the team. Bressoud was the first player drafted by the Houston expansion club. On April 18, 1958, at Seals Stadium in San Francisco, Cimoli became California's first major league batter. Brown was the first draft choice of the Padres. Thomas was the first to play for all three California teams in the National League. Landrith was the expansion Mets' first draft choice (although the first player signed to a New York contract was infielder Ted Lepcio). When the Giants bought Keefe and Dude Esterbrook from the American Association Mets, it was the last straw for association owners convinced that the Giants were using their neighbors as a farm team; the Mets were immediately drummed out of the American Association.

3 American League Franchises

Next, we present an all-time all-star team for every franchise in the junior circuit. Separate teams for the Philadelphia, Kansas City, and Oakland versions of the Athletics; for both the Washington teams and their successors in Minnesota and Texas; for the Seattle Pilots and the modern Milwaukee Brewers; for the St. Louis Browns and the modern Baltimore Orioles. Also included are the best of two long-forgotten AL entries, the 1901 Milwaukee Brewers and the 1901–02 Baltimore Orioles.

—— BOSTON RED SOX ——

The Red Sox have traditionally had problems with pitching. Even their most famous pitcher had won a mere 88 games before being sold off to the Yankees where he had to make his living with a home run here and there. On the other hand, the hitting has almost always been good—and often spectacular.

    1B—Jimmie Foxx
    2B—Bobby Doerr
    3B—Wade Boggs
    SS—Joe Cronin
    OF—Ted Williams
    OF—Tris Speaker
    OF—Carl Yastrzemski
     C—Carlton Fisk
     P—Roger Clemens

Honorable mentions to Jimmy Collins, Vern Stephens, Harry Hooper, Jim Rice, Joe Wood, and Mel Parnell. Manager: Bill Carrigan.

—— BALTIMORE ORIOLES I ——

The first American League version of the Orioles was a charter member of the junior circuit. After one mediocre season and one poor one, the franchise was moved to New York, where it eventually became the Yankees.

1B—Dan McGann
2B—Jimmy Williams
3B—John McGraw
SS—Bill Keister
OF—Mike Donlin
OF—Cy Seymour
OF—Kip Selbach
 C—Wilbert Robinson
 P—Joe McGinnity

McGraw was the player-manager.

—— NEW YORK YANKEES ——

The most astonishing thing about this team is that two of its members are not in the Hall of Fame.

1B—Lou Gehrig
2B—Tony Lazzeri
3B—Graig Nettles
SS—Phil Rizzuto
OF—Babe Ruth
OF—Joe DiMaggio
OF—Mickey Mantle
 C—Bill Dickey
 P—Whitey Ford

Honorable mentions to Bobby Richardson, Red Rolfe, Bob Meusel, Earle Combs, Reggie Jackson, Yogi Berra, Red Ruffing, Herb Pennock, Lefty Gomez, and Ron Guidry. Manager: Casey Stengel.

—— PHILADELPHIA ATHLETICS ——

The old Athletics (1901–54) certainly had their ups and downs. Although no team finished last as often, the Athletics also won more AL pennants than anyone but the Yankees.

1B—Jimmie Foxx
2B—Eddie Collins
3B—Frank Baker
SS—Joe Boley
OF—Al Simmons
OF—Mule Haas
OF—Bing Miller
 C—Mickey Cochrane
 P—Lefty Grove

Honorable mentions to Rube Waddell, Eddie Plank, Chief Bender, and George Earnshaw. Manager: Connie Mack.

—— KANSAS CITY ATHLETICS ——

The Kansas City version of the Athletics (1955–67) seems to have existed only as a resting place on the franchise's journey from one coast to the other. They finished sixth in their first year and, despite expansion, never climbed that high again.

1B—Vic Power
2B—Jerry Lumpe
3B—Ed Charles
SS—Dick Howser
OF—Gus Zernial
OF—Norm Siebern
OF—Bob Cerv
 C—Hal Smith
 P—Bud Daley

Manager: Lou Boudreau.

—— OAKLAND ATHLETICS ——

This squad is a combination of the Oakland dynasties of the mid-1970s and the late 1980s.

1B—Mark McGwire
2B—Dick Green
3B—Sal Bando
SS—Bert Campaneris
OF—Rickey Henderson
OF—Jose Canseco
OF—Reggie Jackson
 C—Gene Tenace
 P—Catfish Hunter

Honorable mentions to Joe Rudi, Dennis Eckersley, and Dave Stewart. Manager: Tony LaRussa.

—— CHICAGO WHITE SOX ——

In true White Sox fashion, this lineup would have to scratch for every run. Note that Fisk is the all-time White Sox home run leader—and that he hit more with the Red Sox.

1B—Dick Allen
2B—Eddie Collins
3B—Buck Weaver
SS—Luke Appling
OF—Joe Jackson
OF—Minnie Minoso
OF—Harold Baines
 C—Carlton Fisk
 P—Ted Lyons

Honorable mentions to Ed Walsh, Ray Schalk, Hap Felsch, Nellie Fox, and Luis Aparicio. Manager: Al Lopez.

—— CLEVELAND INDIANS ——

The Indians have been dedicated to playing below .500 for so long that it is difficult to remember that they were once the Yankees' chief rivals. In fact, the most recent player in this line-up is Doby, who retired in 1959.

1B—Hal Trosky
2B—Nap Lajoie
3B—Al Rosen
SS—Lou Boudreau
OF—Larry Doby
OF—Tris Speaker
OF—Charlie Jamieson
C—Steve O'Neill
P—Bob Feller

Honorable mentions to Stan Coveleski, Jim Bagby, Sr., Ken Keltner, Bob Lemon, Early Wynn, Jim Hegan, and Rocky Colavito. Manager: Al Lopez.

—— DETROIT TIGERS ——

The strength of this team is revealed by the fact that the only non-Hall of Famers are Trammell, who is still active, and Newhouser, who turned in an 80–27 record over three years.

1B—Hank Greenberg
2B—Charlie Gehringer
3B—George Kell
SS—Alan Trammell
OF—Ty Cobb
OF—Harry Heilmann
OF—Al Kaline
C—Mickey Cochrane
P—Hal Newhouser

Honorable mentions to Sam Crawford, George Mullin, Tommy Bridges, Harvey Kuenn, Lance Parrish, and Jack Morris. Manager: Hughie Jennings.

—— MILWAUKEE BREWERS I ——

Milwaukee's first AL team lasted only one year, 1901, and then moved to St. Louis. One hopes that the players on this team had nicknames since five of the starting nine were named Bill or Billy.

1B—John Anderson
2B—Billy Gilbert
3B—Bill Friel
SS—Wid Conroy
OF—Bill Hallman
OF—Irv Waldron
OF—Hugh Duffy
 C—Billy Maloney
 P—Bill Reidy

Manager: Hugh Duffy.

—— ST. LOUIS BROWNS ——

If you remember more than two or three of the players on this team (1901–53), you should run to the nearest quiz show. But not if you forgot that Eddie Gaedel should be the pinch-hitter.

1B—George Sisler
2B—Marty McManus
3B—Harlond Clift
SS—Bobby Wallace
OF—Ken Williams
OF—Baby Doll Jacobson
OF—Jack Tobin
 C—Hank Severeid
 P—Urban Shocker

Honorable mentions to Jack Kramer and Vern Stephens. Manager: Luke Sewell.

—— BALTIMORE ORIOLES II ——

Within a decade the doormat Browns became the contender Orioles; then they evolved into the late 1960s and early 1970s powerhouse making up the nucleus of this selection.

        1B—Eddie Murray
        2B—Davey Johnson
        3B—Brooks Robinson
        SS—Cal Ripken
        OF—Frank Robinson
        OF—Paul Blair
        OF—Ken Singleton
         C—Gus Triandos
         P—Jim Palmer

Honorable mentions to Rick Dempsey, Mark Belanger, Mike Cuellar, and Dave McNally. Manager: Earl Weaver.

—— WASHINGTON SENATORS I ——

These original Senators (1901–60) made Washington famous for being first in war, first in peace, and last in the American League. Still, the composite batting average for this team is .295—not bad for a legendary loser.

        1B—Mickey Vernon
        2B—Bucky Harris
        3B—Eddie Yost
        SS—Joe Cronin
        OF—Heinie Manush
        OF—Goose Goslin
        OF—Sam Rice
         C—Muddy Ruel
         P—Walter Johnson

Honorable mentions to Joe Judge and Ossie Bluege. Manager: Bucky Harris.

—— MINNESOTA TWINS ——

For some reason, the Twins have never had a dearth of good hitters. The problem, however, is that until recently these hitters were disposed of as soon as they asked for raises.

    1B—Kent Hrbek
    2B—Rod Carew
    3B—Gary Gaetti
    SS—Zoilo Versalles
    OF—Harmon Killebrew
    OF—Tony Oliva
    OF—Kirby Puckett
     C—Earl Battey
     P—Jim Kaat

Honorable mentions to Jim Perry and Bob Allison. Manager: Sam Mele.

—— CALIFORNIA ANGELS ——

Gene Autry's money bought an expansion franchise in 1961 and lots of expensive free agents after that. Nonetheless, the history of the Angels' pitching is still divided into three periods—before Nolan Ryan, Nolan Ryan, and after Nolan Ryan.

    1B—Rod Carew
    2B—Bobby Grich
    3B—Doug DeCinces
    SS—Jim Fregosi
    OF—Don Baylor
    OF—Reggie Jackson
    OF—Al Downing
     C—Bob Boone
     P—Nolan Ryan

Honorable mention to Leon Wagner and Alex Johnson. Manager: Jim Fregosi.

—— WASHINGTON SENATORS II ——

These expansion Senators existed during the Vietnam War between 1961 and 1971; they made Washington last in war, last in peace, and last in the American League.

    1B—Mike Epstein
    2B—Bernie Allen
    3B—Ken McMullen
    SS—Eddie Brinkman
    OF—Frank Howard
    OF—Del Unser
    OF—Chuck Hinton
     C—Paul Casanova
     P—Dick Bosman

Manager: Ted Williams.

—— TEXAS RANGERS ——

When Bob Short moved the Senators to Arlington, he created a quandry. There must be, deep in the heart of Texas, a reason why this team has never produced the winners it should have; that reason certainly hasn't been a lack of talent.

    1B—Mike Hargrove
    2B—Julio Franco
    3B—Buddy Bell
    SS—Toby Harrah
    OF—Al Oliver
    OF—Jeff Burroughs
    OF—Ruben Sierra
     C—Jim Sundberg
     P—Ferguson Jenkins

Honorable mentions to Bump Wills and Larry Parrish. Manager: Billy Martin.

—— SEATTLE PILOTS ——

There are only two possible reasons for the one-year (1969) existence of the Pilots: Either it was to give pitcher Jim Bouton the chance to recount the Pilots' woes in *Ball Four*, or it was to get Diego Segui into the trivia books for playing on both the Pilots and the Mariners.

    1B—Don Mincher
    2B—John Donaldson
    3B—Tommy Harper
    SS—Ray Oyler
    OF—Wayne Comer
    OF—Tommy Davis
    OF—Steve Hovley
     C—Jerry McNertney
     P—Diego Segui

Manager: Joe Schultz.

—— MILWAUKEE BREWERS II ——

If most of this lineup is familiar, it means that you recall the 1982 World Series.

    1B—Cecil Cooper
    2B—Jim Gantner
    3B—Paul Molitor
    SS—Robin Yount
    OF—Ben Oglivie
    OF—Gorman Thomas
    OF—Larry Hisle
     C—B. J. Surhoff
     P—Teddy Higuera

Honorable mentions to George Scott, Ted Simmons, Rollie Fingers, and Don Money. Manager: Harvey Kuenn.

—— KANSAS CITY ROYALS ——

Aside from the pitcher, all these players were part of the teams that regularly lost the American League Championship Series to the Yankees in the late 1970s.

    1B—John Mayberry
    2B—Frank White
    3B—George Brett
    SS—Freddie Patek
    OF—Hal McRae
    OF—Amos Otis
    OF—Willie Wilson
     C—Darrell Porter
     P—Dan Quisenberry

Honorable mentions to Dennis Leonard and Bret Saberhagen. Manager: Whitey Herzog.

—— SEATTLE MARINERS ——

This is definitely a team of the future—if for no other reason than that it has no past. Since it entered the AL as an expansion franchise in 1977, Seattle has yet to compile a .500 record for any single season.

    1B—Alvin Davis
    2B—Harold Reynolds
    3B—Jim Presley
    SS—Craig Reynolds
    OF—Phil Bradley
    OF—Tom Paciorek
    OF—Ken Griffey, Jr.
     C—Dave Valle
     P—Mark Langston

Honorable mentions to Floyd Bannister and Richie Zisk. Manager: Jim Lefebvre.

—— TORONTO BLUE JAYS ——

After five years of expansion blues, the Blue Jays became respectable in the mid-1980s. Even so, they have developed a reputation for losing the important games despite exceptional talent.

1B—Fred McGriff
2B—Damaso Garcia
3B—Kelly Gruber
SS—Tony Fernandez
OF—George Bell
OF—Lloyd Moseby
OF—Jesse Barfield
 C—Ernie Whitt
 P—Dave Stieb

Honorable mentions to Rico Carty, Bob Bailor, and Tom Henke. Manager: Bobby Cox.

—— ODDS AND ODDS ——

Some American League franchise trivia:

    1B—Don Mincher (Career)
    2B—Chico Garcia (1954 Orioles)
    3B—John McGraw (1900 Cardinals)
    SS—Bob Bailor (1977 Blue Jays)
    OF—Elmer Valo (Career)
    OF—Lou Sockalexis (Career)
    OF—Ruppert Jones (1977 Mariners)
    C—Phil Roof (Career)
    P—Al Fitzmorris (Career)

Mincher spent his entire career with expansion or transferred franchises: the two Washingtons, their successors in Minnesota and Texas, the Angels, Oakland Athletics, and Pilots. Garcia was the first minor leaguer drafted by the St. Louis Browns for its shifted Baltimore operation. It was McGraw's derisive reference to the Athletics as "those white elephants" that ultimately led Philadelphia to adopt the animal as its symbol. Bailor was the first player selected by the expansion Toronto club. Valo moved with three franchises—with the Athletics from Philadelphia to Kansas City, with the Dodgers from Brooklyn to Los Angeles, and with the Senators from Washington to Minnesota. Sockalexis, the first Native American in the majors, was the inspiration for renaming the Cleveland franchise the Indians. Jones was the first player drafted by the Mariners. Roof was on the first-year squads of the Oakland Athletics, Milwaukee Brewers, and Toronto Blue Jays. Fitzmorris was selected twice in expansion drafts—by the Royals in 1969 and Blue Jays in 1977. (Bobby Shantz is the only other player chosen in two expansion drafts—by the Astros and Senators.)

4   Decades

This chapter focuses on all-star teams for every 10 years from the 1880s to the 1990s with no distinction between leagues.

—— THE 1880s ——

The 1880s were a decade of turbulence in professional baseball: The National League matured. The American Association was born. The Union Association was born and died in the same year. And, great players abounded.

    1B—Cap Anson
    2B—Hardy Richardson
    3B—Ezra Sutton
    SS—Monte Ward
    OF—Tip O'Neill
    OF—Pete Browning
    OF— King Kelly
     C—Buck Ewing
     P—Tim Keefe

Dan Brouthers, one of the greatest hitters of all time, can't make this team because of Anson. And a galaxy of pitchers with extraordinary credentials—John Clarkson, Pud Galvin, Charlie Radbourn, and Mickey Welch—come out as also-rans. Five Hall of Famers—Anson, Ward, Kelly, Ewing, and Keefe—form the nucleus of this stellar combination. Add Sutton and Richardson, both .300 hitters; O'Neill, who had perhaps baseball's greatest season in 1887, and Browning, probably the best hitter of the decade, and this remote era compares favorably with any other. The manager is Anson, whose Cubs won five pennants.

—— THE 1890s ——

With the failure of the Players' League in 1890 after only one year and the demise of the American Association a year later, the National League expanded to 12 teams for the remainder of the decade. Baltimore baseball—stealing bases, playing hit and run, and scrapping—became the standard of play from 1894 on. The Orioles won three pennants and placed four players on this team. But the Cleveland Spiders put two players on the team of the decade and won no pennants, while Boston won five pennants with only a single entry here.

    1B—Cap Anson
    2B—Cupid Childs
    3B—John McGraw
    SS—Hughie Jennings
    OF—Jesse Burkett
    OF—Ed Delahanty
    OF—Willie Keeler
      C—Wilbert Robinson
      P—Kid Nichols

The four Orioles are McGraw, Jennings, Keeler, and Robinson. The two Spiders: Childs and Burkett. Boston has many runners-up: Billy Hamilton, the stolen base champion; Bobby Lowe, who hit four home runs in one game; and Hugh Duffy, whose .438 in 1894 was the highest NL batting average ever. And, it has Nichols, who won 30 or more games in seven seasons. Honorable mention also to third baseman Denny Lyons, pitcher Cy Young, shortstop Ed McKean, and outfielder George Van Haltren. The manager is Frank Selee of the Braves.

—— THE 1900s ——

The birth of the American League in 1901 ended the monopoly of the National League, which cut back from 12 to 8 teams at the onset of the 20th century. The World Series began in 1903 and became a fixture in 1905. The Pirates, with four pennants, and the Cubs, with three, dominated the NL. The Tigers won three in a row in the AL.

    1B—Jake Beckley
    2B—Nap Lajoie
    3B—Jimmy Collins
    SS—Honus Wagner
    OF—Ty Cobb
    OF—Ginger Beaumont
    OF—Sam Crawford
     C—Johnny Kling
     P—Christy Mathewson

Of the four American Leaguers here, Lajoie, Collins, and Crawford were recruits from the National League; only Cobb was an original product. Although he didn't arrive until 1905, Cobb still managed to snag three batting titles. Lajoie also won three batting crowns, and his .422 in 1901 is still the AL record. Wagner never batted below .329. Crawford hit over .300 six times. Collins managed three .300 seasons. And Mathewson won 30 or more games four times. The least familiar names in this lineup are Beaumont, who had a batting championship and six .300 seasons; Beckley, who hit .300 every year from 1900 to 1904; and Kling, who was part of the powerhouse Cubs from 1902 on. The manager is Fred Clarke of the Pirates.

—— THE 1910s ——

The fact that eight of the nine players of this decade were American Leaguers demonstrates that the new league had become a fixture.

1B—George Sisler
2B—Eddie Collins
3B—Frank Baker
SS—Honus Wagner
OF—Tris Speaker
OF—Joe Jackson
OF—Ty Cobb
C—Ray Schalk
P—Walter Johnson

This could be the best decade of them all. When Sisler joined the Browns in 1915, he immediately established himself as the best first baseman around. Collins and Baker were half of Connie Mack's $100,000 infield until Mack got tired of winning pennants and sent Collins to the White Sox and Baker to the Yankees. Wagner was a fading star but still the premier shortstop until 1916. Speaker batted over .300 nine times and took the only AL batting championship Cobb didn't win. Jackson hit over .300 in every year of the decade. All Cobb did was hit an astonishing .387 over the 10 years. Schalk was the backstop for the sterling White Sox pitching staff that dominated the AL in the latter part of the decade. And Johnson? Well, he won 264 games with Washington teams that ranged from mediocre to terrible. The manager is John McGraw of the Giants, who won four pennants, and not Connie Mack because Mack broke up the team that had by 1914 also won four.

—— THE 1920s ——

The Golden Age of Baseball—and a dramatically different kind of baseball as a result of the booming bat of Babe Ruth, who led the Yankees to seven pennants during the decade.

1B—Lou Gehrig
2B—Rogers Hornsby
3B—Pie Traynor
SS—Joe Sewell
OF—Ty Cobb
OF—Tris Speaker
OF—Babe Ruth
  C—Mickey Cochrane
  P—Dazzy Vance

Gehrig was the boy wonder of the second half of the decade. Hornsby batted an absolutely astounding .402 over five seasons (1921–25) and .381 for the decade. Traynor was a rookie when the decade began and a .321 lifetime hitter when it ended. Sewell was a underrated hitter who almost never struck out. Cobb and Speaker were aging stars—but still stars. Ruth hit 467 home runs and batted .355 with an average of more than 140 RBI for the decade. Though a rookie in 1925, Cochrane batted .314 over the next five years. Vance had a few bumpy years but won 20 or more games three times with teams that finished sixth just about every year. The manager is Miller Huggins, as much for being able to contain Ruth's excesses and channel his energies as for winning those seven pennants.

—— THE 1930s ——

A hitters' decade all the way! The decade began with a bang as nine teams hit over .300 in 1930—and the entire National League batted .303. To put that in perspective, note that only one team has hit over .300 since 1937.

> 1B—Lou Gehrig
> 2B—Charlie Gehringer
> 3B—Pie Traynor
> SS—Joe Cronin
> OF—Paul Waner
> OF—Mel Ott
> OF—Joe Medwick
> C—Bill Dickey
> P—Lefty Grove

Gehrig gets the first base spot here over Bill Terry (.401 in 1930) and Jimmie Foxx (two batting titles and four league-leading home run titles) on the basis of his .329 average and 119 or more RBI for eight consecutive seasons. Gehringer hit .331 and for six seasons more than 100 RBI. Traynor was declining but still managed a .316 average. Cronin hit .307 and topped 100 RBI seven times. The competition for the outfield slots is fierce, but we'll take Waner (more than .300 eight times), Ott (five home run titles), and Medwick (414 RBI in three years and a triple crown in 1937) over Al Simmons (two batting titles) and Chuck Klein (three home run titles and a batting crown). Dickey (.320) drove in more than 100 runs and exceeded 20 homers four times each. Grove (199–72 for the decade) led the AL in earned run average seven times. The manager is Joe McCarthy, who won five pennants with the Yankees.

—— THE 1940s ——

Some have called the 1940s the worst ten years in baseball history. Even though the Second World War interrupted most of these players' careers and limited their lifetime statistics, there are no embarrassments here.

    1B—Johnny Mize
    2B—Bobby Doerr
    3B—Stan Hack
    SS—Luke Appling
    OF—Ted Williams
    OF—Joe DiMaggio
    OF—Stan Musial
     C—Ernie Lombardi
     P—Bob Feller

Mize (40 or more homers four times) was the most feared power hitter of his day. Doerr was a steady hitter whose average rose as high as .325. Even though Hack faded as the 1940s wore on, he was still a dangerous hitter. This was Appling's last hurrah, but it was loud enough for him to hit over .300 in seven full seasons and to lead the AL once. Williams won four batting championships (with a high of .406 in 1941), as well as leading the AL in RBI six of the seven seasons he played. Williams' lowest home run total was 23 and he led the league in that category four times; this combination produced two triple crowns. DiMaggio hit .325 with four 100-plus RBI seasons. Musial won three batting crowns and batted .346 in the decade. Lombardi won a batting championship in 1942 and hit more than .300 in three other seasons as well. Meanwhile, Feller was striking out everyone in sight. The manager is Billy Southworth, winner of three pennants with the Cardinals and one with the Braves.

—— THE 1950s ——

Although the Yankees and the Dodgers dominated the 1950s, the decade's most successful players were far more widely distributed. Such period stars as Duke Snider, Roy Campanella, Whitey Ford, Ralph Kiner, Hank Aaron, Al Kaline, and Robin Roberts can't break into this lineup.

1B—Stan Musial
2B—Jackie Robinson
3B—Eddie Mathews
SS—Ernie Banks
OF—Ted Williams
OF—Mickey Mantle
OF—Willie Mays
 C—Yogi Berra
 P—Warren Spahn

Musial hit .330, good enough for four batting crowns. Robinson lasted only through 1956, batting more than .300 five times. Mathews stroked 299 home runs in eight seasons. In six-and-a-half years Banks hit 228 out of the park and won two Most Valuable Player Awards. Williams (.336, 227 homers, two batting crowns), Mantle (280 homers, a triple crown, and two MVPs), and Mays (.317, 250 homers, one MVP) earn their berths over Aaron, Kaline, Kiner, and Snider. Berra won three American League Most Valuable Player Awards in the course of driving in more than 100 runs five times. And as for Spahn, his record between 1950 and 1959 was 202 wins and 131 losses. Casey Stengel's Yankees won eight pennants in the 1950s.

—— THE 1960s ——

A decade of turbulence for the nation and of expansion for the national pastime. Each league added four new teams in the 1960s, forcing the creation of divisional play and the League Championship Series in the final year of the decade.

1B—Harmon Killebrew
2B—Bill Mazeroski
3B—Brooks Robinson
SS—Luis Aparicio
OF—Frank Robinson
OF—Willie Mays
OF—Hank Aaron
 C—Joe Torre
 P—Sandy Koufax

A superb fielding infield—except for Killebrew, who played first, third, and the outfield equally badly yet had to be in this lineup somewhere on the basis of his five league-leading home run totals and 393 round-trippers for the decade. Defense gives Brooks Robinson and Luis Aparicio the edge over Ron Santo and Maury Wills, who both had superior offensive stats. Frank Robinson hit 316 home runs and won a triple crown in 1966. Mays had 350 homers and led the NL in that category three times. Aaron had 375 homers. Torre's best year was 1971, but his .293 average for the 1960s earns him the nod over Elston Howard. Between 1962 and 1966 Koufax led the NL in ERA five times, struck out more than 300 three times, pitched four no-hitters, and won 118 and lost only 34 for a .776 percentage. The manager is Ralph Houk, who was in charge when the Yankees won three of their five pennants in the decade.

—— THE 1970s ——

Baseball's greatest decade of change since the 1920s brought Astroturf, multipurpose stadiums, domes, the designated hitter, further expansion, and most importantly, free agency and the explosion of big money.

      1B—Rod Carew
      2B—Joe Morgan
      3B—Mike Schmidt
      SS—Dave Concepcion
      OF—Willie Stargell
      OF—Reggie Jackson
      OF—Pete Rose
       C—Johnny Bench
       P—Tom Seaver

Four of the nine players in this lineup (Morgan, Concepcion, Rose, and Bench) played together for the better part of the decade on the Cincinnati Reds, which won six division titles, four pennants, and two world championships. And the team's chief pretender is George Foster, the Big Red Machine's left fielder. The qualifying stats of the others: Carew, a .343 average and six batting championships; Schmidt, five of seven seasons with more than 35 home runs; Stargell, 296 home runs; Jackson, 292 homers and participation in seven AL Championship Series. Seaver (178–101) wins out over Jim Palmer (186–103) and Steve Carlton (178–126) because he was saddled with mediocre teams for most of the decade. The manager is Sparky Anderson of the Reds.

—— THE 1980s ——

Four commissioners, drug scandals, two player strikes, and collusion by the owners to keep salaries down dominated baseball off the field. On the field, there was parity with only the Dodgers winning more than one World Series in the decade.

    1B—Don Mattingly
    2B—Ryne Sandberg
    3B—Wade Boggs
    SS—Cal Ripken
    OF—Rickey Henderson
    OF—Andre Dawson
    OF—Dale Murphy
      C—Lance Parrish
      P—Dwight Gooden

Mattingly became a standout player only in 1984, but his .323 average after that edges out Eddie Murray and Kent Hrbek. Sandberg (.285) blossomed into a superstar. Boggs's .352 average would qualify in any decade. Ripken wins out on the basis of offense, but Ozzie Smith may be the best defensive shortstop in baseball history. Tony Gwynn, Dave Winfield, and Robin Yount deserve honorable mention; even so, Henderson (three seasons with 100 or more stolen bases), Dawson (250 home runs), and Murphy (308 homers, 2 MVPs) beat them out. Gary Carter gets honorable mention, too, but Parrish (225 home runs) gets the spot. Like Mattingly, Gooden arrived late, as did his only real competition, Roger Clemens. Although Nolan Ryan and Jack Morris were consistently good, Gooden (100–39, 2.64 ERA) was better. The manager is Whitey Herzog of the Cardinals.

—— THE 1990s ——

Even though the decade has barely begun, we won't shy away from a glance into our crystal ball.

```
1B—Will Clark
2B—Roberto Alomar
3B—Matt Williams
SS—Barry Larkin
OF—Bo Jackson
OF—Ken Griffey, Jr.
OF—Ruben Sierra
 C—Sandy Alomar, Jr.
 P—Dwight Gooden
```

Mark Grace, Dave Magadan, and Mark McGwire are possibilities at first base; Shawon Dunston at shortstop; Gregg Jefferies at third; and Benito Santiago behind the plate. The assumption in the outfield is that Bo will heal (and will abandon his hobby so that he can realize his full potential in baseball). If he doesn't, we may have to turn to one of the other outfielders who should shine in the 1990s—Ellis Burks, Barry Bonds, and Bobby Bonilla. Where is Jose Canseco in this list? Fast living and a bad back may keep him out of the select circle. Alomar appears to have no competition at second base, but Ryne Sandberg didn't peak until 1984. The pitchers are the hardest to predict. With no obvious choice available we'll go with Gooden, the veteran of this team. After all, he'll only be 34 when the decade ends. Otherwise, Jose Rijo and Ramon Martinez are possibilities.

5 The Best

When all is said and done, these are the players who come out on top. Some teams have a pinch or designated hitter; others have a pitcher who excelled at preventing opponents from accomplishing what their eight teammates did so well.

—— CAREER BATTING AVERAGE ——

Hitting a baseball is probably the most difficult feat in sports. Using a tapered, cylindrical stick of wood, a batter must redirect a nine-inch sphere coming at him between 75 and 100 miles per hour. He must hit the ball within a range of 90 degrees and have it elude nine opponents eager to stop it. Only for batters does failure two-thirds of the time amount to incredible success.

> 1B—Dave Orr (.352)
> 2B—Rogers Hornsby (.358)
> 3B—Wade Boggs (.346)
> SS—Honus Wagner (.329)
> OF—Ty Cobb (.367)
> OF—Joe Jackson (.356)
> OF—Pete Browning (.354)
> C—Mickey Cochrane (.320)
> P—Dwight Gooden (.721 W–L Pct.)

Sabermetricians have adjusted 19th-century records in recent years. If we were to accept these adjustments, Orr might have to be replaced by Bill Terry (.341) and Browning by Lefty O'Doul (.349). Gooden's 119–46 career record is the best for pitchers with 100 or more victories.

— SINGLE SEASON BATTING AVERAGE —

Modern baseball began in 1893 when the pitcher's mound was moved from 50 feet to 60 feet, six inches away from home plate. The highest batting averages for a single year since then are

> 1B—George Sisler (1922 Browns) .420
> 2B—Rogers Hornsby (1924 Cardinals) .424
> 3B—George Brett (1980 Royals) .380
> SS—Hughie Jennings (1896 Baltimore) .398
> OF—Hugh Duffy (1894 Braves) .438
> OF—Willie Keeler (1897 Baltimore) .432
> OF—Jesse Burkett (1895 Cleveland) .423
> C—Babe Phelps (1936 Dodgers) .367
> P—Elroy Face (1959 Pirates) .947 W—L Pct.

For the purists who prefer an all-20th-century team, put Luke Appling (.388, 1936 White Sox) at shortstop and Ty Cobb (.420, 1911 Tigers; .410, 1912 Tigers), Joe Jackson (.408, 1911 Indians), and Ted Williams (.406, 1941 Red Sox) in the outfield. Phelps is the catcher, even though he batted only 319 times, because that was a sufficient number of at bats to qualify for the batting championship in 1936. Face's record of 18 wins and a single loss was all in relief. The best season at the plate by a pitcher was Walter Johnson's .440 average in 1925. Honorable mention to Nap Lajoie; while playing second base for the Athletics in the very first year of the American League's existence, he hit .422, a mark no American Leaguer has been able to top.

—— BEST HITTERS ——

The greatest hitter in the history of the game wasn't Babe Ruth or Ty Cobb or any of those 19th-century monsters who batted .400. No, the greatest hitter in the history of the game can be found in this lineup, whose members were all perfect for however brief a stretch.

> 1B—Roy Gleason (1963 Dodgers)
> 2B—Steve Biras (1944 Indians)
> 3B—Heinie Odom (1925 Yankees)
> SS—Al Wright (1933 Braves)
> OF—John Paciorek (1963 Astros)
> OF—Ty Pickup (1918 Phillies)
> OF—John Mohardt (1922 Tigers)
>   C—Mike Hopkins (1902 Pirates)
>   P—Ben Shields (1924–25 Yankees, 1930 Red Sox, 1931 Phillies)

The best hitter of all time is Paciorek, who went three-for-three in his only major league game. Gleason and Hopkins both had two hits in two at bats. The rest of these perfect position players had hits in their only major league at bats. Shields took 13 appearances over four seasons to achieve his perfect 4–0 record—and he did it with a lifetime ERA of 8.34! Honorable mention to the perfect hitting pitchers: Hal Deviney (1920 Red Sox), Fred Schemanske (1923 Senators), and Chet Kehn (1942 Dodgers), each of whom went two-for-two. And especially to the player who achieved perfection in two areas, John Kull of the 1909 Athletics, who was one-for-one as a batter and won one and lost none as a pitcher.

—— CHAMPIONS IN PLACE ——

From this list of players who won the most batting championships at their positions, try to guess the team that has won the most batting crowns in the 20th century.

    1B—Rod Carew (3)
    2B—Rogers Hornsby (7)
    3B—Wade Boggs (5)
    SS—Honus Wagner (7)
    OF—Ty Cobb (12)
    OF—Ted Williams (6)
    OF—Stan Musial (6)
     C—Ernie Lombardi (2)
     P—Lefty Grove (5)

Carew won in 1975, 1977, and 1978. (He also won titles in 1969 and 1972–74, when he played second base for the Twins.) Hornsby (1920–25 Cardinals, 1928 Braves); Boggs (1983, 1985–88 Red Sox); and Wagner (1903–04, 1906–09, 1911 Pirates) complete the infield. The Tigers' Cobb is in a class by himself: He led the AL in every season from 1907 to 1919, except 1916. Williams took his titles for the Red Sox in 1941–42, 1947–48, and 1957–58 . Musial (1943, 1946, 1948, 1950–52 Cardinals) added a seventh in 1957 when he played first base. Lombardi had the highest NL averages in 1938 (Reds) and 1942 (Braves). Grove led the AL in won-lost percentage five times (1929–31, 1933 Athletics; 1939 Red Sox). Honorable mention to Billy Goodman, the only utility player ever to win a batting crown. In 1950, when he batted .354, he played 45 games in the outfield, 27 at third base, 21 at first, 5 at second, 1 at short, and 11 as a pinch hitter. Oh, the answer to the question is the Pirates, who have had nine players lead the NL a total of 23 times.

—— CAREER HOME RUNS ——

The top power hitters at each position are

1B—Lou Gehrig (493)
2B—Joe Morgan (266)
3B—Mike Schmidt (509)
SS—Ernie Banks (277)
OF—Babe Ruth (692)
OF—Hank Aaron (661)
OF—Willie Mays (643)
 C—Carlton Fisk (332)
 P—Wes Ferrell (37)

The numbers don't look familiar? That's because they don't include home runs hit while playing other positions. The full career totals for those who are different: Morgan, 268; Schmidt, 548; Banks, 512; Ruth, 714; Aaron, 755; Mays, 660; Fisk, 354; and Ferrell, 38

—— CAREER HOME RUN RATIO ——

Among those with 4,000 or more at bats, these players hit the long ball most often.

1B—Jimmie Foxx (15.23 at bats)
2B—Joe Gordon (22.55 at bats)
3B—Harmon Killebrew (14.22 at bats)
SS—Ernie Banks (18.40 at bats)
OF—Babe Ruth (11.76 at bats)
OF—Ralph Kiner (14.11 at bats)
OF—Dave Kingman (14.65 at bats)
 C—Roy Campanella (17.38 at bats)
PH—Joe Adcock (12.75 at bats)

Honorable mention for Mike Schmidt's 15.24. Adcock's ratio is for pinch-hitting appearances only; his overall career ratio is one home run every 19.66 at bats.

—— SINGLE SEASON HOME RUNS ——

We had to exclude three of the most deserving heavy hitters from this lineup.

1B—Hank Greenberg (1938 Tigers) 58
2B—Davey Johnson (1973 Braves) 42
3B—Mike Schmidt (1980 Phillies) 48
SS—Ernie Banks (1958 Cubs) 47
OF—Roger Maris (1961 Yankees) 61
OF—Babe Ruth (1927 Yankees) 60
OF—Hack Wilson (1930 Cubs) 56
C—Roy Campanella (1953 Dodgers) 40
P—Wes Ferrell (1931 Indians) 9

The first difficulty is that, by all rights, Babe Ruth should be in this lineup twice—the second time for the 59 home runs he hit in 1921. The second difficulty is that there is no room for Jimmie Foxx, who hit 58 home runs with the Athletics in 1932. Even though Foxx played most of that season at first base, he did play 13 games at third and hit a few of his homers while playing there. The third difficulty is that Johnny Bench (1970 Reds) hit 45 home runs and might have been the catcher here except that he hit six of them while playing the outfield and one while playing first base. Campanella also hit one additional homer as a pinch hitter, raising his season total to 41. Rogers Hornsby (1922 Cardinals) tied Johnson's total of 42, but Johnson hit an additional one as a pinch hitter. Honorable mention to Allen Sothoron (1921 Indians), who holds the record for pitching 178 innings without giving up a home run.

—— SINGLE GAME HOME RUNS ——

Although 11 players have hit four home runs in a game, only 6 of them make this team.

>   1B—Lou Gehrig (1932 Yankees)
>   2B—Bobby Lowe (1894 Braves)
>   3B—Bob Horner (1986 Braves)
>   SS—Ernie Banks (1957 Cubs)
>   OF—Chuck Klein (1936 Phillies)
>   OF—Willie Mays (1961 Giants)
>   OF—Rocky Colavito (1959 Indians)
>   C—Gary Carter (1985 Mets)
>   P—Jim Tobin (1942 Braves)

Gehrig (June 3), Lowe (May 30), and Colavito (June 10) hit theirs consecutively. So too did Mike Schmidt (April 17, 1976 Phillies), but he did it in a 10-inning game, so Horner (July 6) gets the third-base slot. Mays (April 30) wins the second outfield spot, and Klein (July 10) beats out Pat Seerey (July 18, 1948 White Sox) because the former hit his four in a 10-inning game and the latter hit his in 11 innings. The other three players in the record book for this feat are Joe Adcock (July 31, 1954 Braves), Gil Hodges (August 31, 1950 Dodgers), and Ed Delahanty (July 13, 1896 Phillies), who was ordinarily an outfielder but who was playing first base that day. Banks is the only shortstop who has twice hit three home runs in a single game (September 14, 1957 Cubs and May 29, 1962 Cubs). Carter is the most recent (September 9) catcher to hit three in a game—and the only one to do it twice (April 20, 1977 Expos). Tobin is the only pitcher to stroke three in a game (May 13).

—— CAREER GRAND-SLAMS ——

The only way to get four runs with one swipe of the bat is by hitting a home run with the bases loaded.

        1B—Lou Gehrig (23)
        2B—Rogers Hornsby (12)
        3B—Harmon Killebrew (11)
        SS—Ernie Banks (12)
        OF—Willie McCovey (18)
        OF—Ted Williams (17)
        OF—Babe Ruth (16)
         C—Johnny Bench (11)
         P—Jim Palmer (0)

Killebrew, Banks, and McCovey played more than one position, but that is no reason to exclude them. In his 18 years in the big leagues, Palmer never gave up a grand slam. Honorable mention to Hank Aaron (16), Dave Kingman (16), and Gary Carter (11).

—— BATTING STREAKS ——

Getting at least one hit every day, day after day isn't easy. This lineup includes the players with the longest batting streaks.

        1B—George Sisler (1922 Browns) 41 games
        2B—Rogers Hornsby (1922 Cardinals) 33 games
        3B—Pete Rose (1978 Reds) 44 games
        SS—Bill Dahlen (1894 Cubs) 42 games
        OF—Joe DiMaggio (1941 Yankees) 56 games
        OF—Willie Keeler (1897 Baltimore) 44 games
        OF—Ty Cobb (1911 Tigers) 40 games
         C—Benito Santiago (1987 Padres) 34 games
         P—Carl Hubbell (1936–37 Giants) 24 wins

Hubbell won 24 consecutive games. Honorable mention to Paul Molitor (1987 Brewers), whose 39-game hitting streak came while he was, for the most part, a designated hitter.

—— GAME STREAKS ——

These players had the longest streaks for doing something game after game.

> 1B—Ray Grimes (1922 Cubs)
> 2B—Bid McPhee (1882–89 Cincinnati AA, 1890–96 Reds)
> 3B—George Brett (1976 Royals)
> SS—Joe Sewell (1929 Indians)
> OF—Billy Hamilton (1894 Phillies)
> OF—Paul Waner (1927 Pirates)
> OF—Rip Repulski (1954 Cardinals)
> C—Al Todd (1937 Pirates)
> P—Carl Hubbell (1936–37 Giants)

Grimes drove in at least one run in 17 consecutive games. McPhee played about 1,700 games in the major leagues before he thought it necessary to wear a glove. Brett had six consecutive three-hit games. Sewell avoided striking out in 115 consecutive contests. Hamilton scored at least one run in 24 successive contests. Waner had at least one extra-base hit in 14 straight games. Repulski had 10 consecutive two-hit games. Todd caught 128 consecutive games in one season without allowing a passed ball. Hubbell recorded 24 consecutive victories. Honorable mention to Roy Cullenbine (1947 Tigers) for working pitchers for at least one base on balls in 22 consecutive games.

—— OTHER STREAKS ——

These players kept various kinds of streaks going the longest.

> 1B—Don Hurst (1929 Phillies)
> 2B—Eddie Stanky (1950 Giants)
> 3B—Pinky Higgins (1938 Red Sox)
> SS—Cal Ripken (1982–87 Orioles)
> OF—Vince Coleman (1988–89 Cardinals)
> OF—Ted Williams (1957 Red Sox)
> OF—Elmer Smith (1921 Indians)
> C—Johnny Blanchard (1961 Yankees)
> P—Jim Barr (1972 Giants)

Hurst had six consecutive hits that were home runs. Stanky walked in seven consecutive plate appearances. (Billy Rogell, 1938 Tigers, and Mel Ott, 1943 Giants, also walked seven times in a row.) Higgins had 12 consecutive hits, interrupted only by two walks. (Walt Dropo of the Tigers also had 12 consecutive hits in 1952; his were uninterrupted.) Ripken appeared in every inning of every game from June 5, 1982, through September 14, 1987, for a total of 8,243 innings over 904 games. Coleman stole 50 consecutive bases without being thrown out. Williams reached base in 16 consecutive plate appearances (four home runs, two singles, nine walks, and one hit by a pitch). Smith had seven consecutive extra base hits (three doubles and four homers, broken up only by two walks). Earl Sheely, 1926 White Sox, also had seven in a row (six doubles and a homer broken by a sacrifice). Blanchard hit four consecutive home runs—over three games. And, Barr retired 41 consecutive batters over two games. Honorable mention to Dave Philley (1958–59 Athletics) for nine consecutive successful pinch-hitting appearances.

—— CAREER HITS ——

The 3,000-hit club has 16 members, 7 of whom make this team. If you can name the other nine, go to the head of the trivia class.

    1B—Stan Musial (3,630)
    2B—Eddie Collins (3,311)
    3B—Pete Rose (4,256)
    SS—Honus Wagner (3,430)
    OF—Ty Cobb (4,191)
    OF—Hank Aaron (3,771)
    OF—Tris Speaker (3,515)
     C—Yogi Berra (2,150)
    PH—Manny Mota (150)

The other nine are Carl Yastrzemski, 3,419; Willie Mays, 3,283; Nap Lajoie, 3,251; Paul Waner, 3,152; Rod Carew, 3,053; Cap Anson, 3,041; Lou Brock, 3,023; Al Kaline, 3,007; and Roberto Clemente, 3,000. The most by a pitcher? Cy Young's 623.

—— SEASON HITS ——

The standard for a good season is 200 hits.

    1B—George Sisler (1920 Browns) 257
    2B—Rogers Hornsby (1922 Cardinals) 250
    3B—Wade Boggs (1985 Red Sox) 240
    SS—Cecil Travis (1941 Senators) 218
    OF—Lefty O'Doul (1929 Phillies) 254
    OF—Al Simmons (1925 Athletics) 253
    OF—Chuck Klein (1930 Phillies) 250
     C—Ted Simmons (1975 Cardinals) 193
    PH—Jose Morales (1976 Expos) 25

The batting averages that went with these totals: Sisler, .407; Hornsby, .401; Boggs, .368; Travis, .359; O'Doul, .398; Al Simmons, .384; Klein, .386; Ted Simmons, .332; and Morales, .321 as a pinch hitter.

—— CAREER RUNS BATTED IN ——

The highest lifetime totals for driving in runs are

    1B—Lou Gehrig (1,990)
    2B—Nap Lajoie (1,599)
    3B—Mike Schmidt (1,595)
    SS—Honus Wagner (1,732)
    OF—Hank Aaron (2,297)
    OF—Babe Ruth (2,211)
    OF—Ty Cobb (1,961)
     C—Yogi Berra (1,430)
     P—Ed Walsh (1.82 ERA)

RBI weren't counted at all until 1907, so some of the preceding were not counted until decades after they were driven in and represent after-the-fact research. Walsh's ERA is the lowest for all pitchers with 1,500 or more innings pitched.

—— SEASON RUNS BATTED IN ——

And the high marks for a single season are

    1B—Lou Gehrig (1931 Yankees) 184
    2B—Rogers Hornsby (1922 Cardinals) 152
    3B—Al Rosen (1953 Indians) 145
    SS—Vern Stephens (1949 Red Sox) 159
    OF—Hack Wilson (1930 Cubs) 190
    OF—Babe Ruth (1921 Yankees) 171
    OF—Chuck Klein (1930 Phillies) 170
     C—Johnny Bench (1970 Reds) 148
     P—Dutch Leonard (1914 Red Sox) 1.01 ERA

Other season totals over 170 are Hank Greenberg's 183 with the 1937 Tigers and 170 with the 1935 Tigers; Jimmie Foxx's 175 with the 1938 Red Sox; and Lou Gehrig's 175 with the 1927 Yankees and 174 with the 1930 Yankees.

—— CAREER DOUBLES ——

The two-base hit was a neglected weapon for years until the Kansas City Royals started racking up doubles in the late 1970s.

        1B—Stan Musial (725)
        2B—Nap Lajoie (648)
        3B—Pete Rose (746)
        SS—Honus Wagner (651)
        OF—Tris Speaker (793)
        OF—Ty Cobb (724)
        OF—Carl Yastrzemski (646)
          C—Ted Simmons (477)
          P—Rollie Fingers (341 saves)

Honorable mention to Hank Aaron (624) and Paul Waner (603), the only players with more than 600 doubles who do not make this team.

—— SINGLE SEASON DOUBLES ——

These players took two most often in a single season.

        1B—George Burns (1926 Indians) 64
        2B—Charlie Gehringer (1936 Tigers) 60
        3B—George Kell (1950 Tigers) 56
        SS—Joe Cronin (1938 Red Sox) 51
        OF—Earl Webb (1931 Red Sox) 67
        OF—Joe Medwick (1936 Cardinals) 64
        OF—Paul Waner (1932 Pirates) 62
          C—Mickey Cochrane (1930 Athletics) 42
          P—Bobby Thigpen (1990 White Sox) 57 saves

Hank Greenberg (63, 1934 Tigers), the only other player with more than 60 doubles in a season, is squeezed out of this lineup. Terry Kennedy (1982 Padres) tied Cochrane's total.

—— CAREER TRIPLES ——

The most recent triple by a member of this lineup dates back to 1936.

1B—Jake Beckley (244)
2B—Bid McPhee (189)
3B—Tommy Leach (172)
SS—Honus Wagner (252)
OF—Sam Crawford (312)
OF—Ty Cobb (297)
OF—Tris Speaker (223)
C—Buck Ewing (178)
P—Cy Young (751 complete games)

Other players with more than 200 triples are Roger Connor, 233; Fred Clarke, 223; and Dan Brouthers, 206.

—— SINGLE SEASON TRIPLES ——

The most recent triple here goes all the way back to 1912, with only Wagner and Ewing as repeaters.

1B—Dave Orr (1881 New York AA) 31
2B—Heinie Reitz (1894 Baltimore) 31
3B—Harry Davis (1897 Pirates) 28
SS—Honus Wagner (1900 Pirates) 22
OF—Owen Wilson (1912 Pirates) 36
OF—Sam Thompson (1894 Phillies) 27
OF—George Treadway (1894 Dodgers) 26
C—Buck Ewing (1884 Giants) 20
P—Will White (1879 Cincinnati) 75 Complete Games

Joe Jackson (1912 Indians), Sam Crawford (1914 Tigers), and Kiki Cuyler (1925 Pirates) later tied Treadway.

—— CAREER TOTAL BASES ——

One for a single, two for a double, three for a triple, and four for a homer:

    1B—Stan Musial (6,134)
    2B—Rogers Hornsby (4,712)
    3B—Pete Rose (5,752)
    SS—Honus Wagner (4,888)
    OF—Hank Aaron (6,856)
    OF—Willie Mays (6,066)
    OF—Ty Cobb (5,863)
     C—Yogi Berra (3,643)
     P—Nolan Ryan (6.54 hits per game)

Ryan is the stingiest pitcher in the number of hits he has given up per nine innings. And honorable mention to the rest of the 5,000 club: Babe Ruth, 5,793; Carl Yastrzemski, 5,539; Frank Robinson, 5,373; Tris Speaker, 5,105; Lou Gehrig, 5,059; and Mel Ott, 5,041.

—— SINGLE SEASON TOTAL BASES ——

The standard for an exceptional season is 400 total bases.

    1B—Lou Gehrig (1927 Yankees) 447
    2B—Rogers Hornsby (1922 Cardinals) 450
    3B—Eddie Mathews (1953 Braves) 363
    SS—Ernie Banks (1958 Cubs) 379
    OF—Babe Ruth (1921 Yankees) 457
    OF—Chuck Klein (1930 Phillies) 445
    OF—Stan Musial (1948 Cardinals) 429
     C—Johnny Bench (1970 Reds) 355
     P—Nolan Ryan (1972 Angels) 5.26 hits per game

Gehrig topped 400 four other times; Klein, twice more; and Hornsby and Ruth, one additional time each. Eight others join them: Jimmie Foxx (twice), Joe DiMaggio, Jim Rice, Hal Trosky, Hack Wilson, Babe Herman, Joe Medwick, and Hank Aaron.

—— CAREER SLUGGING AVERAGE ——

The standard for inclusion here is 4,000 at bats.

    1B—Lou Gehrig (.632)
    2B—Rogers Hornsby (.577)
    3B—Dick Allen (.534)
    SS—Ernie Banks (.500)
    OF—Babe Ruth (.690)
    OF—Ted Williams (.634)
    OF—Joe DiMaggio (.579)
      C—Roy Campanella (.500)
      P—Cy Young (511 wins)

Honorable mention to Jimmie Foxx, whose .609 is the fourth highest ever.

—— SINGLE SEASON ——
SLUGGING AVERAGE

Even though some of the hitters' totals are in the stratosphere, no one is likely to top the pitcher on this team.

    1B—Lou Gehrig (1927 Yankees) .765
    2B—Rogers Hornsby (1925 Cardinals) .756
    3B—George Brett (1980 Royals) .664
    SS—Ernie Banks (1958 Cubs) .614
    OF—Babe Ruth (1920 Yankees) .847
    OF—Ted Williams (1941 Red Sox) .735
    OF—Hack Wilson (1930 Cubs) .723
      C—Gabby Hartnett (1930 Cubs) .630
      P—Charlie Radbourn (1884 Providence) 60 wins

Ruth slugged .700 or better nine times, including the astonishing 1920 season and 1921 when he slipped to .846. Only seven other players have topped the .700 plateau: Gehrig, five times; Williams and Jimmie Foxx, three times each; Hornsby twice; and Wilson, Mickey Mantle, and Stan Musial, once each.

—— CAREER RUNS SCORED ——

The object of the game is to circle the bases and cross the plate. The following did that the most times:

    1B—Stan Musial (1,949)
    2B—Eddie Collins (1,818)
    3B—Pete Rose (2,165)
    SS—Honus Wagner (1,740)
    OF—Ty Cobb (2,245)
    OF—Babe Ruth (2,174)
    OF—Hank Aaron (2,174)
     C—Yogi Berra (1,175)
     P—Walter Johnson (110 shutouts)

Pitchers try to stop runners from scoring and Johnson holds the career record for shutouts. Honorable mention to Willie Mays (2,062), the only player with more than 2,000 runs who fails to make this team.

—— SINGLE SEASON RUNS SCORED ——

Some gargantuan numbers from the last century—and a few from this century:

    1B—Lou Gehrig (1936 Yankees) 167
    2B—Fred Dunlap (1884 St. Louis UA) 160
    3B—Arlie Latham (1887 St. Louis AA) 163
    SS—Hughie Jennings (1895 Baltimore) 159
    OF—Billy Hamilton (1894 Phillies) 196
    OF—Babe Ruth (1921 Yankees) 177
    OF—Tom Brown (1891 Boston AA) 177
     C—King Kelly (1886 Cubs) 155
     P—Grover Alexander (1916 Phillies) 16 ShO

Gehrig and Ruth were the only two 20th-century players to cross the plate more than 160 times in a season—and each of them did it twice.

—— SINGLE GAME RUNS SCORED ——

Eight of the players in this lineup scored six runs in one game; the ninth scored seven.

1B—Frank Torre (September 2, 1957, Braves)
2B—Bobby Lowe (May 3, 1895, Braves)
3B—Ezra Sutton (August 27, 1887, Braves)
SS—Johnny Pesky (May 8, 1946, Red Sox)
OF—Mel Ott (August 4, 1934, and April 30, 1944, Giants)
OF—Ginger Beaumont (July 22, 1899, Pirates)
OF—Jimmy Ryan (July 25, 1894, Cubs)
 C—King Kelly (August 27, 1887, Braves)
 P—Guy Hecker (August 15, 1886, Louisville AA)

Hecker is the only one to ever score seven. Ott is the only one to score six twice. And, four honorable mentions—Mike Tiernan, Cap Anson, Jim Whitney, and Spike Owen—for six in a game.

— CAREER BASE ON BALLS AVERAGE —

This lineup is based on walks divided by plate appearances.

1B—Earl Torgeson (.165)
2B—Max Bishop (.204)
3B—Eddie Yost (.180)
SS—Eddie Joost (.157)
OF—Ted Williams (.208)
OF—Babe Ruth (.197)
OF—Mickey Mantle (.176)
 C—Gene Tenace (.183)
 P—Deacon Phillippe (1.25 BB per game)

Torgeson is a surprise, but the real sleeper is Joost, a .239 career hitter whose walks bring his on-base percentage up to .358. Phillippe issued the lowest number of walks per nine innings of all pitchers with 2,500 or more innings pitched.

—— CAREER WALKS ——

If a walk is as good as a hit, this lineup is very good indeed.

1B—Carl Yastrzemski (1,845)
2B—Joe Morgan (1,865)
3B—Eddie Yost (1,614)
SS—Luke Appling (1,302)
OF—Babe Ruth (2,056)
OF—Ted Williams (2,019)
OF—Mickey Mantle (1,734)
 C—Gene Tenace (984)
 P—Juan Marichal (3.27 K/BB ratio)

Only two pitchers who worked more than 3,500 innings have struck out three times as many batters as they walked. Marichal's ratio (2,302 K, 704 BB) is approached only by Ferguson Jenkins' 3.20 (3,192 K, 997 BB).

—— SINGLE SEASON WALKS ——

It's a wonder that some of these players didn't go directly from the on-deck circle to first base.

1B—Harmon Killebrew (1969 Twins) 145
2B—Eddie Stanky (1945 Dodgers) 148
3B—Eddie Yost (1956 Senators) 151
SS—Eddie Joost (1949 Athletics) 149
OF—Babe Ruth (1923 Yankees) 170
OF—Ted Williams (1947, 1949 Red Sox) 162
OF—Jim Wynn (1969 Astros) 148
 C—Gene Tenace (1977 Padres) 125
 P—Babe Adams (1920 Pirates) 18 BB

Adams gave up the fewest walks per nine innings (.616) in the annals of the game. Christy Mathewson (1913 Giants) came close, though, with .618 walks per game. It is worth noting that for the years cited Tenace batted a mere .233 and Yost .231.

—— CAREER STOLEN BASES ——

A single isn't always a single; to some players first base is merely a way station to second base.

1B—Frank Chance (405)
2B—Eddie Collins (743)
3B—Tommy Leach (361)
SS—Honus Wagner (703)
OF—Rickey Henderson (936)
OF—Lou Brock (938)
OF—Ty Cobb (892)
 C—Buck Ewing (336)
PR—Herb Washington (31)

The odd man out is Billy Hamilton, the 19th-century speed-ster who is officially credited with 937 stolen bases. In those days, however, a runner was credited with a stolen base for taking an extra base on a base hit. No one knows how many of Hamilton's steals actually saw him go from first to third on a single.

—— SINGLE SEASON STOLEN BASES ——

Obviously the stolen base wasn't much of an offensive priority between the dead ball era and Maury Wills.

1B—Frank Chance (1903 Cubs) 67
2B—Eddie Collins (1910 Athletics) 81
3B—Fritz Maisel (1914 Yankees) 74
SS—Maury Wills (1962 Dodgers) 104
OF—Rickey Henderson (1982 Athletics) 130
OF—Vince Coleman (1985 Cardinals) 110
OF—Lou Brock (1974 Cardinals) 118
 C—John Wathan (1982 Royals) 36
 P—Herb Washington (1974 Athletics) 29

Henderson also stole 100 bases in 1980 and 108 in 1983. Coleman swiped 107 in 1986 and 109 in 1987.

—— CAREER STRIKEOUT RATIO ——

Nobody could top these players at putting the ball in play. They struck out only once every . . .

    1B—Frank McCormick (30.28 at bats)
    2B—Nellie Fox (42.74 at bats)
    3B—Andy High (33.85 at bats)
    SS—Joe Sewell (62.56 at bats)
    OF—Lloyd Waner (44.92 at bats)
    OF—Tommy Holmes (40.92 at bats)
    OF—Sam Rice (33.71 at bats)
     C—Mickey Cochrane (23.32 at bats)
     P—Nolan Ryan (9.57 Ks per game)

Strikeouts weren't regularly recorded until 1913 so much fabled contact hitters as Lave Cross, Stuffy McInnis, and Willie Keeler are excluded because of incomplete statistics. Ryan has struck out the most batters per nine innings since 1913.

—— FEWEST STRIKEOUTS IN A ——
SINGLE SEASON

The marks for fewest whiffs with at least 400 at bats are

    1B—Stuffy McInnis (1922 Indians) 5 in 537 at bats
    2B—Emil Verban (1947 Phillies) 0 in 540 at bats
    3B—Joe Sewell (1932 Yankees) 3 in 503 at bats
    SS Lou Boudreau (1948 Indians) 0 in 560 at bats
    OF—Lloyd Waner (1936 Pirates) 5 in 414 at bats
    OF—Don Mueller (1956 Giants) 7 in 453 at bats
    OF—Tris Speaker (1927 Senators) 8 in 523 at bats
     C—Mickey Cochrane (1927 Athletics) 7 in 432 at bats
     P—Nolan Ryan (1973 Angels) 383 Ks

Actually, Matt Kilroy (1886 Baltimore) struck out 505 batters, but he had a few advantages Ryan never imagined—a mound only 50 feet from the plate and a rule that required seven balls for a walk.

—— CAREER RECORD HOLDERS ——

Each of the following holds a career record:

1B—Johnny Mize
2B—Eddie Collins
3B—Pete Rose
SS—Honus Wagner
OF—Don Baylor
OF—Sam Crawford
OF—Ty Cobb
C—Ray Schalk
P—Addie Joss

Mize hit three home runs in a game six times. Collins is credited with 511 sacrifices. Rose has both the most singles (3,215) and the most at bats (14,103). Wagner hit higher than .300 for the first 17 years of his career—from 1897 to 1913. Baylor was hit by a pitch 267 times. Crawford hit 50 inside-the-park home runs. Cobb stole home 50 times. Schalk flashed the signs in four no-hit games. Joss is significantly ahead of the next best pitcher at keeping runners off the bases: he gave up 1,893 hits and 370 walks in 2,336 innings, an average of 8.73 runners per nine innings. (The runner-up is Ed Walsh, who allowed exactly 9.00 runners per game.) Honorable mentions to Hank Aaron (131 sacrifice flies and 1,477 extra base hits), Rickey Henderson (45 lead-off home runs), Tim Raines (an .853 stolen base percentage), Tommy Davis (a .320 batting average as a pinch hitter), and Cliff Johnson (20 pinch-hit homers).

— SINGLE SEASON RECORD HOLDERS —

And each of the members of this lineup holds a single-season record.

     1B—Don Mattingly (1987 Yankees)
     2B—Ron Hunt (1971 Expos)
     3B—Bill Bradley (1907 Indians)
     SS—Dale Berra (1983 Pirates)
     OF—Willie Keeler (1898 Baltimore)
     OF—Max Carey (1922 Pirates)
     OF—Willie Wilson (1980 Royals)
      C—Clyde McCullough (1945 Cubs)
      P—Dick Radatz (1964 Red Sox)

Mattingly socked six home runs with the bases loaded. Hunt was hit by pitches 50 times. Bradley sacrificed himself 46 times. Berra reached base on catcher's interference an astounding seven times. Keeler's mark of 202 singles has endured for more than nine decades. Carey has the highest stolen base percentage of all players with 50 or more attempted steals; he was successful 51 out of 53 times, a .961 percentage. Wilson recorded 705 official at bats. McCullough holds the record for the fewest games played during the regular season and then appearing in the World Series—none; he got back from military service only in time to strike out in his only Series at bat that year. Radatz struck out more batters—181 in 157 innings—than any other relief pitcher. Honorable mentions to Gil Hodges (1954 Dodgers) for 19 sac flies; Babe Ruth (1923 Yankees) for getting on base 379 times; Augie Galan (1935 Cubs) for the most at bats (646) without grounding into a double play; and John Frederick (1932 Dodgers) for six pinch-hit home runs.

—— SINGLE GAME RECORD HOLDERS ——

An eclectic collection of single-game record holders:

1B—Jim Bottomley (1924 Cardinals)
2B—Bobby Knoop (1966 Angels)
3B—Gary Gaetti (1990 Twins)
SS—Tommy Corcoran (1903 Reds)
OF—Mike Griffin (1890 Philadelphia PL)
OF—Tom McCreery (1897 Louisville)
OF—Harold Baines (1984 White Sox)
C—Duke Farrell (1897 Washington)
P—Roger Clemens (1986 Red Sox)

Bottomley drove in 12 runs (September 16). Knoop participated in six double plays on May 1. On July 17 Gaetti became the only player to start two triple plays in the same game. Corcoran recorded more assists (14) than any other player in a nine-inning game (August 7). Griffin (June 23) is still the only player in history to reach base on errors four times in a game. McCreery hit three inside-the-park home runs on July 12. Baines won the longest game ever broken up by a home run, a 25-inning contest that began on May 8 and continued the next day. Farrell caught eight would-be base stealers on May 11. Clemens struck out 20 batters on April 29, the only time a pitcher has notched that many Ks in a nine-inning contest. Honorable mention to Pat Collins (1910 Browns), who appeared in the same game as both a pinch runner and a pinch hitter, and to Ed Fitzgerald (1952 Pirates), who actually returned to catch in a game in which he had already pinch hit.

—— UNLIKELY LEADERS ——

This lineup of leaders celebrates the fact that not only during the Second World War years and the split 1981 season did unexpected players emerge to lead the league in key offensive categories. Remember what these men leds in?

1B—Wally Pipp (1916–17 Yankees)
2B—Billy Gardner (1957 Orioles)
3B—Lee Handley (1939 Pirates)
SS—Eddie Miller (1947 Reds)
OF—Fred Odwell (1905 Reds)
OF—Harry Lumley (1906 Dodgers)
OF—Beau Bell (1937 Browns)
 C—Tim McCarver (1966 Cardinals)
 P—Bob Porterfield (1953 Senators)

Pipp, largely remembered today as the first baseman displaced by Lou Gehrig, led the AL in home runs in both seasons. Gardner, a lifetime .237 hitter, led the AL in doubles. Although he only stole 17, Handley was the NL's chief thief on the bases. Like Gardner, Miller overcame a puny lifetime average (.230) to lead in two base hits. Odwell was around for only four years and accumulated only 10 homers, but 9 of them came in 1905—enough to lead the NL. Lumley played for seven seasons, but made the most of them: In 1906, he led in slugging average; in 1904, he led in both doubles and triples; and in 1907, he hit home runs with more frequency than any other National Leaguer. Bell led the AL in both hits and doubles. McCarver undermined the image of catchers being slow-footed by leading in triples. Porterfield posted a record of 22–10 for the most victories in the league; otherwise he never won more than 13 and ended up with a record of 87–97. Honorable mention to Ray Herbert of the 1962 White Sox who parlayed a 20–9 mark into the best winning percentage (his career record was 104–107).

—— LOW LEADERS ——

Circumstances have sometimes conspired to let a player lead the league in a major category with a figure that in other years would have relegated him to the middle of the pack.

> 1B—Fred Merkle (1918 Cubs)
> 2B—Pedro Garcia (1973 Brewers)
> 3B—Ned Williamson (1885 Cubs)
> SS—Honus Wagner (1906 Pirates)
> OF—Carl Yastrzemski (1968 Red Sox)
> OF—Del Unser (1969 Senators)
> OF—Hack Wilson (1926 Cubs)
>   C—Frankie Pytlak (1934 Indians)
>   P—Early Wynn (1950 Indians)

Merkle's league-leading 71 runs batted in came in a season abbreviated by the First World War. Garcia had the most doubles (32). Williamson's league-leading fielding average was .891! Wagner led the NL with 237 total bases. Yastrzemski's .301 batting crown symbolized the year of the pitcher. Unser led the AL with eight triples. Wilson's 21 homers for the Cubs have been the lowest league-leading total since the arrival of the lively ball in 1921. (The absolute lowest total compiled by a league leader were the three homers hit by Orator Shaffer in 1877.) Pytlak led all AL players in being hit by pitches (five times). Wynn is one of five pitchers to lead a league with an ERA over 3.00; in addition to his all-time high of 3.20, there have been Rosy Ryan (1922 Giants) with 3.00, Bill Walker (1929 Giants) with 3.08, Lefty Grove (1938 Red Sox) with 3.07, and Warren Spahn (1961 Braves) with 3.01.

—— GREATEST CAREERS ——

Now that all the numbers are in, we can provoke a controversy or two by offering what, in our estimation, is *the* all-time all-star team.

    1B—Lou Gehrig
    2B—Rogers Hornsby
    3B—Mike Schmidt
    SS—Honus Wagner
    OF—Ty Cobb
    OF—Babe Ruth
    OF—Willie Mays
     C—Bill Dickey
     P—Walter Johnson

Runnersup? Jimmie Foxx, George Sisler, Cap Anson, and Bill Terry to Gehrig. Nap Lajoie, Eddie Collins, Frankie Frisch, and Charlie Gehringer to Hornsby. Pie Traynor and John McGraw to Schmidt. Hughie Jennings, Luke Appling, and Ozzie Smith to Wagner. Ted Williams, Pete Browning, Jesse Burkett, Hank Aaron, Joe DiMaggio, Mickey Mantle, Stan Musial, Tris Speaker, and Ed Delahanty to Cobb-Ruth-Mays. King Kelly, Mickey Cochrane, Yogi Berra, Roy Campanella, and Johnny Bench to Dickey. Cy Young, Grover Alexander, Christy Mathewson, Lefty Grove, Warren Spahn, Whitey Ford, Sandy Koufax, Tom Seaver, and Steve Carlton to Johnson. Our choice for a manager is Casey Stengel, with John McGraw and Joe McCarthy close behind.

—— GREATEST SEASONS ——

Everyone may have a personal choice for an all-time, all-star team, but how about the greatest single season by a player at each position?

    1B—Lou Gehrig (1927 Yankees)
    2B—Rogers Hornsby (1924 Cardinals)
    3B—George Brett (1980 Royals)
    SS—Ernie Banks (1958 Cubs)
    OF—Ty Cobb (1911 Tigers)
    OF—Babe Ruth (1921 Yankees)
    OF—Hack Wilson (1930 Cubs)
     C—Johnny Bench (1970 Reds)
     P—Walter Johnson (1913 Senators)

We don't ordinarily propose a batting order for our selections, but this lineup cries out for one. So how about: Cobb (.420 batting average, 83 stolen bases); Hornsby (.424); Ruth (.378, 59 home runs, 171 RBI, .846 slugging average); Gehrig (.373, 47 home runs, 175 RBI); Wilson (56 home runs, 190 RBI); Bench (45 home runs, 148 RBI); Banks (47 home runs); Brett (.390); and Johnson (36–7, 1.09 ERA). Of course, if Johnson had had this lineup on his side, it's hard to see how he could have lost a single game. Honorable mention to Tip O'Neill (1887 St. Louis AA), who batted .492 (when walks counted as hits) and also led the league in doubles, triples, home runs, runs, slugging average, total bases, and hits. He is the only player who has ever led his league in doubles, triples, and homers in the same year.

—— GREATEST DAYS ——

These players had no reason to regret a scheduled double-header or, in one case, even a tripleheader.

1B—Nate Colbert (1972 Padres)
2B—Max Bishop (1930 Athletics)
3B—Clyde Barnhart (1920 Pirates)
SS—Herman Long (1894 Braves)
OF—Stan Musial (1954 Cardinals)
OF—Mel Almada (1937 Senators)
OF—Joe Kelley (1894 Baltimore)
  C—Hank Severeid (1920 Browns)
  P—Ed Reulbach (1908 Cubs)

Both Colbert (August 1) and Musial (May 2) cracked five home runs in a double-bill. Colbert also set records by driving in 13 runs and amassing 22 total bases. Bishop (May 12) walked eight times—and then matched this total four years later (July 8, 1931) while playing for the Red Sox. Barnhart is the only player in major league history to get at least one hit in three games on the same day (October 2). Long (May 30) and Almada (July 25) must have had a lot of hitting behind them; each of them scored nine runs in a twin bill. Kelley cracked out nine consecutive hits on September 9. Severeid handled 27 chances, 21 of them on strikeouts in the two games on July 13. Reulbach pitched two complete-game shutouts against the Dodgers on September 26. Honorable mention to Hank Majeski, who hit six doubles in the Athletics' doubleheader on August 27, 1948. And also to Tim Keefe, who won both ends of a doubleheader for New York (AA) on July 4, 1883; he gave up only three hits that day but managed to yield a run in the process.

—— GREATEST GAMES ——

Every player has his day, but some have compressed a week of achievement into a single game.

        1B—Joe Adcock (1954 Braves)
        2B—Rennie Stennett (1975 Pirates)
        3B—Kevin Seitzer (1987 Royals)
        SS—Johnny Burnett (1932 Indians)
        OF—Piggy Ward (1893 Reds)
        OF—Max Carey (1922 Pirates)
        OF—Ty Cobb (1925 Tigers)
          C—Wilbert Robinson (1892 Baltimore)
          P—Harvey Haddix (1959 Pirates)

Adcock (July 31) collected 18 total bases on four home runs and a double. Stennett stroked seven hits—four singles, two doubles, and a triple—in seven at bats in a nine-inning game on September 16. Seitzer went six-for-six with two home runs, a double, and four runs scored on August 2. Burnett had seven singles and two doubles in 11 at bats in the 18-inning game on July 10. Ward holds the record for getting on base the most times in a nine-inning game (two singles, five walks, and one hit by a pitch on June 18). Carey shares the record for extra-inning games with Burnett: He had five singles, a double, and three walks in 18 innings on July 7. Cobb responded to a taunt that he could not hit the long ball by bashing three homers and adding a double and two singles (May 5). Robinson set the standard for Stennett by stroking six singles and a double in nine innings (June 10). Haddix pitched a perfect game for 12 1/3 innings before losing on an error, an intentional pass, and Joe Adcock's home run that became a double when he passed Hank Aaron on the bases.

—— GREATEST INNINGS ——

Some players did a full day's work in a single inning:

  1B—Ed Cartwright (1890 St. Louis AA)
  2B—Fred Pfeffer (1883 Cubs)
  3B—Ned Williamson (1883 Cubs)
  SS—Tom Burns (1883 Cubs)
  OF—Jim Lemon (1959 Senators)
  OF—Andre Dawson (1985 Expos)
  OF—Dale Murphy (1989 Braves)
   C—Joe Astroth (1950 Athletics)
   P—Tippy Martinez (1983 Orioles)

On September 6, 1883, the Cubs exploded for 18 runs in the seventh inning, the most ever in the major leagues. Among the record 18 hits they racked up in that inning were Pfeffer's two singles and a double, Williamson's two singles and a double, and Burns's two doubles and a home run. Cartwright drove in seven runs with grand slam and a three-run blast in the third inning on September 23. Lemon (September 5, third inning), Dawson (September 24, fifth inning), and Murphy (July 27, sixth inning) are the only three players to clout two homers good for six RBI in the same inning. Astroth (September 23, sixth inning) is the only catcher to drive in six runs in one frame. And Martinez picked off three Blue Jay runners in the 10th inning on August 24. (Infielder Lenn Sakata had been pressed into service behind the plate and the Blue Jays were taking big leads off him; besides, Martinez's enthusiasm for throwing to Sakata was under control. Sakata, however, hit a three-run homer in the bottom of the 10th to win the game.) Honorable mention to Gene Stephens, the only other player to collect three hits in an inning—two singles and a double—for the Red Sox in the seventh inning on June 18, 1953. Also to the only two catchers to hit two homers in an inning—Andy Seminick (eighth inning, June 2, 1949 Phillies) and John Boccabella (sixth inning, first game, July 6, 1973 Expos).

—— ALL-TIME SWITCHERS ——

These players both switched and fought.

        1B—Eddie Murray
        2B—Frankie Frisch
        3B—Pete Rose
        SS—Maury Wills
        OF—Mickey Mantle
        OF—Reggie Smith
        OF—Max Carey
          C—Ted Simmons
          P—Tony Mullane

Switch-hitting records held by these players include Frisch's .316 lifetime batting average, Rose's 230 hits with the Reds in 1973, and Carey's 140 runs scored with the 1922 Pirates. Mantle holds several switch-hitting records: 536 lifetime homers, 54 home runs in a season (1961), 130 RBIs in a season (1956), and highest slugging average (.705 in 1956). Mullane was both a switch-hitter and ambidextrous. On July 18, 1882, he started a game for Louisville (AA) throwing right-handed. For reasons lost to posterity, he switched to his left arm in the fourth inning—and won the game. This is the only time a pitcher threw with both arms in a game. Some notables who do not make this team are Rip Collins, George Davis, and Tommy Tucker, as well as Willie Wilson and Garry Templeton, the only players to collect 100 or more hits from each side of the plate in a single season. Templeton accomplished this with the Cardinals in 1979; Wilson did it the following year while playing for the Royals.

—— COMBINATIONS ——

The combination of offensive categories that has received the most attention in recent years is 40 home runs and 40 stolen bases. Some others are equally rare:

    1B—Jim Bottomley (1928 Cardinals)
    2B—Juan Samuel (1984–87 Phillies)
    3B—Eddie Mathews (1953, 1959 Braves)
    SS—Ernie Banks (1958–59 Braves)
    OF—Babe Ruth (1921 Yankees)
    OF—Ty Cobb (1911 Tigers)
    OF—Jose Canseco (1988 Athletics)
      C—Thurman Munson (1975–77 Yankees)
      P—Sandy Koufax (1963 Dodgers)

Bottomley is the only player ever to rack up more than 40 doubles, more than 30 home runs, and more than 20 triples in the same season. Samuel is the only player to reach double numbers in doubles, triples, home runs, and stolen bases in four consecutive seasons. Mathews is the only third baseman to hit 40 or more homers and bat over .300 twice. (The only other third baseman to do this was Al Rosen with the 1953 Indians.) Banks is the only shortstop to reach 40/.300 and he did it in two consecutive seasons. Who but Babe Ruth could have driven in and scored more than 170 runs in a single season? No one since Cobb has even approached 80 stolen bases and 140 RBI. Canseco is, of course, the charter—and only—member of the 40HR/40SB club. Campanella is the only catcher to reach 40/.300. Koufax is the only pitcher to combine 25 or more wins good for a won-lost percentage over .800 with more than 300 strikeouts and an earned run average below 2.00.

—— 100 WALKS, 100 HITS ——

Only 10 players have had more walks than hits with at least 100 of each in a season.

> 1B—Roy Cullenbine (1947 Tigers) 137 BB, 104 H
> 2B—Max Bishop (1929 Athletics) 128 BB, 110 H
> 3B—Eddie Yost (1956 Senators) 151 BB, 119 H
> SS—Eddie Joost (1947 Athletics) 114 BB, 111 H
> OF—Jimmy Wynn (1969 Astros) 148 BB, 133 H
> OF—Ted Williams (1954 Red Sox) 136 BB, 133 H
> OF—Mickey Mantle (1968 Yankees) 106 BB, 103 H
> C—Gene Tenace (1977 Padres) 125 BB, 102 H
> P—Elroy Face (1959 Pirates) 18 W, 10 Sv

Bishop accomplished this feat in four other seasons. Joost, Wynn, Mantle, and Tenace repeated once each. The only other players in this category are Eddie Stanky (1945 and 1946 Dodgers) and Hank Greenberg (1947 Pirates). Face had more wins than saves in relief—with both figures in double numbers.

—— BACK TO BACK MVPs ——

Only nine players have won the Most Valuable Player Award in back-to-back seasons—one for each position.

> 1B—Jimmie Foxx (1932–33 Athletics)
> 2B—Joe Morgan (1975–76 Reds)
> 3B—Mike Schmidt (1980–81 Phillies)
> SS—Ernie Banks (1958–59 Cubs)
> OF—Mickey Mantle (1956–57 Yankees)
> OF—Roger Maris (1960–61 Yankees)
> OF—Dale Murphy (1982–83 Braves)
> C—Yogi Berra (1954–55 Yankees)
> P—Hal Newhouser (1944–45 Tigers)

Foxx (1938 Red Sox), Mantle (1962 Yankees), Berra (1951 Yankees), and Schmidt (1986 Phillies) each won a third award.

6 The Worst

They tried, but they simply weren't up to it.

—— THE WORST CAREER HITTERS ——

The worst hitter in big league history for players having at least 1,000 at bats was catcher Bill Bergen, who toiled for the Reds and Dodgers between 1901 and 1911. His teammates are

      1B—John Boccabella (1963–74) .219
      2B—Rich Morales (1967–74) .195
      3B—Jackie Hernandez (1965–73) .208
      SS—Ray Oyler (1965–70) .175
      OF—Dave Nicholson (1960–67) .212
      OF—Rusty Torres (1971–80) .212
      OF—Vic Harris (1972–80) .217
        C—Bill Bergen (1901–11) .170
        P—Hugh Mulcahy (1935–1947) 45–89 (.336)

Bergen achieved his distinction in more than 3,000 at bats, almost twice as many as runnerup Harris. The only other major leaguers with at least 1,000 at bats and batting averages below .200 are catchers Fritz Buelow (.189) and Mike Ryan (.193). Insofar as all these position players were active during an expansion period (the creation of the American League in the cases of Bergen and Buelow), the chief villain here appears to be the general lowering of the major league talent pool. Among pitchers with at least 100 decisions, Rollie Naylor's career record of 42 wins and 83 losses gives him an identical winning percentage of .336.

—— THE WORST ——
SINGLE SEASON HITTERS

Although he turned in such glamorous yearly batting averages as .132, .139, and .159, Bill Bergen never quite managed the plate appearance minimum that would have qualified him for a batting title. The worst in an individual season are

    1B—Dave Kingman (1982 Mets) .204
    2B—Pete Childs (1902 Phillies) .194
    3B—Jerry Kenney (1970 Yankees) .193
    SS—John Gochnaur (1902 Indians) .185
    OF—Willie Kirkland (1962 Indians) .200
    OF—Curt Blefary (1968 Orioles) .200
    OF—Charlie Jamieson (1918 Athletics) .202
     C—Billy Sullivan (1908 White Sox) .191
     P—Jack Nabors (1916 Athletics) 1–21

Gochnaur has the most competition: His average was .18519, as against .18527 for Eddie Joost (1943 Braves) and .18547 for Ed Brinkman (1965 Senators). Mention should also be made of Dal Maxvill, who, although he failed to come up with a qualifying 400 at bats for the 1969 Cardinals, used his 372 plate appearances to compile an impressively unimpressive average of .175. Among the pitchers, Nabors's neighbors are Joe Harris, who put together a record of 2–21 for the 1906 Red Sox; John Coleman, who won 12 but who set the single-season loss record with 48 for the 1883 Phillies; and Gene Garber, whose 16 losses for the 1979 Braves are the most ever suffered by a relief pitcher.

—— THE VERY WORST ——

Randy Tate, a 1975 pitcher for the Mets, went hitless in 41 at bats to establish himself as the worst batter statistically in baseball history. But not all absolute zeroes were pitchers.

        1B—Red Gust (1911 Browns) 0–12
        2B—Ed Samcoff (1951 Athletics) 0–11
        3B—Ramon Conde (1962 White Sox) 0–16
        SS—Ceylon Wright (1916 White Sox) 0–18
        OF—Mike Potter (1976–77 Cardinals) 0–23
        OF—Jim Riley (1921 Browns, 1923 Senators) 0–14
        OF—Larry Littleton (1981 Indians) 0–23
         C—Roy Luebbe (1925 Yankees) 0–15
         P—Terry Felton (1979–82 Twins) 0–16

Felton's numbers are his won-lost record, the worst by a pitcher without a win. Honorable mention to Paul Dicken for his 0–13 strictly as a pinch hitter for the 1964 and 1966 Indians.

—— OUT OF SEASON ——

This is a lineup of players who went hitless for an entire season.

        1B—Frank Leja (1962 Angels)
        2B—Jim Driscoll (1972 Rangers)
        3B—Herman Bronkie (1912 Indians)
        SS—Ceylon Wright (1916 White Sox)
        OF—Cliff Carroll (1000 Pirates)
        OF—Fred Tauby (1937 Phillies)
        OF—Dave Bergman (1975 Yankees)
         C—Hal Finney (1936 Pirates)
         P—Bob Buhl (1962 Braves-Cubs)

Hitless at bats: Leja, 16; Driscoll, 18; Bronkie, 16; Wright, 18; Carroll and Tauby, 20; Bergman, 17; and Finney, 35. Also a nod to Bill McNulty (1969 Athletics), who matched Bergman's 17 fruitless appearances. Buhl's 0–70 makes it worth including a pitcher's offensive statistic.

—— NEGATIVE CAREER RECORDS ——

Some of these players were good enough to last, so they lasted long enough to be bad. The others were just bad.

        1B—Carl Yastrzemski
        2B—Rob Picciolo
        3B—Pete Rose
        SS—George McBride
        OF—Lou Brock
        OF—Hank Aaron
        OF—Tony Armas
         C—Ray Schalk
         P—Earl Whitehill

Yastrzemski's .285 career average is the lowest among players with 3,000 hits. Picciolo's mere 25 walks in 1,628 at bats is the worst ratio for players with at least 1,500 plate appearances. While he was compiling the most hits in baseball history, Rose was also making more outs (9,797) than anyone else. McBride has both the lowest lifetime batting average (.218) and the lowest slugging average (.264) among players with 4,000 at bats. Brock has the record for being thrown out stealing—307 times. Aaron has the mark for grounding into double plays—328 times. Armas owns the highest ratio of strikeouts (1,114) to walks (238) among players with 4,000 or more at bats—better than four and one-half to one. Schalk's .253 average is the lowest among nonpitchers in the Hall of Fame. Whitehill's 4.36 is not only the highest lifetime ERA for a pitcher with at least 3,500 innings pitched but it is also the only one over 4.00. Honorable mention to a pair of shortstops: Herman Long for his 1,037 errors, the most of any player at any position, and Tommy Thevenow, whose only homers in 4,164 at bats were inside the park job. This gives Thevenow the lowest total of four-baggers of any kind for players with 4,000 at bats and absolute primacy for players who never hit the ball out of the park.

—— NEGATIVE SEASON RECORDS ——

A potpourri of being the best at the worst.

1B—Ken Phelps (1984 Mariners)
2B—Tony Taylor (1964 Phillies)
3B—Piano Legs Hickman (1900 Giants)
SS—Dal Maxvill (1970 Cardinals)
OF—Mickey Rivers (1976 Yankees)
OF—Jim Rice (1984 Red Sox)
OF—Rickey Henderson (1982 Athletics)
C—Gene Tenace (1974 Athletics)
P—Dave Stewart (1988 Athletics)

Phelps's mere 51 runs batted in on 24 home runs established a new mark for wasting power. Taylor had only 350 assists. Hickman recorded the lowest fielding average (.836) of any player who appeared in at least 100 games. Maxvill's five doubles, seven extra base hits, and 89 total bases are all low-water marks for players appearing in at least 150 games. Rivers walked fewer times (13) than anyone else who has ever played in 150 games. Rice broke the record for hitting into the most double plays (36). Henderson was caught stealing 42 times. Tenace's 58 singles is the lowest total for any player appearing in 150 games. In the year of the balk, Stewart moved runners around a generous 16 times. Dishonorable mention to Larry Gardner (1920 Indians), whose 3 for 23 set the record for the lowest stolen base percentage (.130) for players who attempted at least 20 steals.

—— POWER SHORTAGE ——

A lineup of players who never hit a home run despite the ample number of at bats indicated.

    1B—Charlie Babb (1,180)
    2B—Irv Hall (1,904)
    3B—Mick Kelleher (1,081)
    SS—Tim Johnson (1,269)
    OF—Tom Oliver (1,931)
    OF—Rip Cannell (913)
    OF—Marty Callaghan (767)
     C—Roxy Walters (1,426)
     P—Robin Roberts (505 HRs allowed)

Roberts holds the mark for home runs yielded. Others who have batted 1,000 times without a homer are catcher Benny Bengough, and infielders Luis Gomez, Red Shannon, and Gil Torres.

—— HELPLESS HANDS ——

When it comes to runs batted in for a season, these players have been the most unproductive during a minimum of 400 at bats:

    1B—Ivy Griffin (1920 Athletics) 20
    2B—Don Blasingame (1965 Senators) 18
    3B—Bobby Byrne (1908 Cardinals) 14
    SS—Enzo Hernandez (1971 Padres) 12
    OF—Goat Anderson (1907 Pirates) 12
    OF—Clyde Milan (1909 Senators) 15
    OF—Jack Smith (1919 Cardinals) 15
     C—Oscar Stanage (1914 Tigers) 25
     P—Les Sweetland (1930 Phillies) 7.71 ERA

Sweetland's ERA is the highest for any pitcher who ever qualified for the category title. Just missing this team is the otherwise legendary Willie Keeler, who drove in a mere 17 runs for the 1907 Yankees.

—— BIBLE HITTERS ——

These players said "thou shalt not pass" more often than any others in a season, and so rarely walked during 400 at bats:

 1B—George Stovall (1909 Indians) 6
 2B—Whitey Alperman (1909 Dodgers) 2
 3B—Ollie O'Mara (1918 Dodgers) 7
 SS—Virgil Stallcup (1951 Reds) 6
 OF—Rube Oldring (1907 Athletics) 7
 OF—Shano Collins (1922 Red Sox) 7
 OF—Jesus Alou (1968 Giants) 7
  C—Ossee Schreckengost (1905 Athletics) 3
  P—Bob Feller (1938 Indians) 208 BBs

Feller's 208 walks in 278 innings is the single-season wildness mark. Despite their lack of discrimination at the plate, Oldring, Schreckengost, Collins, and Alou all batted higher than .260 in the years indicated.

—— LEAD FEET ——

A lineup of players with the fewest stolen bases for 1,000 games or more:

 1B—Dick Stuart (2–1,112)
 2B—Hal Lanier (11–1,106)
 3B—Rico Petrocelli (10–1,553)
 SS—Dal Maxvill (7–1,423)
 OF—Willie Horton (8–2,028)
 OF—Frank Howard (8–1,895)
 OF—Deron Johnson (11–1,765)
  C—Gus Triandos (1–1,206)
 *PRD—Spud Davis (6–1,458)

*Pinch Rundown. Honorable mentions to catcher Ernie Lombardi (8–1,853), first baseman Walt Dropo (5–1,288), and utility man Gary Sutherland (11–1,031).

—— MOST CAREER STRIKEOUTS ——

Strikeouts kill rallies, but not necessarily careers.

    1B—Tony Perez (1,867)
    2B—Bobby Grich (1,148)
    3B—Mike Schmidt (1,883)
    SS—Ernie Banks (1,236)
    OF—Reggie Jackson (2,597)
    OF—Willie Stargell (1,936)
    OF—Dave Kingman (1,816)
     C—Johnny Bench (1,278)
     P—Nolan Ryan (257 wild pitches)

Ryan's errant tosses are the major league mark. A dishonorable mention goes to Lou Brock, whose 1,730 strikeouts make him one of baseball's most curious leadoff men.

—— MOST SEASON STRIKEOUTS ——

As with career strikeout victims, the position players here are of relatively recent vintage.

    1B—Cecil Fielder (1990 Tigers) 182
    2B—Juan Samuel (1984 Phillies) 168
    3B—Mike Schmidt (1975 Phillies) 180
    SS—Zoilo Versalles (1965 Twins) 122
    OF—Bobby Bonds (1970 Giants) 189
    OF—Rob Deer (1987 Brewers) 186
    OF—Pete Incaviglia (1986 Rangers) 185
     C—Gary Alexander (1978 Athletics, Indians) 166
     P—Bill Stemmeyer (1886 Braves) 64 WPs.

Stemmeyer needed only 41 games to uncork his record number of wild pitches. Bonds not only holds the single-season mark but also occupies second place with his 187 whiffs for the 1969 Giants.

—— HIGHEST STRIKEOUT AVERAGE ——

The percentages next to these names are not batting averages, but strikeout averages during a minimum 4,000 at bats.

　1B—Dave Kingman (.272)
　2B—Juan Samuel (.237)
　3B—Dick Allen (.246)
　SS—Woodie Held (.235)
　OF—Gorman Thomas (.286)
　OF—Reggie Jackson (.263)
　OF—Bobby Bonds (.249)
　　C—Gene Tenace (.227)
　　P—Tom Zachary (.788)

Only five pitchers have issued more walks than strikeouts over at least 3,000 innings, and Zachary's 914 walks and 720 strikeouts is by far the worst. Kingman, Jackson, and Thomas all closed their careers with more strikeouts than hits.

—— WHAT DID THEY DO RIGHT? ——

Strikeouts per at bats? Try this team of players who went quickly from rookies to has beens.

　1B—Tom Brown (1963 Senators) 45–116
　2B—Al Lefevre (1920 Giants) 13–27
　3B—Jim Woods (1960–61 Phillies) 28–82
　SS—Ray Busse (1971–74 Astros) 54–155
　OF—Horace Speed (1975 Giants, 1978 Indians) 40–135
　OF—Jackie Warner (1966 Angels) 55–123
　OF—Jay Van Noy (1951 Cardinals) 6–7
　　C—Paul Ratliff (1963, 1970–71 Twins, 1971–72 Brewers)
　　　　119–297
　　P—Bruno Haas (1915 Athletics) 28 BBs in 14.1 innings

Haas holds the mark for walks per innings pitched. The highest batting average among the position players was Speed's .215.

—— ZERO ——

Not a number that appears in the record book very often, but these players managed to get one next to their names.

> 1B—Don Mattingly (1986 Yankees)
> 2B—Juan Samuel (1984 Phillies)
> 3B—Pete Rose (1975 Reds)
> SS—Rabbit Maranville (1922 Pirates)
> OF—Bill Holbert (1879 Syracuse, Troy)
> OF—Kirby Puckett (1985 Twins)
> OF—Herb Washington (1974 Athletics)
>   C—Choo Choo Coleman (1963 Mets)
>   P—Steve Bedrosian (1985 Braves)

Mattingly did not attempt a steal in 677 at bats. Samuel never sacrificed in 701 at bats. Rose had more at bats (662) than any other player with a .000 stolen-base percentage; he was zero for one. Maranville's zero home runs in 672 at bats is the all-time record for lack of power. Holbert had 244 at bats without a single extra-base hit. Puckett wasn't walked intentionally in 691 at bats. Washington played in the most games, 91, without ever coming to bat or playing in the field; he was, of course, the designated runner. Coleman batted 247 times without a double. Bedrosian started 37 games and required a relief pitcher in every one of them. Honorable mention to Cal Ripken (1989 Orioles), zero triples in 646 at bats; Craig Robinson (1973 Phillies), zero walks in 146 at bats; Sandy Alomar, Sr. (1971 Angels), zero hit-by-pitch in 689 at bats; Mike Phillips (1977 Mets-Cardinals), zero hits in 24 pinch-hit at bats; and Rose (1973 Reds), Puckett (1986 Twins), and Frank Taveras (1979 Pirates, Mets), zero sacrifice flies in 680 at bats.

7 What's in a Name?

Just some fun. The criteria for inclusion in these line-ups have little or nothing to do with ability. And, because this is all in fun, we took lots of liberties with positions; a single game at a position is sufficient to qualify.

—— THE NAME OF THE GAME ——

We would love to tell you that there was once a ballplayer named Barney Baseball. But we can't. Nor has there ever been a major leaguer named Nestor NoHit or Harry Homerun. Until there is, we'll go with:

```
1B—Vic Power
2B—Neal Ball
3B—Stan Jok
SS—Gene Alley
OF—Lee Walls
OF—John Strike
OF—Charlie Spikes
 C—Matt Batts
 P—Early Wynn
```

Bob Walk would be in the bullpen, but his name hardly inspires confidence. The reserves would, of course, be led by Johnny Bench. Cecil Fielder could come in for defensive purposes. Of course, Herb Score would be up in the announcers' booth doing the play by play.

—— EATING ——

An absolutely delicious ensemble:

    1B—Jackie Mayo
    2B—Coot Veal
    3B—Gene Leek
    SS—Joe Bean
    OF—Darryl Strawberry
    OF—Tony Curry
    OF—George Gerken
     C—Harry Sage
     P—Eddie Bacon

Bob Lemon is the manager. And, he has a well-balanced pitching staff with which to work: Herb Hash, Laurin Pepper, Hap Collard, Harry Colliflower, Frank Pears, Earl Huckleberry, and Mark Lemongello. And what about Johnny Grubb?

—— FISH ——

Quite a catch:

    1B—Lefty Herring
    2B—Chico Salmon
    3B—Ed Whiting
    SS—Bobby Sturgeon
    OF—Lip Pike
    OF—Kevin Bass
    OF—George Haddock
     C—Bert Blue
     P—Harry Eels

And, the Trout family (Dizzy and Steve), Clarence Pickrel, Thornton Kipper, and Preacher Roe round out the pitching staff.

—— BIRDS ——

Let's see how this lineup flies.

1B—George Crowe
2B—Jay Partridge
3B—Sammy Drake
SS—Alan Storke
OF—Bill Eagle
OF—Cannonball Crane
OF—Tom Parrott
C—Johnny Peacock
P—Joey Jay

The bullpen would include Craig Swan and Ed Hawk. And, honorable mention to all the Blue Jays of Toronto, Cardinals of St. Louis, and Orioles of Baltimore.

—— ANIMALS ——

Some ferocious, some tame, even a rodent:

1B—Fenton Mole
2B—Nellie Fox
3B—Bert Hogg
SS—Chicken Wolf
OF   Rob Deer
OF—Joe Rabbit
OF—Lyman Lamb
C—Bill Hart
P—Jim Panther

Panther barely beats out Lerton Pinto, Bob Moose, Al Doe, and Joe Gibbon. And, honorable mention to the Tigers of Detroit and the Cubs of Chicago.

—— COUNTRIES ——

The only thing more comprehensive than an all-star team is a United Nations team. For example:

    1B—Frank Brazill
    2B—Blas Monaco
    3B—Tim Ireland
    SS—Rafael Santo Domingo
    OF—Bob Holland
    OF—Buck Jordan
    OF—Moe Solomon
     C—Hugh Poland
     P—Osman France

And, in the bullpen, Mark Portugal throwing to Gus Brittain.

—— FOREIGN CITIES ——

While we're speaking internationally, you might want to consider:

    1B—Hal Danzig
    2B—Kelly Paris
    3B—Rudy York
    SS—Al Naples
    OF—Clyde Milan
    OF—Luis Medina
    OF—Gus Bergamo
     C—Benito Santiago
     P—Alex Madrid

Or even Lee Delhi, Bill Bergen, or Tom Oran.

—— NATURAL FORMATIONS ——

And on the eighth day, there was created this team:

    1B—Lester Rock
    2B—Elias Peak
    3B—Heinie Sand
    SS—Frank Mountain
    OF—John Stone
    OF—Tom Gulley
    OF—Paul Strand
     C—Marc Hill
     P—Jose Mesa

And a solid team it is—especially with Whitey Ford, Ernie Shore, Hub Knolls, and Luis Arroyo to round out the pitching staff.

—— WATER, WATER, EVERYWHERE ——

We don't think we're all wet with this one.

    1B—Boomer Wells
    2B—Pete Runnels
    3B—Hubie Brooks
    SS—Freddy Marsh
    OF—Harlin Pool
    OF—Ralph Pond
    OF—Mickey Rivers
     C—Steve Lake
     P—Jack Spring

No reserves because this isn't a very deep team.

—— THE GARDEN ——

Some of the following blossomed into pretty good players.

1B—Fred Stem
2B—Jake Flowers
3B—Pete Rose
SS—Donie Bush
OF—Jim Lillie
OF—Bob Seeds
OF—George Daisey
 C—Les Moss
 P—Dave Vineyard

Charlie Root, Billy Bowers, Bob Vines, Bob Sprout, and Jim Greengrass are also part of this squad.

—— THE MUSICAL ONES ——

An organ isn't the only musical instrument you'll find around the ballpark.

1B—Sam Horn
2B—Steve Sax
3B—Jim Tabor
SS—Les Bell
OF—Bill Sharp
OF—Jack Reed
OF—Charlie Chant
 C—Fred Carroll
 P—Frank Viola

If Viola runs into trouble there is always Bob Fife.

—— THE GOD SQUAD ——

If prayer helps, this team might never lose a game.

1B—Fred Abbott
2B—Johnny Priest
3B—Jimmy Sexton
SS—Max Bishop
OF—Maurice Archdeacon
OF—Dave Pope
OF—Bob Christian
 C—Bert Chaplin
 P—Howie Nunn

Jiggs Parson is in the bullpen; Harry Shriver is the manager and Johnny Podres the pitching coach. Honorable mention to all the St. Louis Cardinals and San Diego Padres. Could Jose Pagan make this team? Bless our souls, no.

—— THE OLD TESTAMENT ——

You can probably guess the genesis of this team.

1B—Jake Daniel
2B—Mike Eden
3B—Stan Benjamin
SS—Amado Samuel
OF—Babe Ruth
OF—Hank Aaron
OF—Moe Solomon
 C—Gerry Moses
 P—Bob Cain

The slugging of Ruth and Aaron would undoubtedly attract a lot of fans and provide the owners of the team with a tidy prophet.

—— ROYALTY ——

This lineup could become a dynasty.

1B—Walter Prince
2B—Lee King
3B—Ray Knight
SS—Harry Lord
OF—Bob Marquis
OF—Al Kaiser
OF—Mel Queen
C—Billy Earle
P—Martin Duke

Art Rebel just wouldn't fit in at this team's home park, the Kingdome. Honorable mention to all the Royals of Kansas City.

—— AROUND THE CASTLE ——

This team is subordinate to the previous one.

1B—Mike Squires
2B—Jimmy Stewart
3B—Pete Coachman
SS—Joe Chamberlain
OF—Mike Page
OF—Brett Butler
OF—Bob Usher
C—Darrell Porter
P—Vergil Jester

Joe Bowman and Bob Groom throw to Smokey Burgess and Jimmy Archer in the bullpen. But Joe Tinker and Tom Poorman can't break in.

—— MONEY PLAYERS ——

These days, financial information plays almost as large a role on the sports pages as hits, runs, and errors. So, this team was probably inevitable.

        1B—Norm Cash
        2B—John Happeny
        3B—Don Money
        SS—Ernie Banks
        OF—Elmer Pence
        OF—Art Ruble
        OF—Bobby Bonds
         C—Dick Rand
         P—John Sterling

Herman Franks is the manager. And honorable mention to Jim Shilling, Chet Nichols, Gary Fortune—and all the Bucs of Pittsburgh.

—— THE BARD ——

Name the Shakespearean plays in which the characters with the same names as these players appear, and you win the literary trivia prize.

        1B—Rudy York
        2B—Bill Regan
        3B—Fred Lear
        SS—Willie Miranda
        OF—John Titus
        OF—Carl Warwick
        OF—Pat Duncan
         C—Bruce Benedict
         P—Frank Bushey

Our revels now are ended.

—— THE BEST NAMES ——

Baseball seems to have had more than its share of colorful names:

1B—Peek-a-Boo Veach
2B—Creepy Crespi
3B—Coco Laboy
SS—Yats Wuestling
OF—Bevo LeBourveau
OF—Bingo Binks
OF—Gavvy Cravath
 C—Yam Yaryan
 P—Heinie Meine

Honorable mention to Putsy Caballero, Rivington Bisland, Pickles Dilhoeffer, Clyde Kluttz, Boots Poffenberger, Sig Jakucki, Cannonball Titcomb, Emil Bildilli, Garland Buckeye, Pea Ridge Day, Dooley Womack, and the ever lyrical Van Lingle Mungo.

—— WHO??? ——

If Alfred Pesano were to choose an all-star team, he could do far worse than:

1B—Harold Troyavesky
2B—Casimir Kwietniewski
3B—Andrew Nordstrom
SS—John Paveskovich
OF—Maximilian Carnarius
OF—Leopold Hornschmeyer
OF—Aloysius Szymanski
 C—Cornelius McGillicuddy
 P—Sanford Braun

Billy Martin would, in fact, have chosen Hal Trosky, Cass Michaels, Andy Carey, Johnny Pesky, Max Carey, Lee Magee, Al Simmons, Connie Mack, and Sandy Koufax.

—— THE ROBINSONS ——

It's possible to create teams out of Smiths, Johnsons, and Jacksons, but none can compare to:

    1B—Eddie Robinson
    2B—Jackie Robinson
    3B—Brooks Robinson
    SS—Craig Robinson
    OF—Frank Robinson
    OF—Floyd Robinson
    OF—Bill Robinson
     C—Wilbert Robinson
     P—Don Robinson

Ron, Hank, two Jeffs, and Humberto in the bullpen.

—— THE WILLIAMSES ——

The chief pretenders to the Robinsons would appear to be:

    1B—Billy Williams
    2B—Davey Williams
    3B—Matt Williams
    SS—Dib Williams
    OF—Ted Williams
    OF—Ken Williams
    OF—Cy Williams
     C—Earl Williams
     P—Stan Williams

The bullpen is headed by Mitch, the bench by Dick, Gus, Walt, and Jimmy.

—— NICKNAMES ——

No prizes for figuring out the real names here.

    1B—The Iron Horse
    2B—The Fordham Flash
    3B—The Wild Horse of the Osage
    SS—The Scooter
    OF—The Splendid Splinter
    OF—The Georgia Peach
    OF—The Sultan of Swat
     C—The Duke of Tralee
     P—The Big Train

The names are, of course, Lou Gehrig, Frankie Frisch, Pepper Martin, Phil Rizzuto, Ted Williams, Ty Cobb, Babe Ruth, Roger Bresnahan, and Walter Johnson.

—— LETTERS IN THE DIRT ——

Anyone can devise all-star teams by the letters of the alphabet, but how about a literally alphabetical lineup?

    1B—Jewel Ens
    2B—Frank Emmer
    3B—Roy Ellam
    SS—Shorty Dee
    OF—Walter Kay
    OF—Cecil Espy
    OF—Tommie Agee
     C—Jose Azcue
     P—Johnny Gee

The bullpen would include Joey Jay, Hod Eller, and Mark Esser, the bench Charlie See and Mike Ivie. A manager? How about one from Japan? . . . Oh, no. Forget it.

—— THE MENDOZA LINEUP ——

With his .200 or lower average, Mario Mendoza was usually at the cutoff point for the batting statistics printed on Sunday. This inspired George Brett to refer to .200-plus hitters as being across the Mendoza Line. Other players who have contributed their names to baseball expressions are:

    1B—Jake Stahl
    2B—Arlie Latham
    3B—George Moriarty
    SS—Mario Mendoza
    OF—Babe Ruth
    OF—Ted Williams
    OF—Russ Snyder
      C—Sam Brenegan
      P—Grover Lowdermilk

Stahl's refusal to play one day because of a foot injury was the first time someone was accused of jaking it. An Arlie Latham was once an infielder who couldn't catch up to a bleeder of a hit. To do a moriarty was to take a wild swing. Ruthian shots may still be seen at your local ballpark. When three infielders play between first and second, they are using Lou Boudreau's Williams shift. Four decades of Baltimore players have referred to rally-killing grounders to second as snyders. In his only major league game Brenegan couldn't nail a base stealer because he let the pitcher's throw hit him on the back of his hand; thus, to do a brenegan was to embarrass oneself in a debut. A lowdermilk was a pitcher without control, as in Grover's lifetime mark over nine seasons of 296 strikeouts and 376 walks.

8 Transactions

Trades, sales, waiver purchases, free agents, and everything else connected to the itinerant ways of major leaguers.

—— ONE FOR LESS THAN ONE ——

The following is a lineup of players traded straight up for other players, no third bodies or money involved. Guess the players for whom these were dealt:

1B—Don Hurst (1934 Phillies to Cubs)
2B—Randy Asadoor (1985 Rangers to Padres)
3B—Steve Demeter (1960 Tigers to Indians)
SS—Dick Tracewski (1965 Dodgers to Tigers)
OF—Ed Morgan (1938 Dodgers to Phillies)
OF—Gil Coan (1954 Senators to Orioles)
OF—Bris Lord (1910 Indians to Athletics)
 C—Joe Tipton (1949 White Sox to Athletics)
 P—Bob Chakales (1954 Indians to Orioles)

Both Hurst and Morgan were swapped for slugger Dolf Camilli. Asadoor went for future bullpen ace Mitch Williams. Demeter netted the Tigers batting champion Norm Cash. Tracewski was Los Angeles's payment for relief ace Phil Regan. Coan went to Baltimore for Roy Sievers, who quickly became Washington's main power source for many years. In exchange for Lord, the Indians received no less than Shoeless Joe Jackson. Tipton's cost to the Athletics was Nellie Fox. Without Chakales, the Indians would have never had Vic Wertz. Dishonorable mention to the Chicago Cubs' front office of 1917 for acquiring Dode Paskert from the Phillies for the exhorbitant price of Cy Williams.

—— FIRSTS ——

These players all represented firsts of one transaction kind or another. Remember what they were?

    1B—Dick Gernert (1959 Red Sox to Cubs)
    2B—Davey Johnson (1977 Phillies)
    3B—Ron Santo (1973 Cubs to Angels)
    SS—Johnny Peters (1880 Cubs to Providence)
    OF—Rick Monday (1965 Athletics)
    OF—Joel Youngblood (1982 Mets to Expos)
    OF—Kirk Gibson (1988 Tigers to Dodgers)
     C—King Kelly (1887 Cubs to Braves)
     P—Keith Comstock (Career)

Gernert's swap for Jim Marshall and Dave Hillman was the first modern interleague trade not requiring waivers. Johnson was the first to return to the majors from Japan. Santo was the first 5-and-10 player to refuse a trade; he eventually went to the White Sox instead of the Angels. Peters was the very first "player to be named later," in a trade for catcher Lew Brown. Monday was the first player to be chosen in the college draft. Youngblood was the first player to get hits for two teams in two different cities on the same day. Gibson was the first second-look free agent to switch teams after a collusion settlement between owners and players. Kelly was the first player to be sold—for $10,000. Comstock has no rivals for having been released—by teams in the National League, the American League, various AAA and AA minor leagues, Japan, Mexico, and Venezuela. Honorable mention to Dick Wakefield of the 1941 Tigers, baseball's first bonus baby, and Dick Woodson of the 1974 Twins, the first player to go to salary arbitration, which he won.

—— ON THE ROAD ——

A lineup of players who changed uniforms most often. Note that it does not include Dick Littlefield or Bob Miller.

>   1B—Jack Doyle (12 times)
>   2B—Joe Quinn (12 times)
>   3B—Jim Donnelly (11 times)
>   SS—Bones Ely (8 times)
>   OF—Tommy Davis (12 times)
>   OF—Tom Brown (11 times)
>   OF—Deron Johnson (10 times)
>   C—Deacon McGuire (14 times)
>   P—Bobo Newsom (17 times)

Doyle played for Columbus (AA); Baltimore, Washington (twice), Cleveland, Brooklyn, Philadelphia, Chicago, and New York (3 times) in the NL; and the Yankees in the AL. Quinn labored for St. Louis (UA); the Cardinals (4 times), Baltimore, Cleveland, Braves (twice), and Reds in the NL; Boston (PL); and Washington (AL). Donnelly was with Kansas City (UA); Indianapolis, St. Louis, Columbus (AA); Kansas City, Detroit, Washington, Baltimore, Pittsburgh, New York, St. Louis (NL). Ely was with Louisville and Syracuse (AA); the NL's Buffalo, Brooklyn, St. Louis, Pittsburgh; Philadelphia and Washington in the AL. After 8 seasons with the Dodgers, Davis moved to the Mets, Astros, Cubs (twice), White Sox, Pilots, A's (twice), Orioles, Angels, and Royals. Brown played for Baltimore, Columbus, Pittsburgh, Boston (AA); Boston (PL); and Indianapolis, Louisville, Washington, Pittsburgh, Boston, St. Louis (NL). Johnson labored for the Yankees, KC A's, Oakland A's, Brewers, White Sox, Red Sox (twice), Reds, Braves, Phillies. McGuire was with Toledo, Cleveland, Rochester, Washington (AA); NL's Detroit (twice), Washington, Philadelphia, Brooklyn; AL's Detroit (twice), New York, Boston, Cleveland. Newsom played for Brooklyn (twice), Browns (three times), Senators (five times), Cubs, Giants, Red Sox, Tigers, Athletics (twice), and Yankees.

—— STAYING HOME ——

Players who spent lengthy careers with just one team include:

        1B—Cap Anson (22 years Cubs)
        2B—Charlie Gehringer (19 years Tigers)
        3B—Brooks Robinson (23 years Orioles)
        SS—Luke Appling (20 years White Sox)
        OF—Carl Yastrzemski (23 years Red Sox)
        OF—Mel Ott (22 years Giants)
        OF—Al Kaline (22 years Tigers)
         C—Johnny Bench (17 years Reds)
         P—Walter Johnson (21 years Senators)

Robinson and Yastrzemski share the record for the longest career with just one club. Bill Dickey of the Yankees and Ted Lyons of the White Sox tie Bench and Johnson, respectively, but they played fewer games than the battery selected.

—— ELEPHANT CEMETERY ——

Identified with one team during their entire careers, these players put on other uniforms for their very last seasons.

        1B—Harmon Killebrew (21 years Senators, Twins)
        2B—Dave Concepcion (18 years Reds)
        3B—Ron Santo (14 years Cubs)
        SS—Mark Belanger (17 years Orioles)
        OF—Sam Rice (19 years Senators)
        OF—Zack Wheat (18 years Dodgers)
        OF—Yogi Berra (18 years Yankees)
         C—Gabby Hartnett (19 years Cubs)
         P—Bob Friend (15 years Pirates)

Killebrew closed out with the Royals; Concepcion with the Angels; Santo, the White Sox; Belanger, the Dodgers; Rice, the Indians; Wheat, the Athletics; Berra, the Mets; Hartnett, the Giants; and Friend, the Mets and Yankees.

—— RENT-A-CHAMPION ——

Because of trades, free-agency opportunities, and franchise shifts, some players have spent only one season with particular teams—but led the league in offensive categories while waiting to move on.

> 1B—Deacon White (1877 Braves)
> 2B—Rogers Hornsby (1928 Braves)
> 3B—Tommy Harper (1969 Pilots)
> SS—Paul Radford (1887 New York AA)
> OF—Reggie Jackson (1976 Orioles)
> OF—Ron Leflore (1980 Expos)
> OF—Tom Brown (1891 Boston AA)
>   C—Ernie Lombardi (1942 Braves)
>   P—Mark Baldwin (1889 Columbus AA)

Both White and Hornsby captured twin batting and slugging titles. Harper spent his only year in Seattle leading the league in stolen bases. Radford walked more than anybody else in the American Association. Jackson led up to his free-agency deal with the Yankees by winning the slugging crown. LeFlore stole more bases than any other National Leaguer. Brown was first in triples, runs scored, and plate appearances. Lombardi won the batting title. Baldwin led the league in both strikeouts and game appearances. Among those deserving honorable mention are George Case (1946 Indians) for leading the AL in steals; Hank Greenberg (1947 Pirates) for most walks; and Joe Start (1878 Cubs) for most hits. Albie Pearson was the Senators' Rookie of the Year in 1958, but was traded to the Orioles only a few games into 1959.

—— LEAGUE LEADERS ——

Even being traded in the middle of a season has not prevented the following players from leading the league in important categories:

1B—Dale Alexander (1932 Red Sox, Tigers)
2B—Red Schoendienst (1957 Giants, Braves)
3B—Heinie Zimmerman (1916 Cubs, Giants)
SS—Pop Smith (1889 Pirates, Braves)
OF—Harry Walker (1947 Phillies, Cardinals)
OF—Gus Zernial (1951 White Sox, Athletics)
OF—Willie McGee (1990 Cardinals, Athletics)
C—Frankie Hayes (1945 Athletics, Indians)
P—Rick Honeycutt (1983 Rangers, Dodgers)

Alexander and Walker are the only players to have won batting championships for combined teams in the same league. McGee sat on his league-leading average in the NL while playing in the AL. Schoendienst led the NL in hits, Zimmerman in runs batted in. Zernial not only matched Zimmerman's feat but also led in home runs. Hayes was the AL leader for most double plays by a catcher. Honeycutt, like McGee, switched leagues in midseason and so was something of a bystander during the final weeks of his ERA crown. On the negative side, Smith didn't allow his trade to Boston to prevent him from leading the NL in strikeouts. Honorable mentions to: John Anderson (1090 Dodgers and Washington) for leading in both slugging average and triples; Roy Cullenbine (1945 Indians and Tigers) for walking the most in the AL; Red Barrett (1945 Braves and Cardinals) for most complete games; and Ron Herbel (1970 Padres and Mets) for most appearances by a pitcher.

—— FAST SHUFFLES ——

Or, how to sell the Brooklyn Bridge to your rivals.

    1B—Dixie Walker (1948 Dodgers to Pirates)
    2B—Jimmy Jordan (1933 Cardinals to Dodgers)
    3B—Garvin Hamner (1947 Phillies to Browns)
    SS—Rey Quinones (1989 Mariners to Pirates)
    OF—Johnny Rizzo (1938 Cardinals to Pirates)
    OF—Mark Chartak (1942 Yankees to Senators)
    OF—Jim Greengrass (1955 Reds to Phillies)
     C—Don Padgett (1941 Cardinals to Dodgers)
     P—Dizzy Dean (1938 Cardinals to Cubs)

Branch Rickey persuaded his front office counterparts that the over-the-hill Walker's only problem was that he didn't want to play on an integrated team; that the anemic-hitting Jordan's only problem was St. Louis manager Frankie Frisch; that it wasn't Rizzo, but another farmhand named Slaughter, who had a sore arm; that Padgett wouldn't be drafted by the Army when he already had been; and that the seriously injured Dean was worth Curt Davis, Clyde Shoun, and $200,000. The Browns thought they were obtaining Granny Hamner because the Phillies had listed the lesser brother simply as "G. Hamner." The Mariners did not dwell on Quinones's emotional problems; Pittsburgh released him three weeks after surrendering three players for him. Hearing that the Yankees were about to deal Chartak to St. Louis for $14,000, Clark Griffith sounded the patriotic note that wartime Washington needed an able first baseman-outfielder, got him for $12,000, then passed him on to the Browns for the original $14,000. Cincinnati neglected to mention that Greengrass had phlebitis and was barely able to walk.

—— BEST INTERESTS ——

The following players donned or did not don uniforms because of the "best interests of baseball":

1B—Jason Thompson (1981 Pirates to Yankees)
2B—Benny McCoy (1943 Tigers to Athletics)
3B—Johnny Berardino (1947 Browns to Senators)
SS—Steve Mesner (1943 Reds to Dodgers)
OF—Joe Rudi (1976 Athletics to Red Sox)
OF—Minnie Minoso (1990 White Sox)
OF—Kip Selbach (1904 Senators to Red Sox)
C—Bennie Warren (1942 Phillies to Pirates)
P—Vida Blue (1976 Athletics to Yankees)

Bowie Kuhn detected irregularities in a planned three-way deal among the Pirates, Yankees, and Angels and said no to Thompson's swap for Jim Spencer. Kuhn also scotched Charlie Finley's intentions of selling Rudi and Blue for $1 million each. Judge Landis ruled that the Tigers had been keeping McCoy in their farm system illegally and so had no right to exchange him for Wally Moses. Landis also killed the sales of Mesner and Warren because their prospective buyers were unaware that the players had been drafted into the Army. Berardino got Happy Chandler to cancel his trade to Washington for Gerry Priddy by saying he was going to retire to become an actor; as soon as the deal was scratched, Berardino unretired himself to go off to Cleveland where Bill Veeck's blandishments included a screen test. Fay Vincent ruled that the aged Minoso's plan to appear as a six-decade player was merely a stunt. After suspending the talented Selbach for inert play with the last-place Senators, American League President Ban Johnson encouraged his trade to Boston so Selbach could flourish and the fledgling league as a whole would look more competitive against the NL.

—— MET THIRD BASEMEN ——

Nolan Ryan for Jim Fregosi and Amos Otis for Joey Foy weren't the only trades the Mets made for third basemen. Others given away in that quest (with the players received following) were

　　1B—Richie Hebner (Phil Mankowski)
　　2B—Manny Lee (Ray Knight)
　　3B—Don Zimmer (Cliff Cook)
　　SS—Felix Mantilla (Pumpsie Green)
　　OF—Amos Otis (Joey Foy)
　　OF—Dave Kingman (Bobby Valentine)
　　OF—Frank Thomas (Wayne Graham)
　　C—Joe Nolan (Leo Foster)
　　P—Nolan Ryan (Jim Fregosi)

The Knight deal paid dividends in 1986. And then there was the 1985 swap of Walt Terrell to Detroit for Howard Johnson.

— NEW YORK, NEW YORK, NEW YORK —

Until Brooklyn is granted another franchise, this is likely to remain as the lineup of players on three New York teams.

　　1B—Fred Merkle (Giants, Dodgers, Yankees)
　　2B—Tony Lazzeri (Giants, Dodgers, Yankees)
　　3B—Dude Esterbrook (Giants, Dodgers, New York AA)
　　SS—Candy Nelson (Giants, Brooklyn AA, New York AA)
　　OF—Willie Keeler (Giants, Dodgers, Yankees)
　　OF—Lefty O'Doul (Giants, Dodgers, Yankees)
　　OF—Benny Kauff (Giants, Yankees, Brooklyn FL)
　　C—Zack Taylor (Giants, Dodgers, Yankees)
　　P—Burleigh Grimes (Giants, Dodgers, Yankees)

Honorable mentions to Jack Doyle and Sal Maglie, who played for the Giants, Dodgers, and Yankees. Manager: Casey Stengel, who played for the Dodgers and Giants and who managed the Dodgers, Yankees, and Mets.

—— MORE BLUE THAN ORANGE ——

When it came to former Ebbets Field and Polo Grounds players, the Mets showed a preference for ex-Dodgers over ex-Giants.

1B—Gil Hodges
2B—Charlie Neal
3B—Don Zimmer
SS—Chico Fernandez
OF—Duke Snider
OF—Willie Mays
OF—Eddie Bressoud
C—Joe Pignatano
P—Roger Craig

Only Mays (who came many years later) and Bressoud (who played only one game in the outfield in his career) had been on the New York Giants prior to the Mets. The reliever is another Ebbets Field alumnus, Clem Labine.

—— YANKEES, NO HOME ——

Not all the players who wore Yankee pinstripes have a right to be called Bronx Bombers.

1B—Bob Oliver
2B—Fernando Gonzalez
3B—Bill Sudakis
SS—Eddie Brinkman
OF—Alex Johnson
OF—Bobby Bonds
OF—Walt Williams
C—Ed Herrmann
P—Cecil Upshaw

This is, of course, a lineup of players who never wore a Yankee uniform in Yankee Stadium because they toiled at Shea Stadium in 1974 and/or 1975 while the Bronx park was being revamped. Manager: Bill Virdon.

—— THE RIVALS ——

Babe Ruth wasn't the only prize the Yankees swiped off their Red Sox rivals in the good old days.

1B—Babe Dahlgren
2B—Mike McNally
3B—Joe Dugan
SS—Everett Scott
OF—Roy Johnson
OF—Patsy Dougherty
OF—Babe Ruth
 C—Wally Schang
 P—Red Ruffing

For minimal considerations, Boston also yielded to New York Waite Hoyt, Joe Bush, Herb Pennock, Sam Jones, Wilcy Moore, Carl Mays, and Sparky Lyle.

—— THE KC CONNECTION ——

In the 1950s, the Yankees came as close to having a major league farm club as any team ever has. Among the Kansas City Athletics who ended up in New York were

1B—Harry Simpson
2B—Joe DeMaestri
3B—Hector Lopez
SS—Clete Boyer
OF—Bob Cerv
OF—Roger Maris
OF—Enos Slaughter
 C—Wilmer Shantz
 P—Ryne Duren

The pitching staff would also include Bobby Shantz, Art Ditmar, Ralph Terry, Bud Daley, Virgil Trucks, and Duke Maas.

—— LOYAL CANADIANS ——

Since the Expos have been around only since 1969 and the Blue Jays only since 1977, not too many players have worn both Canadian uniforms.

1B—Tommy Hutton
2B—Damaso Garcia
3B—Tom Lawless
SS—Hector Torres
OF—Ron Fairly
OF—Mitch Webster
OF—Al Oliver
 C—Ken Macha
 P—Dale Murray

The bench would feature Tony Solaita, Tony Johnson and Reggie Williams.

—— HUBBER—HUBBERS ——

For all its deficiencies behind the plate, this lineup of men who wore the uniforms of both the Braves and Red Sox in Boston has it all over New York and Canada.

1B—Stuffy McInnis
2B—Bucky Walters
3B—Jimmy Collins
SS—Rabbit Warstler
OF—Babe Ruth
OF—Al Simmons
OF—Chick Stahl
 C—Fred Lake
 P—Cy Young

The bench includes Wes Ferrell, Buck Freeman, and Roy Johnson.

—— TRADED NOT TO PLAY ——

Many teams have traded players not to acquire other players or cash, but managers. For example:

    1B—Gil Hodges (1963 Mets to Senators)
    2B—Eddie Stanky (1951 Giants to Cardinals)
    3B—Bucky Harris (1928 Senators to Tigers)
    SS—Solly Hemus (1958 Phillies to Cardinals)
    OF—Chuck Tanner (1976 Athletics to Pirates)
    OF—Pete Rose (1984 Expos to Reds)
    OF—Frank Robinson (1974 Angels to Indians)
    C—Mickey Cochrane (1933 Athletics to Tigers)
    P—Christy Mathewson (1916 Giants to Reds)

Hodges cost the Senators Jimmy Piersall. (Five years later, the Mets surrendered pitcher Bill Denehy to get Hodges back to manage them.) Stanky cost the Cardinals pitcher Max Lanier and outfielder Chuck Diering. Harris went for infielder Jack Warner. Hemus was swapped for infielder Gene Freese. Tanner, the only member of this lineup already retired when he was swapped, brought the A's catcher Manny Sanguillen. Rose went home in a deal for infielder Tom Lawless. Robinson, who had to wait out the final two weeks of the 1974 season before taking over in Cleveland the following year, was exchanged for catcher Ken Suarez and outfielder Rusty Torres. Cochrane's move to the Tigers cost them catcher Johnny Pasek and $100,000. Mathewson, infielder Bill McKechnie, and outfielder Edd Roush (all three of them future Hall of Famers) were swapped for infielder Buck Herzog and outfielder Red Killefer. Honorable mention to the 1960 trade that saw Cleveland manager Joe Gordon and his coach Jo-Jo White sent to the Tigers in exchange for manager Jimmy Dykes and coach Luke Appling.

—— NO, THANKS ——

Some players have just said no when they've been traded.

1B—Donn Clendenon (1969 Expos to Astros)
2B—Jackie Robinson (1956 Dodgers to Giants)
3B—Billy Cox (1955 Orioles to Indians)
SS—Joe Tinker (1913 Dodgers to Reds)
OF—Jake Stahl (1907 Senators to White Sox)
OF—Mike Donlin (1912 Pirates to Phillies)
OF—Ray Powell (1923 Braves to Phillies)
C—Sammy White (1960 Red Sox to Indians)
P—Preacher Roe (1954 Dodgers to Orioles)

Robinson, Cox, Donlin, Powell, White, and Roe retired rather than go. Clendenon was replaced in the deal and then traded to the Miracle Mets. Stahl was placated only when the White Sox immediately redealt him to the Yankees. Tinker demanded money and jumped to the Federal League when he didn't get it.

—— NO RESPECT ——

Some recent stars had to wait a very long time before their names were picked at the annual amateur draft.

1B—Keith Hernandez (1971 Cardinals) 42d rnd.
2B—Glenn Hubbard (1975 Braves) 20th rnd.
3B—Vance Law (1978 Pirates) 38th rnd.
SS—Ryne Sandberg (1978 Phillies) 20th rnd.
OF—Bill Russell (1966 Dodgers) 37th rnd.
OF—Ken Griffey, Sr. (1969 Reds) 29th rnd.
OF—Brett Butler (1979 Braves) 23d rnd.
C—Bob Boone (1969 Phillies) 20th rnd.
P—Bruce Sutter (1970 Senators) 21st rnd.

Figure it this way: In 1971, there were 41 rounds of 24 teams picking players before St. Louis grabbed Hernandez. That's almost 1,000 players deemed better than the future MVP.

—— HARD TO GET ——

Not all college players have been swept off their feet by the annual major league draft. In fact, some of them made mini-careers out of saying no before accepting big league offers.

1B—Luis Medina
2B—Al Newman
3B—Craig Worthington
SS—Scott Fletcher
OF—Hubie Brooks
OF—Greg Vaughn
OF—Oddibe McDowell
C—Charlie O'Brien
P—Scott Ruskin

Medina said no to the Mets twice, and the Yankees, Reds, Athletics, and Astros before signing with the Indians. Newman preferred the Expos to the Angels, Rangers, and Mets. Worthington rejected the Mets, Astros, and Cubs before saying yes to the Orioles. The Dodgers, Athletics, and Astros preceded Fletcher's choice of the Cubs. For Brooks it was the Mets, not the Expos, Royals, White Sox (twice), or Athletics. Vaughn changed his mind about the Brewers after having rejected them, the Cardinals, Pirates, and Angels. McDowell said no to the Cardinals, Rangers, Yankees, Blue Jays, and Twins before accepting a second Texas offer. O'Brien went with the Brewers rather than the Rangers, Mariners, or Athletics. Ruskin landed with the Pirates after turning down the Reds, Rangers, Indians, and Expos.

9 Where or When

This chapter focuses not so much on what happened as on in which city or ballpark it happened or under what circumstances.

—— HISTORIC FIRSTS ——

A relatively easy way of getting into the record book is to have been around for the first major league game.

> 1B—Tim Murnane (1876 Braves)
> 2B—Ross Barnes (1876 Cubs)
> 3B—Ned Williamson (1884 Cubs)
> SS—George Wright (1876 Braves)
> OF—Jim O'Rourke (1876 Braves)
> OF—Ollie Pickering (1901 Indians)
> OF—Babe Herman (1935 Reds)
>   C—Tim McGinley (1876 Braves)
>   P—Lou Knight (1876 Philadelphia)

In the very first National League game on April 22, 1876, between Boston and Philadelphia, Murnane stole the first base; Wright, the very first batter of all, grounded out to short; and O'Rourke was the first to get a hit (a two-out single in the first inning). McGinley was the first both to strike out and to score a run, and Knight was the first to deliver a pitch. Ten days later, Barnes became the first player to hit a home run. On May 30, 1884, Williamson went into the books as the first player to hit three homers in a single contest. Pickering was the first American Leaguer to stand up at home plate in the AL inaugural between Cleveland and Chicago on April 24, 1901. Herman hit the first homer in a major league night game on July 10, 1935.

—— UNFAMILIAR SETTINGS ——

Teams sometimes moved home games to escape Sunday blue laws, poor attendance, or bizarre situations.

        1B—Roger Connor (1881 Troy)
        2B—Hobe Ferris (1902 Red Sox)
        3B—Roger Bresnahan (1902 Orioles)
        SS—Monte Ward (1889 Giants)
        OF—Patsy Dougherty (1904 Yankees)
        OF—Buck Freeman (1903 Red Sox)
        OF—Elmer Flick (1903 Indians)
         C—Chief Zimmer (1903 Phillies)
         P—George Mullin (1903 Tigers)

Connor hit the first major league grand slam home run in a Troy home game played across the Hudson River in Albany. Ferris went four for five to help spoil one of Cleveland's two home games played in Ft. Wayne. Bresnahan homered to ruin another Cleveland home-away-from-home game, this time in Dayton's only major league game. In 1889 New York City evicted the Giants from the Polo Grounds to build a road through the stadium; led by Ward, their captain, the Giants won the post-season championship against Brooklyn (AA) at the St. George Cricket Grounds on Staten Island in the only Staten Island Ferry World Series. Dougherty contributed three hits toward a New York victory over the Tigers in Newark's only American League game. Freeman's homer, triple, three singles, and six RBI buried Cleveland in the third and last game the Indians played in Canton. Flick stroked three hits including a triple as the Indians beat the Yankees in their second Columbus home game. Manager Zimmer was two for three and stole a base at the age of 42, but the "hometown" Braves won the only 20th-century major league game played in Providence. Mullin won Detroit home games in both Toledo, his hometown, and Grand Rapids.

—— BOTH LEAGUES ——

Frank Robinson was the first black manager in both the National and American leagues, but that is only one of his accomplishments in both circuits. Trivia experts will know what these players succeeded in doing in both major leagues.

1B—Bob Watson
2B—Nap Lajoie
3B—Darrell Evans
SS—Bill Almon
OF—Frank Robinson
OF—Sam Crawford
OF—Ron LeFlore
C—Gus Triandos
P—Jim Bunning

Watson is the only player to have hit for the cycle in both leagues (1977 Astros and 1979 Red Sox). Lajoie led the league in RBI while playing for the 1898 Phillies, the 1901 Athletics, and the 1904 Indians. Evans is the only one to have belted 40 homers in a season in each league (1973 Braves and 1985 Tigers). On a negative note, Almon led both leagues in errors (1977 Padres and 1982 White Sox in a tie with Alfredo Griffin). Robinson did just about everything in both leagues—being named MVP (1961 Reds and 1965 Orioles), leading each league in slugging (1960–62 Reds and 1966 Orioles), and leading the league in runs scored (1956, 1962 Reds and 1966 Orioles). In the pre-Ruth era, Crawford led each league in homers (1901 Reds and 1908 Tigers). LeFlore is the only one to have led each league in stolen bases (1978 Tigers and 1980 Expos). Triandos was the first to catch no-hitters in both leagues, Hoyt Wilhelm (1958 Orioles) was first in the AL and Jim Bunning (1964 Phillies) in the NL. (Jeff Torborg subsequently did it with Sandy Koufax and Nolan Ryan.) Bunning, the pitching equivalent of Robinson, won more than 100 games, pitched no-hitters (1958 Tigers and 1964 Phillies), and struck out more than 1,000 batters for both the Nationals and the Americans.

—— BALLPARK BAPTISMS (NL) ——

Civic leaders love to celebrate the opening of ballparks. These players had an extra reason for celebrating:

  1B—Vic Saier (April 20, 1916) Cubs
  2B—Otto Knabe (April 9, 1913) Phillies
  3B—Dick Allen (April 12, 1965) Phillies
  SS—Ed Spiezio (April 8, 1969) Padres
  OF—Wally Post (April 10, 1962) Reds
  OF—Willie Stargell (April 17, 1964) Pirates
  OF—Rico Carty (June 30, 1970) Braves
   C—Joe Torre (April 12, 1966) Braves
   P—Sam Jones (April 12, 1960) Giants

Saier's 11th-inning hit was Chicago's margin of difference over Cincinnati in the Wrigley Field opener. Knabe's double and an error in the outfield provided the only run for Johnny Seaton's opening day shutout at Ebbets Field in Brooklyn. Allen hit the first indoors home run at the Astrodome, and it gave Philadelphia a win over Houston. The unlikely Spiezio christened Jack Murphy Stadium with San Diego's first hit and first home run, enough to give the Padres a 2–1 win. Post dampened the Dodger Stadium opener by hitting a decisive three-run homer. Stargell went four for five with a homer to ruin the Mets' opener at Shea Stadium. Carty's homer and four runs batted in made the Reds wish they had opened Riverfront Stadium the next day. Despite Torre's long ball hitting, Atlanta went down to defeat in its first home opener; Torre's two solo blasts came up against a two-run shot from the same Stargell who had left Shea Stadium fans dejected two years before. Jones won a masterful 3–1 game over the Cardinals in the first game ever played in Candlestick Park.

—— BALLPARK BAPTISMS (AL) ——

Players who have distinguished themselves in inaugural games in American League ballparks include:

1B—Pop Dillon (April 25, 1901) Tigers
2B—Steve Yerkes (April 20, 1912) Red Sox
3B—Vern Stephens (April 15, 1954) Orioles
SS—Mark Belanger (April 17, 1968) Orioles
OF—Babe Ruth (April 18, 1923) Yankees
OF—George Stone (July 1, 1910) Browns
OF—Ty Cobb (April 20, 1912) Tigers
  C—Mickey Cochrane (July 31, 1932) Athletics
  P—Andy Messersmith (April 7, 1970) Angels

Dillon saved the opening of old Bennett Field with a double in the bottom of the ninth that climaxed a 10-run comeback and a 14–13 victory for the Tigers. Yerkes had five hits to help the Red Sox win the Fenway Park opener. Stephens hit a big homer to help Baltimore open Memorial Stadium on a winning note. Belanger homered to help spoil the opening game at the Big A in Anaheim. Ruth hit the first of his many Yankee Stadium homers in the first game in the Bronx. Stone helped dampen the spirits of Chicago fans by collecting a single, double, and triple to boost St. Louis to a victory in the Comiskey Park opener. Cobb worked two double steals with Sam Crawford, including a steal of home, in the first Tiger Stadium game. Cochrane batted in the lone run in the eighth inning of Lefty Grove's 1–0 masterpiece over Cleveland in the first Municipal Stadium contest. Messersmith hurled a four hitter against the Brewers in California's grim 12–0 win in Milwaukee's first AL County Stadium game. Honorable mention to John Mayberry, who homered and drove in four runs in Kansas City's 12–1 victory over Texas in the 1973 inaugural at Royals Stadium and to Joe Rudi of the Angels who had three hits and four RBI in the 1977 indoor opener at the Seattle Kingdome.

—— THE BEST YEAR OF THEIR LIVES ——

In 1945, these players were the cream of the crop. Two years later, with the last veteran home from the Second World War, not one of them was even on a major league roster.

1B—Nick Etten (Yankees)
2B—Dutch Meyer (Indians)
3B—Chuck Workman (Braves)
SS—Glenn Crawford (Cardinals, Phillies)
OF—Buster Adams (Phillies, Cardinals)
OF—Jimmy Wasdell (Phillies)
OF—Bobby Estalella (Athletics)
 C—Frank Mancuso (Browns)
 P—Roger Wolff (Senators)

Etten hit .285 with 18 home runs and 111 RBI. Meyer batted .292. Workman worked 25 homers and 87 RBI into his steady .274 average. Crawford, who split his time between the outfield and shortstop, came in at .292 and struck out only 15 times in more than 300 at bats. Adams hit .287 with 22 home runs, 109 RBI, and 104 runs scored. Wasdell batted an even .300 and drove in 60 runs. Estalella finished one point below the magic circle at .299, but he also walked 74 times. Mancuso contributed a solid .268 for a catcher. The knuckleballer Wolff won 20 and lost 10.

—— FOUR DECADES ——

Only 21 players have appeared in box scores throughout four different decades. Two of them—Nick Altrock and Minnie Minoso—also appeared in a fifth decade, if only as publicity stunts.

1B—Bill Buckner (1960s–1990s)
2B—Kid Gleason (1880s–1910s)
3B—John Ryan (1880s–1910s)
SS—Eddie Collins (1900s–1930s)
OF—Jim O'Rourke (1870s–1900s)
OF—Ted Williams (1930s–1960s)
OF—Minnie Minoso (1940s–1980s)
C—Carlton Fisk (1960s–1990s)
P—Nick Altrock (1890s–1930s)

Also: Jack Quinn, Bobo Newsom, Mickey Vernon, Jim Kaat, Early Wynn, Rick Dempsey, Nolan Ryan, Dan Brouthers, Tim McCarver, Willie McCovey, Jack O'Connor, and Deacon McGuire.

—— FOUR MAJOR LEAGUES ——

It has been categorically impossible for any player who was a rookie after 1891 to appear in the box scores of four different major leagues. The following did just that:

1B—Joe Quinn (UA, NL, PL, AL)
2B—Fred Dunlap (NL, UA, PL, AA)
3B—Lave Cross (AA, PL, NL, AL)
SS—Bill Hallman (NL, PL, AA, AL)
OF—Dummy Hoy (NL, PL, AA, AL)
OF—Hugh Duffy (NL, PL, AA, AL)
OF—Emmett Seery (UA, NL, PL, AA)
C—Duke Farrell (NL, PL, AA, AL)
P—Gus Weyhing (AL, PL, NL, AL)

Cross played for all four loops in the same city, Philadelphia. The manager is Tom Loftus, the only man ever to head teams in four leagues (UA, AA, NL, AL).

—— FORMING HABITS ——

A lineup of players who have been able to do at the end of their careers what they had accomplished as youngsters.

1B—John Miller
2B—Joe Morgan
3B—George Brett
SS—Luis Aparicio
OF—Rusty Staub
OF—Ty Cobb
OF—Ted Williams
C—Joe Torre
P—Nolan Ryan

Miller is the only player to have homered in his first and final big league at bats. Morgan led the NL in walks in 1965 and then again 15 years later. Brett has won the AL batting title in three decades—1976, 1980, and 1990. In the final year of his 18-year career, as in every other season, Aparicio had at least 400 at bats and 400 chances in the field. Staub and Cobb are the only major leaguers to have hit home runs before they reached 20 and after they passed 40. Williams led the AL in RBI in his rookie year of 1939 and in 1958 still saw the ball well enough to lead the junior circuit in hitting. During his playing career, Torre saw action with three clubs—the Cardinals, Braves, and Mets; since his retirement, he has managed three clubs—the Cardinals, Braves, and Mets. Ryan led the AL in strikeouts in 1972 and again 17 years later in 1989.

10 All-Star Game

Time for a midbook break with some lineups related to the annual exhibitions between the National and American leagues.

—— BEST ALL-STAR GAMES ——

Before the television considerations of recent years led to a lot of twilight starting times, the All-Star games occasioned some big hitting.

    1B—Phil Cavarretta (1944 NL)
    2B—Red Schoendienst (1950 NL)
    3B—Al Rosen (1954 AL)
    SS—Arky Vaughan (1941 NL)
    OF—Ted Williams (1941, 1946 AL)
    OF—Stan Musial (1955 NL)
    OF—Johnny Callison (1964 NL)
    C—Gary Carter (1981 NL)
    P—Carl Hubbell (1934 NL)

Cavarretta reached base five times. Schoendienst hit a homer in the 14th inning to down the AL. Rosen had two homers, as did Vaughan though in a losing cause. Williams offset the Vaughan blasts with one of his own in 1941 and then hit two more in 1946 to lead an AL rout of the NL. Musial's 12th-inning homer and Callison's ninth-inning shot brought dramatic victories to the NL. Carter walloped two homers in another NL victory. Hubbell made NL fans forget their team's loss by striking out Babe Ruth, Lou Gehrig, Jimmie Foxx, Al Simmons, and Joe Cronin in succession with his screwball. Honorable mention to Fernando Valenzuela who in 1984 combined with Doc Gooden to break Hubbell's record by whiffing six straight AL hitters and who then in 1986 tied the Hubbell mark for strikeouts by getting Don Mattingly, Cal Ripken, Jesse Barfield, Lou Whitaker, and Teddy Higuera.

—— ALL-STAR FIXTURES ——

A lineup of players with the most All-Star Game appearances:

1B—Stan Musial (24)
2B—Nellie Fox (13)
3B—Brooks Robinson (18)
SS—Ozzie Smith (10)
OF—Hank Aaron (24)
OF—Willie Mays (24)
OF—Ted Williams (18)
 C—Yogi Berra (15)
 P—Tom Seaver (8)

Between 1959 and 1963 there were two All-Star games a year, giving players from that era more opportunity for appearing. Seaver is one of several pitchers who have been in at least eight games.

—— ALL-LEAGUE ALL-STARS ——

With the exception of the first baseman here, these players owe a large debt to interleague trading for being able to say they represented both leagues at All-Star games.

1B—Johnny Mize (Cardinals, Giants, Yankees)
2B—Phil Garner (Athletics, Pirates)
3B—Dick Allen (Phillies, Cardinals, White Sox)
SS—Craig Reynolds (Mariners, Astros)
OF—Hank Aaron (Braves, Brewers)
OF—Frank Robinson (Reds, Orioles, Angels)
OF—Reggie Smith (Red Sox, Cardinals, Dodgers)
 C—Ted Simmons (Cardinals, Brewers)
 P—Jim Bunning (Tigers, Phillies)

No player has ever appeared for one league, then with the other, then reappeared with his original league. The only managers who have called the shots from both dugouts have been Alvin Dark, Sparky Anderson, and Dick Williams.

—— THEY TOO WERE ALL STARS: AL ——

Not everyone picked for the All-Star games has been a future Hall of Famer; for example,

        1B—Harry Simpson (1956 Athletics)
        2B—Billy Moran (1962 Angels)
        3B—Dave Chalk (1974 Angels)
        SS—Billy Hunter (1953 Browns)
        OF—Lou Finney (1940 Red Sox)
        OF—Thurman Tucker (1944 White Sox)
        OF—Oris Hockett (1944 Indians)
         C—Duane Josephson (1968 White Sox)
         P—Bob Keegan (1954 White Sox)

Lifetime averages: Simpson, .266; Moran, .263; Chalk, .252; Hunter, .219; Finney, .287; Tucker, .255; Hockett, .276; and Josephson, .258. The only year in which Keegan won more than 10 games (16–9) was 1954; his lifetime record was 40–36.

—— THEY TOO WERE ALL STARS: NL ——

The senior circuit's unexpected all stars have included:

        1B—Joe Cunningham (1959 Cardinals)
        2B—Pete Coscarart (1940 Dodgers)
        3B—Pinky May (1940 Phillies)
        SS—Woody English (1933 Cubs)
        OF—Hershel Martin (1938 Phillies)
        OF—Morrie Arnovich (1939 Phillies)
        OF—Max West (1940 Braves)
         C—Steve Swisher (1976 Cubs)
         P—Ken Raffensberger (1944 Phillies)

Lifetime averages: Cunningham, .291; Coscarart, .243; May, .275; English, .286; Martin, .285; Arnovich, .287; West, .254; and Swisher, .216. Raffensberger, whose 20 losses led the NL in 1944, had a career record of 119–154.

11   In the Shadows

Even if you've heard of these players, you may have forgotten some of their achievements and misadventures.

— GUESS AGAIN —

The game here is to figure out what these players failed to accomplish in their special talent areas.

    1B—Rusty Staub
    2B—Johnny Evers
    3B—Frank Baker
    SS—Luis Aparicio
    OF—Hank Aaron
    OF—Al Kaline
    OF—Lou Brock
     C—Bill Dickey
     P—Johnny Vander Meer

Although he collected 500 hits for four different teams (Astros, Expos, Mets, Tigers), Staub never had a 200-hit season. Evers never turned more than 58 double plays when he played with Joe Tinker and Frank Chance. "Home Run" Baker never hit more than 12 round-trippers in a season and had only 93 in a 13-year career. Regular leadoff man that he was, Aparicio never scored 100 runs in a season and had a career on-base percentage of only .308. Homer king Aaron never hit 50 in a season, and Kaline never even reached 30. Brock never stole home while with the Cardinals; his one theft of the plate came as part of a delayed double steal while he was with the Cubs in 1964. Offensive threat that he was for so many years, Dickey never led the AL in a single offensive category. Double no-hitter or not, Vander Meer never won 20 games in a season and ended his career two games under .500 at 119–121.

—— THE GOOD AND THE BAD ——

A lineup of players who led the league in one category too many in the same year.

> 1B—Dave Kingman (1982 Mets)
> 2B—Jake Wood (1961 Tigers)
> 3B—Pete Rose (1975 Reds)
> SS—Zoilo Versalles (1965 Twins)
> OF—Bob Bescher (1911 Reds)
> OF—Bobby Bonds (1969 Giants)
> OF—Babe Ruth (1923–24, 1927–28 Yankees)
>   C—Ernie Lombardi (1938, 1942 Reds)
>   P—Nolan Ryan (1972–74, 1976–78 Angels)

Kingman led in homers (37) and in compiling the worst batting average (.204). Wood topped the AL in triples (14) and strikeouts (141). Rose led in doubles (47) and runs scored (112) while also establishing the all-time NL mark for the fewest steals (0) per games played. Versalles was elected AL MVP—but not for setting an all-time strikeout mark for shortstops (122). Bescher led in stolen bases (81), but also in whiffs (78). Bonds scored the most runs (120), but only when he hadn't walked back to the bench on his way to the most strikeouts (187). In all four years, Ruth led the American League in homers, walks, and strikeouts. Lombardi won two batting titles while leading NL catchers in passed balls. For the six seasons cited, Ryan led the AL in walks and strikeouts.

—— THE REST OF THE STORY ——

Forgotten aspects to memorable plays, games, and events:

1B—Fred Merkle (1908 Giants)
2B—Rennie Stennett (1975 Pirates)
3B—Mike Schmidt (1976 Phillies)
SS—Pee Wee Reese (1950 Dodgers)
OF—Babe Ruth (1930 Yankees)
OF—Duke Snider (1947 Dodgers)
OF—Hank Aaron (1974 Braves)
 C—Mickey O'Neil (1926 Dodgers)
 P—Christy Mathewson (1908 Giants)

Merkle's infamous boner (failing to touch second on a game winning hit) came in his very first full game as a starter for the Giants; when the boner forced a makeup pennant-deciding game with the Cubs, Mathewson was deprived of the win that would have made him the all-time NL victories leader. When Stennett tied the record for seven hits in a nine-inning game, he also contributed to baseball's most lopsided shutout, 22–0. Schmidt's four homers in one game helped the Phillies overcome two 11-run deficits—the most ever by a team. Although Cal Abrams has worn the goat horns for being thrown out at the plate in the final 1950 regular season game, he had little choice because Reese was halfway to third behind him. On the same day Gehrig's streak at first base ended, Ruth pitched for the first time in nine years and won a complete-game victory. The same game in which Jackie Robinson broke the color line saw fellow-Hall of Famer Snider make his debut with a pinch-single. In the same game in which Aaron passed Babe Ruth for career homers, he set the NL record for runs scored. O'Neill volunteered to coach at third base for an inning of a Dodgers game—the inning in which Babe Herman doubled into a double play.

—— CLOSE BUT NO CIGAR ——

All the infielders and outfielders on this team lost batting crowns by less than a point, while the catcher finished a distant third, one and a half points behind.

1B—Bill Terry (1931 Giants)
2B—Nap Lajoie (1910 Indians)
3B—Tony Cuccinello (1945 White Sox)
SS—Robin Yount (1982 Brewers)
OF—Ted Williams (1949 Red Sox)
OF—Joe Vosmik (1935 Indians)
OF—Carl Yastrzemski (1970 Red Sox)
C—Chief Meyers (1911 Giants)
P—Gaylord Perry (1972 Indians)

Terry's .34861 lost out to Chick Hafey's .34889, with Jim Bottomley finishing third at .34817. Lajoie is still officially second to Ty Cobb by .00097 even though recent research has shown that Cobb's average was actually .38188 to Lajoie's .38344. Cuccinello's .00009 loss to George Stirnweiss is the closest batting race in baseball history. The other victims: Yount finished second with .33070 to Willie Wilson's .33162. Williams's .34275 trailed George Kell's .04291. Vosmik's .34830 was beaten by Buddy Myer's .34903. Yastrzemski's .32862 was lower than Alex Johnson's .32899. And Meyers finished third with a batting average of .33248, against Honus Wagner's .334 and Doc Miller's .33276. Perry's ERA of 1.9155 was ever so slightly higher than Luis Tiant's 1.9100.

—— WHAT DOES A GUY HAVE TO DO? ——

Over the past 15 years, a period that has seen both Rod
Carew and George Brett flirt with .400, the average batting
champion has had to hit .345. Imagine, then, the chagrin of
these players, who did *not* lead their leagues.

> 1B—Lou Gehrig (1930 Yankees) .379
> 2B—Nap Lajoie (1910 Indians) .384
> 3B—Fred Lindstrom (1930 Giants) .379
> SS—Honus Wagner (1905 Pirates) .363
> OF—Joe Jackson (1911 Indians) .408
> OF—Ty Cobb (1922 Tigers) .401
> OF—Babe Ruth (1923 Yankees) .393
> C—Babe Phelps (1936 Dodgers) .367
> P—Ralph Terry (1961 Yankees) .842 Pct.

Jackson not only finished behind Cobb's .420 in 1911, but
was a runner-up to the same Cobb in 1912 when the Tiger outfielder outhit him, .410 to .395.

The others: Behrig bowed to Al Simmons's .381, Lajoie to
Cobb's .385, Lindstrom to Bill Terry's .401, Wagner to Cy Seymour's .377, Cobb to George Sisler's .420, Ruth to Harry Heilmann's .403 and Phelps to Paul Waner's .373.

Terry's 16–3 record was only second best to fellow Yankee
Whitey Ford's 25–4 (.862).

A tie for manager, since both Frank Chance of the 1909
Cubs and Leo Durocher of the 1942 Dodgers piloted teams that
won 104 games and still finished in second place. Chance's
Cubs wound up six and one-half games behind Pittsburgh and
Durocher's Dodgers finished two games behind St. Louis.

—— WHAT DOES A GUY REALLY ——
HAVE TO DO?

Only serious historians will know why none of the following won batting championships. And it isn't because hitters were better in the old days.

> 1B—Dan Brouthers (1887 Detroit) .419
> 2B—Yank Robinson (1887 St. Louis AA) .426
> 3B—Denny Lyons (1887 Philadelphia AA) .469
> SS—Paul Radford (1887 New York AA) .404
> OF—Bob Caruthers (1887 St. Louis AA) .459
> OF—Pete Browning (1887 Louisville AA) .471
> OF—Tuck Turner (1894 Phillies) .423
> C—George Baker (1884 St. Louis UA) .471
> P—Charlie Buffinton (1884 Braves) 47 Wins

You're probably thinking that 1887 was a tough year for pitchers, but that was the year that bases on balls counted as hits. (Had this rule been in force in 1941, Ted Williams would have batted .549.) Also, it took four strikes to make an out in 1887, and that didn't hurt averages either. A total of 13 players hit better than .400 in 1887, including the two batting champions—Cap Anson (.421 in the NL) and Tip O'Neill (.402 in the AA). Real sympathy must be reserved for Turner and Baker. The former lost the NL batting crown to Hugh Duffy, who hit .438 under modern rules. The latter finished 51 points higher than the league leader but failed to come to bat enough times. Under today's rules, which use plate appearances as the criterion for qualification, Baker would have been given credit for the necessary appearances and he would have won. Buffinton finished considerably behind Charlie Radbourn's record total of 60 wins.

—— REMARKABLE RUNNERS-UP ——

Batting titles aren't the only category that have seen players with tremendous seasons being stymied. Try to figure out what these players finished second in.

        1B—Lou Gehrig (1927 Yankees)
        2B—Billy Herman (1936 Cubs)
        3B—Bill Bradley (1903 Indians)
        SS—Eddie Joost (1949 Athletics)
        OF—Omar Moreno (1980 Pirates)
        OF—Mickey Mantle (1961 Yankees)
        OF—Chuck Klein (1930 Phillies)
         C—Roy Campanella (1953 Dodgers)
         P—Christy Mathewson (1904 Giants)

Gehrig's .765 slugging average fell before Babe Ruth's .772 mark. Herman hit 57 doubles in the same year that Joe Medwick was setting the NL doubles record with 64. Bradley legged out 22 triples, 3 fewer than Sam Crawford. Joost walked 149 times, but Ted Williams managed 13 more passes. Moreno stole 96 bases, but Ron LeFlore stole 97. Mantle was joining the select 50 HR club in the same year that teammate Roger Maris was joining the even more select 60 HR club. Klein has to take first prize for frustration: his 250 hits fell short of Bill Terry's record-establishing 254 and his 170 runs batted in came in the same year that Hack Wilson was tearing up all the record books with 190 RBI. Campanella, the only catcher to hit 40 homers in a season, finished behind both Eddie Mathews and Duke Snider in that power category. Mathewson won 33 games, but his teammate Joe McGinnity won 35. The same thing happened the next year when Mathewson won only 30 to McGinnity's 31.

—— LEADER OF THE PACK ——

Sometimes a player can carry a whole team, but sometimes he can't carry it very far.

    1B—Jimmie Foxx (1935 Athletics)
    2B—Rogers Hornsby (1928 Braves)
    3B—Harmon Killebrew (1959 Senators)
    SS—Ernie Banks (1958 Cubs)
    OF—Wally Berger (1935 Braves)
    OF—Ralph Kiner (1949–52 Pirates)
    OF—Andre Dawson (1987 Cubs)
     C—Ernie Lombardi (1942 Braves)
     P—Steve Carlton (1972 Phillies)

Foxx tied for the league lead in homers with 36 and led the league in RBI (115) and slugging (.636); the Athletics finished last. Hornsby led in batting average with .387 and hit 21 homers with 94 RBI; the Braves finished seventh. Killebrew led with 42 home runs and drove in 105; the Senators were last. Banks led the league in homers (47), RBI (129), and slugging (.614) while batting .313; the best the Cubs could do with all that hitting was finish fifth. Berger led in homers (34) and RBI (130); the rest of the Braves managed only 41 more homers and finished last. Kiner led the league (or tied for the lead) in home runs in all four seasons while the Pirates finished sixth, last, seventh, and last. Dawson's league-leading totals in home runs (49) and RBI (137) couldn't get the Cubs out of last place. Lombardi led the league in hitting (.330); the next highest average on the team was .278 and the Braves finished seventh. Carlton —27–10, a 1.98 ERA, and 310 strikeouts, all league-leading figures—was the entire franchise as the Phils won only 59 games and finished last.

—— OUT OF PROPORTION ——

From a mathematical point of view, some very unlikely achievements:

        1B—Jack Harshman (Career)
        2B—Rod Carew (1969 Twins)
        3B—Fritz Connally (1985 Orioles)
        SS—Freddie Patek (1980 Royals)
        OF—Tip O'Neill (1887 St. Louis AA)
        OF—Tom McCreery (1897 Louisville, Giants)
        OF—Pat Tabler (Career)
          C—Don Leppert (Career)
          P—Virgil Trucks (1952 Tigers)

With 21 homers among his 76 hits, Harshman (who was also a pitcher) has the highest ratio of homers to safeties for players with at least 400 at bats. Carew stole 19 bases in 1969, but 7 of them were home plate. Connally's only three homers of his two-year major league career included two grand slams. Patek hit three homers in a game, but only five for the season. O'Neill led the American Association in doubles, triples, and homers (the only player ever to do this), but never again led the league in any of these categories over his 10-year career. Like Patek, McCreery hit three of five season homers in one game—but all his round-trippers for the contest were inside the park. Through 1990, Tabler was a lifetime .286 hitter, but a .500 hitter (40–80) when he batted with the bases loaded. Leppert hit three homers in a game for the 1963 Senators, but only 15 for his entire career. Trucks finished the season with a 5–19 record, but two of the victories were no-hitters!

—— IT DOESN'T RUN IN THE FAMILY ——

If you can't name the more famous brothers of these players, you're reading the wrong book.

1B—Tommie Aaron
2B—Jim Delahanty
3B—Butts Wagner
SS—Sam Wright
OF—Josh Clarke
OF—John O'Rourke
OF—Vince DiMaggio
 C—Luke Sewell
 P—Henry Mathewson

Aaron was a .229 hitter for the Braves. Delahanty hit .283 as a utility player. Wagner batted .226 in his only season. Harry and George Wright's brother managed only 12 games in parts of three seasons and came up short of deserving a 13th by batting .109. Clarke's .239 was spread over 223 games in five different seasons in three different decades (1898, 1905, 1908–09, and 1911). O'Rourke turned in a commendable .295 in his three years. DiMaggio, probably the most noted in this lineup, hit 125 home runs, but was also one of the all-time strikeout kings (837 whiffs—more than twice as many as Joe and some 300 more than Dom). Sewell was a fixture in the American League for years, but had a better career managing the Browns to their 1944 pennant. In three games for the Giants in 1906 and 1907, the lesser Mathewson won none and lost one. The Wrights (as managers) and the Waners are the only brother combinations in the Hall of Fame.

—— OH, BROTHER ——

Even though their baseball careers were overshadowed by those of their famous brothers, at least in one area—if only for one season in some cases—they earned family bragging rights.

        1B—Amos Cross
        2B—Jimmy Cooney
        3B—Hank Allen
        SS—Yo-Yo Davalillo
        OF—Carlos May
        OF—Vince DiMaggio
        OF—John O'Rourke
         C—Pinky Hargrave
         P—Jesse Tannehill

In his only full season for Louisville (AA) in 1886, Cross walked more times (44) than his brother Lave did for any season in 21 years. Cooney's part-time play in seven years did not prevent him from ending up with as many homers (two) and stolen bases (30) as his brother Johnny accumulated in 20 years. Allen had 19 pinch hits in 7 years, brother Dick had 5 in 15 years. Davalillo batted .293 in his only year, while hitting specialist Vic hit only .279. May ended up with more walks and stolen bases, and even a higher batting average (.274–.267). than his slugging brother Lee. DiMaggio stole 79 bases during his career, while his brother Joe swiped only 30. In his three seasons in the 19th century, O'Rourke managed to lead the NL in slugging once—something his brother Jim could not accomplish in 19 seasons; he also outslugged his brother for a career, .442 to .422. Bubbles Hargrave may have won a hitting title, but brother Pinky ended up with more homers (39 to 29). Aside from being a formidable pitcher, Tannehill hit more homers and had higher batting and slugging averages than his brother Lee.

—— OH, BROTHERS ——

Although the four Delahantys and the three Alous, Boyers, DiMaggios, and Wrights are common knowledge, other families have sent at least three sons to the major leagues. Can you name the brothers of these players:

1B—Jim Paciorek
2B—Mike Edwards
3B—Hector Cruz
SS—Jim O'Neill
OF—Len Sowders
OF—John Mansell
OF—Hank Allen
C—Eddie Sadowski
P—Walter Clarkson

Their brothers: John and Tom; Dave and Marshall; Tommy and Jose; Jack, Mike, and Steve; Bill and John; Mike and Tom; Dick and Ron; Bob and Ted; and John and Dad. Also the Sewells (Luke, Joe, and Tommy) and the Crosses (Amos, Lave, and Frank).

—— LIKE FATHERS, LIKE SONS ——

This lineup not only spans the generations but also lists fathers and sons who played the same position.

1B—George and Dick Sisler
2B—Sandy and Roberto Alomar
3B—Roy Sr. and Roy Jr. Smalley
SS—Maury and Bump Wills
OF—Ken Sr. and Ken Jr. Griffey
OF—Felipe and Moises Alou
OF—Bobby and Barry Bonds
C—Ozzie Sr. and Ozzie Jr. Virgil
P—Dizzy and Steve Trout

The Trouts combined for 254 wins, 30 more than the Jim Bagbys. Honorable mention to Jack Doscher (1903–06) and his father Herm (1879, 1881–82), the first father-son combination in the major leagues.

—— A SEASON DOES NOT A ——
CAREER MAKE

Forty home runs in a season is the mark of a slugger. But what kind of slugger hits 40 once and can't manage 250 in a career?

    1B—Jim Gentile (1961 Orioles)
    2B—Davey Johnson (1973 Braves)
    3B—Al Rosen (1953 Indians)
    SS—Rico Petrocelli (1969 Red Sox)
    OF—Ben Oglivie (1980 Brewers)
    OF—Wally Post (1955 Reds)
    OF—Gus Zernial (1953 Athletics)
     C—Roy Campanella (1953 Dodgers)
     P—Ed Walsh (1908 White Sox)

Their one season and career totals are Gentile, 46 and 179; Johnson, 43 and 136; Rosen, 43 and 192; Petrocelli, 40 and 210; Oglivie, 41 and 235; Post, 40 and 210; Zernial, 42 and 237; and Campanella, 41 and 242. Walsh is here because he is one of only two pitchers to win 40 games in a season and fail to win 200 in his career: his season/career wins are 40 and 195. Some of these can be explained. Campanella and Petrocelli were plagued by injuries. Gentile's big year came at least partly as a result of expansion. And Johnson was not a power hitter at all—except for that one year in the Atlanta launching pad when three members of the Braves hit more than 40 home runs. Only three other hitters have accomplished this: Hal Trosky, 42 homers with the 1936 Indians and 228 lifetime; Dick Stuart, 42 with the 1963 Red Sox and 228 lifetime; and Jeff Burroughs, 41 with the 1977 Braves and 240 lifetime. The other pitcher is Jack Chesbro, 41 victories with the 1904 Yankees and 199 lifetime.

—— MORE WHOLE THAN PARTS ——

These hitters had brilliant career averages, but they never won any batting titles.

        1B—Hank Greenberg (.313)
        2B—Eddie Collins (.333)
        3B—Pie Traynor (.320)
        SS—Cecil Travis (.314)
        OF—Joe Jackson (.356)
        OF—Riggs Stephenson (.336)
        OF—Mike Donlin (.334)
          C—Mickey Cochrane (.320)
          P—Mordecai Brown (.639 Pct.)

The problem for most of these players was, of course, people named Cobb, Hornsby, and Williams. As high as Brown's yearly winning percentage got, those of Ed Reulbach and Christy Mathewson were invariably higher.

—— MORE PARTS THAN WHOLE ——

On the other hand, some players without lifetime .300 marks have silver bats above their fireplaces.

        1B—Norm Cash (1961 Tigers) .271
        2B—George Stirnweiss (1945 Yankees) .268
        3B—Carney Lansford (1981 Red Sox) .292
        SS—Dick Groat (1960 Pirates) .286
        OF—Alex Johnson (1970 Angels) .288
        OF—Sherry Magee (1910 Phillies) .291
        OF—Debs Garms (1940 Pirates) .293
          C—Joe Torre (1971 Cardinals) .297
          P—Ben Cantwell (1933 Red Sox) .413 Pct.

Even though Cantwell led the AL in W–L percentage in 1933 with a 20–10 record, he had only one other winning season, slipped to 4–25 in 1935, and ended his career with 76 wins and 108 losses. Also, Pete Runnels, who won two batting titles for the 1960 and 1962 Red Sox, still ended up at only .291.

—— SO MANY, SO FEW ——

With the exception of the shortstop, these sluggers hit at least 250 homers, but never led the league.

        1B—Norm Cash (377)
        2B—Joe Gordon (253)
        3B—Ron Santo (342)
        SS—Cal Ripken (225)
        OF—Stan Musial (475)
        OF—Billy Williams (426)
        OF—Al Kaline (399)
         C—Yogi Berra (358)
         P—Eddie Plank (305 wins)

Ripken and Rico Petrocelli (210) are the only shortstops to hit 200 homers and never lead the league. Plank had to contend with Cy Young and Jack Chesbro.

—— SO FEW, SO MANY ——

Though not the greatest power hitters of all time, these men managed to lead the league in home runs.

        1B—Nick Etten (1944 Yankees) 22
        2B—Bobby Grich (1981 Angels) 22
        3B—Bill Melton (1971 White Sox) 33
        SS—Vern Stephens (1945 Browns) 24
        OF—Bill Nicholson (1943–44 Cubs) 29–33
        OF—Bob Meusel (1925 Yankees) 33
        OF—Tommy Holmes (1945 Braves) 28
         C—Buck Ewing (1883 Giants) 10
         P—Red Barrett (1945 Braves, Cardinals) 23 wins

Career totals: Etten, 89; Grich, 202; Melton, 160; Stephens, 247; Nicholson, 235; Meusel, 156; Holmes, 88; and Ewing, 70. Barrett had only 69 career wins, the lowest career total for a league leader in wins. Although Stephens and Nicholson were genuine power hitters, they clearly benefited from the absence of the Greenbergs and Kiners during the war.

—— UNEXPECTED POWER SOURCES ——

A new stance, new coach, or new ballpark can suddenly turn the most unlikely players into home-run hitters.

        1B—Ed Morgan (1930 Indians) 26
        2B—Davey Johnson (1973 Braves) 43
        3B—Wade Boggs (1987 Red Sox) 24
        SS—Roy Smalley, Sr. (1950 Cubs) 21
        OF—Tommy Holmes (1945 Braves) 28
        OF—Tommy Harper (1970 Brewers) 31
        OF—Willard Marshall (1947 Giants) 36
         C—Mickey Tettleton (1989 Orioles) 26
         P—Monte Weaver (1932 Senators) 22 wins

The season highs otherwise for these players were: Morgan, 11; Johnson, 18; Boggs, 8; Smalley, 8; Holmes, 13; Harper, 18; Marshall, 17; and Tettleton, 15. Except for 1932, Weaver never won more than 12 games in a nine-year career.

—— ONCE A THIEF ——

For one season they stole everything there was to steal; otherwise, they moped around the bases.

        1B—Bert Haas (1946 Reds) 22
        2B—George Grantham (1923 Cubs) 43
        3B—Jap Barbeau (1909 Pirates, Cardinals) 33
        SS—Barry McCormick (1897 Cubs) 44
        OF—Wally Moses (1943 White Sox) 56
        OF—Wilbur Howard (1975 Astros) 32
        OF—Jerry Mumphrey (1980 Padres) 52
         C—Billy Earle (1889 Cincinnati AA) 26
         P—Jim Lonborg (1967 Red Sox) 246 Ks

The steal highs otherwise for these players were Haas, 9; Grantham, 21; Barbeau, 5; McCormick, 15; Moses, 21; Howard, 11; Mumphrey, 22; and Earle, 6. Except for 1967, Lonborg never struck out even 150 batters in a season.

—— THEY NEVER BUNCHED THEM ——

Out of this team of players with the most career hits, none won any batting crowns.

1B—Jake Beckley (2,931)
2B—Eddie Collins (3,311)
3B—Brooks Robinson (2,848)
SS—George Davis (2,688)
OF—Lou Brock (3,023)
OF—Sam Rice (2,987)
OF—Sam Crawford (2,964)
 C—Yogi Berra (2,150)
 P—Early Wynn (300 wins)

Collins and Brock are the only members of the 3,000-hit club not to win a batting title. Wynn is the only pitcher with 300 wins never to lead the league in won-lost percentage.

—— LOTS OF HITS, LOTS OF AT BATS ——

Players with the most career hits who failed to maintain .300 batting averages.

1B—Carl Yastrzemski (3,419) .285
2B—Nellie Fox (2,663) .288
3B—Brooks Robinson (2,848) .267
SS George Davis (2,683) .296
OF—Lou Brock (3,023) .293
OF—Frank Robinson (2,943) .294
OF—Al Kaline (3,007) .297
 C—Yogi Berra (2,150) .285
 P—Bobo Newsom (211 wins) .487

Newsom lost 222 games. The only other pitcher to win 200 and yet finish with a won-lost record under .500 is Jake Powell (247–254, .493).

—— MAJOR FEATS IN THE MINORS ——

This lineup features players who accomplished things in the minors that have never been duplicated in the majors.

1B—Joe Bauman (1954 Longhorn League)
2B—Bill Alexander (1902 Texas League)
3B—Al Rosen (1948 American Association)
SS—Buzzy Wares (1910 Pacific Coast League)
OF—Walter Malmquist (1913 Nebraska State League)
OF—Gene Rye (1930 Texas League)
OF—Joe Wilhoit (1920 Western League)
 C—Nig Clarke (1902 Texas League)
 P—Ron Necciai (1952 Appalachian League)

Bauman hit 72 homers for Roswell, the highest season total for any professional league. Alexander went eight for eight in a game for Corsicana; in the same game, catcher Clarke also went eight for eight—however, his hits were all home runs! (Clarke drove in 16 runs in a 51–3 rout of Texarkana.) Rosen hit five consecutive homers over two games for Kansas City. Wares had 72 sacrifices on the year for Oakland. Malmquist hit .477 for York—the highest average compiled in a professional league since the founding of the National League in 1876. Rye hit three homers in one inning for Waco. Wilhoit had a 69-game hitting streak for Wichita. Necciai struck out 27 batters in a nine-inning game for Bristol. Honorable mentions to Buzz Arlett, who clouted four home runs in two separate games for the International League Orioles in 1932; Joe Cantley, who hit three grand slams in a 1914 game for Opelika of the Georgia-Alabama League; Bob Crues, whose 254 runs batted in for Amarillo in the West Texas-New Mexico League in 1948 is a professional record.

12 Rookies

This chapter takes a look at the ones who succeeded and the ones who didn't.

—— BEST ROOKIE YEARS ——

In 1987, Mark McGwire hit 49 homers and drove in 118 runs for the Athletics. Impressive, but he can't make this team.

> 1B—Dale Alexander (1929 Tigers)
> 2B—Tony Lazzeri (1926 Yankees)
> 3B—Jimmy Williams (1899 Pirates)
> SS—Johnny Pesky (1942 Red Sox)
> OF—Joe Jackson (1911 Indians)
> OF—George Watkins (1930 Cardinals)
> OF—Ted Williams (1939 Red Sox)
> C—Bill Dickey (1929 Yankees)
> P—Grover Alexander (1911 Phillies)

Dale Alexander hit .343 with 25 homers and 137 runs batted in. Lazzeri had 18 homers and 114 RBI. Jimmy Williams compiled a 27-game hitting streak during a .355 season. Pesky hit .331. Jackson hit an astonishing .408 to set the all-time rookie mark. Watkins has the National League record for his .373 in St. Louis. Ted Williams batted .327 with 31 homers and a record 145 RBI. Dickey's first season mark was .324. Alexander holds several rookie pitching records—most victories (28), most complete games (31), and most shutouts (7). Aside from AL rookie-homer-record-holder McGwire, nods to Wally Berger (1930 Braves) and Frank Robinson (1956 Reds) for the NL rookie home run record (38); to Tony Oliva (1964 Twins) for being the only rookie batting titlist; to Lloyd Waner (1927 Pirates) whose record 223 hits produced a .355 batting average; and to Doc Gooden (1984 Mets) whose 276 strikeouts is a rookie record and whose 11.39 strikeouts per nine innings established a major league record.

—— BEST DEBUTS ——

Talk about getting off to a good start!

1B—Willie McCovey (1959 Giants)
2B—Danny Murphy (1902 Athletics)
3B—Cecil Travis (1933 Senators)
SS—Bert Campaneris (1964 Athletics)
OF—Bob Nieman (1951 Browns)
OF—Fred Clarke (1894 Louisville)
OF—Bobby Bonds (1968 Giants)
 C—Aubrey Epps (1933 Pirates)
 P—Bumpus Jones (1892 Reds)

In their first big league games: McCovey had two triples and two singles. Murphy went six for six, including a home run off Cy Young. Travis had five singles in a 12-inning game. Campaneris had two homers. Nieman went Campaneris one better by being the only player ever to homer in his first two at bats. Clarke had four hits. Bonds hit a grand slam homer; the first to do it was pitcher Bill Duggleby of the 1898 Phillies. Epps got three hits in four at bats and drove in three runs—and never played another big league game. Most amazing of all was Jones, who entered the Cincinnati clubhouse on the last day of the season, proclaimed that he was the best pitcher on the premises, signed a contract, then went out to hurl a no-hitter against the Pirates. The following year, he was batted around in spring training and early season games, moved on to the Giants, and then disappeared. (Bobo Holloman's May 6, 1953, no-hitter for the St. Louis Browns was in his first start but not in his first appearance.

—— YOUNGEST PLAYERS ——

Otherwise known as the Joe Nuxhall team are

  1B—Ed Kranepool (1962 Mets) age 17
  2B—Ted Sepkowski (1942 Indians) age 18
  3B—Putsy Caballero (1944 Phillies) age 16
  SS—Tommy Brown (1944 Dodgers) age 16
  OF—Mel Ott (1926 Giants) age 17
  OF—Al Kaline (1953 Tigers) age 18
  OF—Willie Crawford (1964 Dodgers) age 17
   C—Jimmie Foxx (1925 Athletics) age 17
   P—Joe Nuxhall (1944 Reds) age 15

All these players put in little more than token appearances in their debut years. Nuxhall's initial two-thirds of an inning produced two hits, five walks, and a 07.50 ERA. The youngest starting pitcher was Jim Derrington (1956 White Sox) who at the age of 17 lost his maiden game. He was washed up at 18.

—— YOUNGEST REGULARS ——

Don't blame the Second World War for this lineup:

  1B—Phil Cavarretta (1935 Cubs) age 19
  2B—Larry Doyle (1907 Giants) age 20
  3B—Sibby Sisti (1940 Braves) age 19
  SS—Robin Yount (1974 Brewers) age 18
  OF—Ken Griffey, Jr. (1989 Mariners) age 19
  OF—Al Kaline (1954 Tigers) age 19
  OF—Tony Conigliaro (1964 Red Sox) age 19
   C—Del Crandall (1949 Braves) age 19
   P—Willie McGill (1891 Cincinnati, Milwaukee,
      St. Louis AA) age 17

Cavarretta batted .275; Doyle, .260; Sisti, .251; Yount, .250; Griffey, .264; Kaline, .276; Conigliaro, .290 with 24 homers; and Crandall, .263. McGill won 20 games in his second season. Honorable mention to Les Mann (1913 Braves), who was beaten out by Griffey by only three days; Mann batted .253.

—— JINXED SOPHOMORES ——

These players had good rookie years, fell down a chute the next season, and then rebounded for solid careers.

    1B—Walt Dropo (1950–51 Red Sox)
    2B—Cupid Childs (1890 Syracuse AA, 1891 Cleveland)
    3B—Gil McDougald (1951–52 Yankees)
    SS—Alvin Dark (1948–49 Braves)
    OF—Ira Flagstead (1919–20 Tigers)
    OF—Roy Sievers (1949–50 Browns)
    OF—Al Bumbry (1973–74 Orioles)
     C—Thurman Munson (1970–71 Yankees)
     P—Stan Bahnsen (1968–69 Yankees)

Dropo declined from .332 with 34 homers and a league-leading 144 RBI to .239 with 11 homers and 57 RBI. Childs dipped to .281 after a rookie season of .345. McDougald slipped from a .306 mark to .263, Dark from .322 to .276. Like Dropo, Sievers declined across the board—from .306 with 16 home runs and 91 RBI to .238 with 10 homers and 57 RBI. Flagstead's astonishing 96-point drop from .331 to .235 still fell short of Bumbry's even greater plummet—a 104-point descent to .233 from .337. Munson slipped 51 points from .302 to .251. Bahnsen's debut at 17 wins and 12 losses with an ERA of 2.05 was followed by a 9–16, 3.83 ERA season. Dishonorable mentions to Ginger Beaumont (1899–1900 Pirates) for losing 73 batting points from one season to the next and to Bernie Carbo (1970–71 Reds) for plunging from .310 with 21 homers and 63 runs batted in to .219 with 5 homers and 20 RBI.

—— BRIEFEST REGULARS ——

Go figure this one out: For one season every player in this lineup was good enough to be a regular starter; but only one ever appeared in another game after that one year.

    1B—Dutch Schliebner (1923 Dodgers, Browns)
    2B—Sparky Anderson (1959 Phillies)
    3B—Buddy Blair (1942 Phillies)
    SS—Gair Allie (1954 Pirates)
    OF—Larry Murphy (1891 Washington AA)
    OF—Ernie Sulik (1936 Phillies)
    OF—Goat Anderson (1907 Pirates)
     C—Archie Clarke (1890 Giants)
     P—Bill Sweeney (1884 Baltimore UA)

Schliebner hit .271 in 146 games. Anderson proved that managing was his game by hitting only .218 in 152 games. Blair was much more respectable at .279 for 137 games. Allie's fast exit should have caused little surprise after his .199 effort for 121 games. Murphy came in at .265 for 107 games, Sulik at .287 for 122 games, and Anderson at .206 for 121 games. The main exception to this lineup is catcher Clarke, who did indeed return for a handful of games in 1891 after batting .214 as New York's regular catcher in 101 contests the previous year. Sweeney compiled a splendid 40–21 record before disappearing. His 20th-century counterpart was Harry Schmidt, who went 21–13 for the 1903 Dodgers. Honorable mentions to two more Phillies from the 1940 team: first baseman Art Mahan who hit .244 in 145 games and second baseman Ham Schulte who hit .236 in 120 games.

—— FLASHES ——

In their rookie years, they made everyone sit up and notice them; soon enough, the only thing to notice about these players was that they had become easy outs.

        1B—Bob Hale (1955 Orioles)
        2B—Lou Klein (1943 Cardinals)
        3B—Ted Cox (1977 Red Sox)
        SS—Onix Concepcion (1984 Royals)
        OF—Bob Hazle (1957 Braves)
        OF—Joe Charboneau (1981 Indians)
        OF—Dino Restelli (1949 Pirates)
          C—Mike Stanley (1986–87 Rangers)
          P—Von McDaniel (1957 Cardinals)

Hale's .357 average made him the only Oriole with 100 at bats to reach .300. Klein batted .287 to help win a pennant, went off to war, never won a regular job when he came back, and jumped to Mexico. Cox hit .362 after being called up by the Red Sox in September and almost brought Boston a pennant. Concepcion went from .282 in 1984 to .204 the next season. Hurricane Hazle, the epitome of baseball flashes, led the Braves to a pennant with his .403 average in 43 games. The enigmatic Charboneau went from Rookie of the Year (.289 average, 23 homers, 87 runs batted in) to the minor leagues. Restelli hit eight homers in his first 10 games, but only five in his last 83. Stanley batted .280 in his first two seasons and showed enormous potential defensively. McDaniel filled ballparks around the National League with shutout performances and low-hit games, but barely got out of Florida in 1958.

—— PHENOMS ——

Because of their incredible minor or college league records, all of these men had the media telling them how great they were going to be at a major league level. And then, they took the field.

1B—Bob Nelson (1955 Orioles)
2B—Chris Pittaro (1985 Tigers)
3B—Billy Harrell (1955 Indians)
SS—Harry Chappas (1978 White Sox)
OF—Clint Hartung (1947 Giants)
OF—Carlos Bernier (1953 Pirates)
OF—Bob Lennon (1954 Giants)
 C—Marc Sullivan (1985 Red Sox)
 P—Rube Melton (1941 Phillies)

Nelson, ballyhooed as "the Babe Ruth of Texas," never hit a big league homer and batted .205. Pittaro's .221 came after Detroit manager Sparky Anderson predicted the Hall of Fame for him and tried to displace veteran second baseman Lou Whitaker on his behalf. Harrell stopped hitting even in the minors after averaging only .231 for Cleveland. The diminutive Chappas hit .302 in the minors, but in the majors mainly became a candidate for being, at 5'3", the shortest man in baseball history. Hartung, the phenom prototype, warmed the bench at the Polo Grounds for seven years as a .212 hitter and an even more forgettable pitcher. Bernier's single season at .213 came after he had broken most Pacific Coast League offensive records. Lennon hit 64 homers one season in the Southern Association; in the majors he batted .165 with one homer in 79 at bats. Having his father as Boston's general manager did not help Sullivan bat higher than .186 for his career. Melton's record of 30–50 came after three teams (Phillies, Cardinals, Dodgers) were so attracted to him that they ended up in hot water over a circus series of tamperings and under-the-table deals orchestrated by Branch Rickey.

—— FIRST BLACKS ——

After Moses and Welday Walker were driven out of base-ball in 1884, black players Irwin Sandy and George Treadway tried to pass as Latins or Indians. The first publicly acknowledged black players, however, were

      1B—Jackie Robinson (1947 Dodgers)
      2B—Hank Thompson (1947 Browns, 1949 Giants)
      3B—Ozzie Virgil, Sr. (1958 Tigers)
      SS—Ernie Banks (1953 Cubs)
      OF—Larry Doby (1947 Indians)
      OF—Carlos Paula (1954 Senators)
      OF—Sam Jethroe (1950 Braves)
       C—Elston Howard (1955 Yankees)
       P—Bob Trice (1953 Athletics)

Other first black Americans included: 1951 White Sox, Sam Hairston; 1954 Cardinals, Tom Alston; 1954 Reds, Nino Escalera; 1954 Pirates, Curt Roberts; 1957 Phillies, John Kennedy; and the 1959 Red Sox, Pumpsie Green. Honorable mentions to John Wright, Roy Campanella, Don Newcombe, and Roy Partlow, who were signed by the Dodgers after Robinson but before Doby and Thompson, the American League's first blacks. Also to Dan Bankhead, 1947 Dodgers, the first black pitcher; Gene Baker, 1953 Cubs, who came up with Banks; and Pat Scantlebury, 1956 Reds, the last player to make the jump to the majors from the Negro leagues. And to Frank Robinson, 1975 Indians, the first black manager; and Emmett Ashford, 1966 American League, the first black umpire.

—— GUESS WHAT? ——

If you can figure out what this team is, you deserve to be a baseball writer. (That's a hint.)

1B—Mitchell Page (1977 Athletics)
2B—Dave Stapleton (1980 Red Sox)
3B—Coco Laboy (1969 Expos)
SS—Billy Klaus (1955 Red Sox)
OF—Tom Umphlett (1953 Red Sox)
OF—Roy Foster (1970 Indians)
OF—Steve Henderson (1977 Mets)
 C—Dave Rader (1972 Giants)
 P—Mike Nagy (1969 Red Sox)

All of the preceding finished second in Rookie of the Year balloting. No wonder Boston fans, in particular, seem prone to having their expectations dashed.

—— LEAD STARTS ——

These future stars should have skipped their rookie years.

1B—Rusty Staub (1963 Astros)
2B—Nellie Fox (1950 White Sox)
3B—Mike Schmidt (1973 Phillies)
SS—Pee Wee Reese (1941 Dodgers)
OF—Lou Brock (1962 Cubs)
OF—Roberto Clemente (1955 Pirates)
OF—Reggie Smith (1967 Red Sox)
 C—Ray Schalk (1913 White Sox)
 P—Red Ruffing (1925 Red Sox)

Staub hit .224; Fox, .247 with four steals; Schmidt, .196 with 136 strikeouts; Reese, .229 with 47 errors; Brock, .263 with a mere 16 steals as opposed to 96 strikeouts; Clemente, .255; Smith, .246 with 95 whiffs; and Schalk, .244. Ruffing debuted with a record of 9–18 and an ERA of 5.01. He also walked 75 batters while striking out only 64.

—— WHAT DID THEY DO WRONG? ——

Some players enter the majors, do little, and disappear. Then there are the others who come on the scene, make the best of limited opportunities, but disappear anyway.

1B—Mike Schemer (1945–46 Giants)
2B—Jerry Lipscomb (1937 Browns)
3B—Frank Skaff (1935 Dodgers, 1943 Athletics)
SS—Boob Fowler (1923–25 Reds)
OF—Tripp Sigman (1929–30 Phillies)
OF—Buzz Arlett (1931 Phillies)
OF—Charlie Dorman (1923 White Sox, 1928 Indians)
  C—Jack Cummings (1926–29 Giants, 1929 Braves)
  P—Eddie Yuhas (1952–53 Cardinals)

1932 Balt
Orioles (INT)
p. 144

Schemer went 36–109 (.330); Lipscomb, 31–96 (.326); Skaff, 24–75 (.320); Fowler, 57–175 (.326), Sigman, 42–129 (.326), Dorman, 29–79 (.367) and Cummings, 45–132 (.341). Special mention must be made of Arlett, the minor league hitting sensation whose only season in the majors produced 26 doubles, 18 home runs, 72 runs batted in, and a .313 average in 418 at bats. Despite being the only player ever to finish among the top five sluggers and home run hitters in his sole big league year, Arlett's reputation as an "all-hit no-field" outfielder doomed him to return to the minors. Yuhas compiled a record of 12 wins, 2 losses, and an ERA of 2.73. Honorable mentions to Butch Sanicki (1949 and 1951 Phillies) for a single, double, three homers, eight runs batted in, and five runs scored in 17 at bats; Tom Hughes (1930 Tigers) for 22 hits in 59 at bats; John Gaddy (1938 Dodgers) for starting two games, completing one, winning both, and establishing an ERA of 0.69. Coaches Bill Burwell, Clyde Sukeforth, Andy Cohen, and Jo-Jo White won the only games they managed.

—— MOST VALUABLE ROOKIES ——

Since the institution of the Rookie of the Year award in 1947, 15 players have followed up that honor by also winning recognition as Most Valuable Players.

1B—Orlando Cepeda (1958 Giants, 1969 Cardinals)
2B—Pete Rose (1963 and 1973 Reds)
3B—Dick Allen (1964 Phillies, 1972 White Sox)
SS—Cal Ripken (1982 and 1983 Orioles)
OF—Willie Mays (1951, 1954, and 1965 Giants)
OF—Frank Robinson (1956 and 1961 Reds, 1966 Orioles)
OF—Fred Lynn (1975 Red Sox)
 C—Johnny Bench (1968, 1970, and 1972 Reds)
 P—Don Newcombe (1949 and 1956 Dodgers)

Rose, Allen, and Ripken had changed positions by the time they won their MVPs: Rose from second to the outfield, Allen from third to first, and Ripken from third to short. Lynn and Newcombe deserve special mention—Lynn for being the only one to win both awards in the same year, and Newcombe for being the only player to win not only Rookie of the Year and Most Valuable Player honors but also the Cy Young Award (1956). The other double winners are Jackie Robinson, 1947 and 1949 Dodgers; Willie McCovey, 1959 and 1969 Giants; Rod Carew, 1967 and 1977 Twins; Thurman Munson, 1970 and 1976 Yankees; Andre Dawson, 1977 Expos and 1987 Cubs; and Jose Canseco, 1986 and 1988 Athletics.

13 The End and After

*This chapter tells what they did after hanging up
their gloves. Or, in some cases, why they hung up
their gloves when they did.*

—— THEY DIED WITH THEIR ——
SPIKES ON

Although Lou Gehrig was the most noted player forced to
the sidelines by a fatal disease, he was out of the game two
years before succumbing. The following met quicker ends:

  1B—Harry Agganis (1955 Red Sox)
  2B—Ken Hubbs (1963 Cubs)
  3B—Tony Boeckel (1923 Braves)
  SS—Ray Chapman (1920 Indians)
  OF—Ed Delahanty (1903 Senators)
  OF—Len Koenecke (1935 Dodgers)
  OF—Roberto Clemente (1972 Pirates)
   C—Thurman Munson (1979 Yankees)
   P—Don Wilson (1974 Astros)

Agganis was felled by a pulmonary embolism. Hubbs,
Munson, and Clemente died in plane crashes. Chapman, the
only on-field fatality in the history of major league baseball,
was beaned by Carl Mays. Delahanty went on a bender and
apparently jumped off the International Bridge into the Niagara
River. Wilson asphyxiated himself in his own garage. Boeckel
was hit by an automobile while looking at the wreckage of a
collision he had survived a few minutes before. Koenecke had
been sent home from a road trip because he hadn't been hitting; after taking a train from St. Louis to Detroit, he chartered
a plane and, once in the air, went berserk. Attempts to calm
him included two blows on the head with a fire extinguisher,
and he died of a fractured skull. Additional baseball suicides
include Chick Stahl, Win Mercer, and Willard Hershberger.

—— THE DISABLED ——

Even though Ray Chapman is the only major leaguer ever killed on the diamond, numerous other players have had promising careers shortened or terminated by serious injuries.

1B—Dale Alexander (1934 Red Sox)
2B—Rennie Stennett (1978 Pirates)
3B—John Castino (1984 Twins)
SS—Dickie Thon (1984 Astros)
OF—Pete Reiser (1946 Dodgers)
OF—Bobby Valentine (1973 Angels)
OF—Tony Conigliaro (1967 Red Sox)
C—John Stearns (1980 Mets)
P—Herb Score (1957 Indians)

A year after winning the batting crown, Alexander accepted his club's recommendation for diathermy treatment for a leg injury and developed gangrene. Stennett, Castino, and Valentine suffered broken legs. Thon was beaned by Mets' pitcher Mike Torrez and, although he fought his way back to a starting position, never regained his burgeoning form as an all-star shortstop. Reiser's broken ankle in 1946 was sandwiched between two fractured skulls in 1942 and 1947 that made him the epitome of the hard-luck player. Conigliaro was beaned by Jack Hamilton. Stearns, one of the only things Mets fans had to cheer about, broke an index finger on a Dave Concepcion foul ball and never again caught 100 games. Score's apparently brilliant career came to another might-have-been when he was struck in the face by a line drive off the bat of Gil McDougald.

—— THE EXILES ——

Baseball has had to admit to more dirty laundry than just the 1919 Black Sox.

        1B—Hal Chase (1919 Giants)
        2B—Gene Paulette (1920 Phillies)
        3B—Heinie Zimmerman (1919 Giants)
        SS—Al Nichols (1877 Louisville)
        OF—George Hall (1877 Louisville)
        OF—Benny Kauff (1920 Giants)
        OF—Jimmy O'Connell (1924 Giants)
         C—Bill Craver (1877 Louisville)
         P—Phil Douglas (1922 Giants)

With the exception of Kauff and Craver, all these players were banned for alleged involvement with gamblers and/or throwing games. Even though ultimately cleared, Kauff was indicted for abetting an auto theft ring, and baseball decided that this was enough to keep him off the field forever. Although usually linked with Nichols, Hall, and pitcher Jim Devlin as the "Louisville Crooks," catcher-shortstop Craver was actually banned because he refused to sign a nongambling pledge circulated in the immediate aftermath of the scandal. The manager of this team could be either Pete Rose for his gambling entanglements or Jack O'Connor, the skipper of the 1910 St. Louis Browns who ordered his own third baseman to play deep against Nap Lajoie so that the latter could beat out Ty Cobb for the batting championship. Lajoie went eight for eight, including six bunt singles, but Cobb won anyway and O'Connor was never allowed to manage again. And don't forget umpire Richard Higham, expelled from the National League in 1882 for telling gamblers the probable winners of games he was to officiate.

—— OLDEST PLAYERS ——

Some players have put off retirement as long as possible.

> 1B—Cap Anson (1897 Cubs) age 46
> 2B—Arlie Latham (1909 Giants) age 50
> 3B—Jimmy Austin (1929 Dodgers) age 49
> SS—Bobby Wallace (1918 Cardinals) age 44
> OF—Sam Thompson (1906 Tigers) age 46
> OF—Sam Rice (1934 Indians) age 44
> OF—Carl Yastrzemski (1983 Red Sox) age 44
> C—Jim O'Rourke (1904 Giants) age 52
> P—Satchel Paige (1965 Athletics) age 59

Anson squeaks by Dan Brouthers, who was a month younger when he played two games for the Giants in 1904. Latham played in only two games, Austin in just one. Wallace played 12 games at short, 17 at second base, and 1 at third. Thompson was in the outfield for 8 games, Rice for 78, and Yaz for only 1 (although he was Boston's regular DH). Right up to Bob Boone and Carlton Fisk, over 40 catchers have been a frequent occurrence. Were it not for O'Rourke's extraordinary 52 years, Gabby Street (1931 Cardinals) and Deacon McGuire (1912 Tigers), both of whom caught a game at the age of 48, would have deserved the nod. Paige's age, of course, is only an estimate; in his three scoreless innings for the 1965 A's, he gave up one hit and struck out one. Honorable mention to Charley O'Leary, who singled and scored a run as a pinch-hitter just a few weeks shy of his 53d birthday for the 1934 Browns. The manager is Connie Mack, who was a few months short of his 89th birthday when he managed his last game for the Athletics in 1950.

—— TIMING IS ALL ——

Some players have ended their careers on high notes. Not counting those who never came back because of illness or death, this is a lineup of players with the best final season.

> 1B—Cap Anson (1897 Cubs)
> 2B—Bobby Doerr (1951 Red Sox)
> 3B—Tony Cuccinello (1945 White Sox)
> SS—Art Fletcher (1922 Phillies)
> OF—Dave Kingman (1986 Athletics)
> OF—Ted Williams (1960 Red Sox)
> OF—Ty Cobb (1928 Athletics)
> C—Wilbert Robinson (1902 Orioles)
> P—Sandy Koufax (1966 Dodgers)

Anson batted .302 with 75 runs batted in. Doerr knocked in 73 runs with a .289 average. Cuccinello, told that he was not going to be signed for the following season to make room for returning servicemen, came within a point of winning the AL batting title with his .308. Fletcher turned in a steady .280. Kingman, whose surly personality and strikeouts made him unattractive on the free-agent market, set a final-season record with 35 home runs. Williams not only hit the homer celebrated by John Updike but also 28 others and batted .316. Cobb went out at .323. Robinson pleased himself as manager with a .293 mark. Koufax is the only player ever to lead a league in significant categories in his final season: He did it in ERA, strikeouts, complete games, shutouts, and victories (27).

—— ONE YEAR TOO MANY ——

Then there were the players who hung around longer than they should have. Although others had lower batting averages in their final seasons, those in this lineup showed the biggest differential from their career marks for 300 at bats or more:

    1B—Stan Musial (1963 Cardinals)
    2B—Nap Lajoie (1916 Athletics)
    3B—Bill Werber (1942 Giants)
    SS—Travis Jackson (1936 Giants)
    OF—Ducky Holmes (1905 White Sox)
    OF—Billy Williams (1976 Athletics)
    OF—Ken Singleton (1984 Orioles)
     C—Fred Carroll (1891 Pirates)
     P—Steve Carlton (1985–88 Five teams)

Musial's .255 represented a 76-point drop from his career average. Lajoie closed out at .246—a whopping 93 points below his lifetime mark. Werber was not only off 66 points in batting (.205 to .271), but also managed only one homer and 13 runs batted in. Jackson was off 61 points at .230; Holmes, 81 points at .201, Williams, 79 points at .211; Singleton, 67 points at .215; and Carroll, 66 points at .218. Carlton's last four seasons were a painful lurch from the Phillies to the Giants to the White Sox to the Indians and, finally, to the Twins to find a mastery that had long abandoned him; his record over the period was 16–37. Over a two-year span, Elston Howard of the Red Sox would deserve the nod ahead of Carroll: For the combined 1967–68 period, the once-great Yankees catcher batted a mere .202, 72 points off his lifetime average. Also earning mention is outfielder Jimmy Ryan of the 1903 Senators, whose .245 was 64 points under his career mark.

—— SECOND THOUGHTS ——

Some players have found retirement less than they bargained for and attempted comebacks.

> 1B—Dick Allen (1977 Athletics)
> 2B—Johnny Evers (1922 White Sox, 1929 Braves)
> 3B—Pie Traynor (1937 Pirates)
> SS—Leo Durocher (1943 and 1945 Dodgers)
> OF—Curt Flood (1971 Senators)
> OF—Babe Herman (1945 Dodgers)
> OF—Sam Dungan (1900 Cubs, 1901 Senators)
> C—Jim O'Rourke (1904 Giants)
> P—Dizzy Trout (1957 Orioles)

Two years after quitting, Allen returned to bat .240 in 51 games. Evers, who had retired in 1917, was reactivated for single games by Chicago and Boston. Manager Traynor reactivated himself after a one-year hiatus for five games and a .167 mark. After turning over shortstop to Pee Wee Reese in 1941, manager Durocher returned for six games in 1943 and two more (as a second baseman) in 1945. In the midst of his protest retirement over the reserve clause, Flood was talked into 13 games by Washington owner Bob Short. Eight years after going home, Herman returned to Ebbets Field to bat .265 in 34 at bats. A fair hitter from 1892 to 1894, Dungan failed in his comeback effort with Chicago, but hit .320 for Washington. O'Rourke had been out of the game 11 years when, at the age of 52, he caught a pennant-deciding game and went one for four. Five years after his retirement, Trout was so impressive in an old timers' game that Baltimore gave him another shot. He appeared in two games, got one batter out, and had an ERA of 81.00.

—— OLDEST REGULARS ——

Then there were those who not only refused to take off their uniforms but also took the field at least 100 times at an advanced baseball age.

        1B—Cap Anson (1897 Cubs) age 46
        2B—Rabbit Maranville (1933 Braves) age 41
        3B—Graig Nettles (1986 Padres) age 42
        SS—Luke Appling (1949 White Sox) age 42
        OF—Sam Rice (1931 Senators) age 41
        OF—Stan Musial (1962 Cardinals) age 41
        OF—Ty Cobb (1927 Athletics) age 40
         C—Carlton Fisk (1990 White Sox) age 42
         P—Hoyt Wilhelm (1970 Braves, Cubs) age 47

Cobb hit a dazzling .357, with Anson, Appling, Rice, and Musial also above .300. Wilhelm's record was 6–5 with 13 saves.

—— UMPIRES ——

With umpires entering the big leagues at younger ages and after elaborate training courses, it is unlikely that the job will continue to attract such former players as:

        1B—Jake Beckley
        2B—Bill Summers
        3B—George Moriarty
        SS—Babe Pinelli
        OF—Jocko Conlan
        OF—Frank Secory
        OF—Sherry Magee
         C—Charlie Berry
         P—Lon Warneke

The bullpen would include Firpo Marberry, Ed Rommel, George Pipgras, Bill Kunkel, and Ken Burkhart.

—— OTHER FIELDS OF DREAMS ——

With the debatable exception of Billy Sunday, these players came into their own only after leaving the major leagues.

    1B—Chuck Connors
    2B—Johnny Berardino
    3B—Carmen Fanzone
    SS—Rod Dedeaux
    OF—Bill Sharman
    OF—Billy Sunday
    OF—Fred Brown
     C—Bob Uecker
     P—John Tener

Connors became a movie heavy and television's "Rifleman." Berardino has been practicing in the soap opera "General Hospital" for decades. Fanzone is a trumpet player in the "Tonight" show band. Dedeaux, after two partial seasons with the Dodgers, went on to become the country's most noted college baseball coach. Although he never appeared in a game, future NBA Hall of Famer Sharman was kicked out of one when Dodger manager Charlie Dressen persuaded an umpire that it was the September call-up, not one of his regulars, who had been mocking the men in blue from the bench. Evangelist Sunday became the Billy Graham of his day. Brown became governor of New Hampshire and the national pastime's only member of the U.S. Senate. Uecker parlayed his diamond mediocrity into careers as an announcer, author, comedian, and television sitcom star. Tener became governor of Pennsylvania. Honorable mentions to longtime Vera Cruz mayor Bobby Avila, author Jim Bouton, journalist Pat Jordan, stuntman Ernie Orsatti, and congressmen Jim Bunning and Vinegar Bend Mizell.

—— FOOTBALL PROS ——

Bo Jackson is far from being the first athlete to play professional baseball and football simultaneously; he was, however, the first gridiron star to play in baseball's All-Star Game.

1B—Tom Brown
2B—Chuck Corgan
3B—Charlie Dressen
SS—Jim Levey
OF—Bo Jackson
OF—Evar Swanson
OF—Walt French
 C—Charlie Berry
 P—Garland Buckeye

Brown, the only major leaguer to appear in a Super Bowl, was in the NFL for the 1964–69 seasons. The others: Corgan, 1924–27; Dressen, 1920 and 1922–23; Levey, 1934–36; Jackson, 1987–90; Swanson, 1924–27; French, 1922 and 1925; Berry, 1925–26; and Buckeye, 1920–24. Honorable mentions to Red Badgro, Paddy Driscoll, Ernie Nevers, George Halas, Greasy Neale, Jim Thorpe, and Ace Parker—not particularly memorable as diamond stars but all in the Football Hall of Fame. Others deserving nods include Vic Janowicz, Matt Kinzer, and Sandy Vance, whose three wins and two losses over three fragmented seasons in the American League in the 1930s make him the only footballer-pitcher with a career record over .500.

—— BASKETBALL PROS ——

Some waited until they saw they wouldn't be very good at baseball, others played the sports simultaneously, and still others were on the basketball court before the baseball diamond.

1B—George Crowe
2B—Ralph Miller
3B—Danny Ainge
SS—Dick Groat
OF—Irv Noren
OF—Frankie Baumholtz
OF—Rusty Saunders
C—Del Rice
P—Gene Conley

Crowe played for the NBL in 1948–49, Miller for the ABL in 1925–31, Ainge for the NBA from 1981 to the present, Groat for the NBA in 1952–53, Noren for the NBL in 1946–47, Baumholtz for the NBL in 1945–46 and the BAA in 1946–47, Saunders for the ABL in 1925–31 and the NBL in 1940–41 and 1945–46, Rice for the NBL in 1945–46, and Conley for the NBA in 1952–53 and 1958–64. Among those deserving honorable mention are pitchers Dave DeBusschere, Ron Reed, and Bob Gibson (who spent the 1957–58 season with the Harlem Globetrotters). The manager-coach would have to be Red Rolfe, who piloted the Tigers between 1949 and 1952 and coached in the BAA in 1946–1947.

—— OTHER SPORTS ——

Tennis, anyone? No, but on the other hand . . .

  1B—Jim Thorpe (track and field)
  2B—Buddy Blattner (table tennis)
  3B—Don Hoak (boxing)
  SS—Andre Rodgers (cricket)
  OF—Sammy Byrd (golf)
  OF—Bill Maharg (boxing)
  OF—Wes Schulmerich (wrestling)
   C—Ernie Lombardi (bocce)
   P—Kirk McCaskill (hockey)

Technically, Thorpe and Lombardi did not have the professional status of the other members of this lineup. Thorpe, of course, suffered for the distinction, while Lombardi became so renowned in the Bay Area for his skills in the Italian game that he was known as "Bocce" to fellow National Leaguers. At one point, Blattner was the national table tennis champion. Hoak fought professionally in his native Pennsylvania, Schulmerich wrestled in his native Oregon. Rodgers has been the only Caribbean cricket player to reach the majors. Byrd is one of several retired major leaguers who have taken to the links; the list includes former pitchers Ralph Terry and Lou Kretlow, and outfielder Ken Harrelson. Maharg was one of the teenagers pressed into service by the Tigers in 1912 to replace the players striking in solidarity with the suspended Ty Cobb; he put in another one-game appearance for the Phillies many years later but concentrated more on the ring. McCaskill was drafted by the Winnipeg Jets in 1981 and scored 10 goals and had 12 assists for their Sherbrooke farm club in 1983–84.

14 Nationalities

Italian Americans and Polish Americans could start ethnic baseball halls of fame. And, they're not the only ones.

—— THE ITALIANS ——

The first Italian-American to reach the majors was Louis Pessano Dickerson, an outfielder in the late 1870s and early 1880s; the first with an Italian surname was Ed Abbaticchio, an infielder between 1897 and 1910. Their successors were rather better.

    1B—Dolf Camilli
    2B—Tony Lazzeri
    3B—Joe Torre
    SS—Phil Rizzuto
    OF—Joe DiMaggio
    OF—Dom DiMaggio
    OF—Carl Furillo
     C—Yogi Berra
     P—Ed Cicotte

Although mainly linked today with the Black Sox scandal in the 1919 World Series, Cicotte was among the top pitchers of his era, compiling a record of 211–147. Honorable mentions to Ernie Lombardi, the half-Italian Roy Campanella, Frank Malzone, Rico Petrocelli, Dave Righetti, and Frank Viola, among others. The manager is Billy Martin.

—— THE POLES ——

No Polish jokes here.

1B—Ted Kluszewski
2B—Bill Mazeroski
3B—Whitey Kurowski
SS—Tony Kubek
OF—Stan Musial
OF—Al Simmons
OF—Carl Yastrzemski
C—Carl Sawatski
P—Stan Coveleski

Simmons's real name was Aloysius Syzmanski.

—— THE FRENCH ——

Franco-Americans are not one of the significant ethnic groups in baseball; however, French pride would not be offended by these selections.

1B—Del Bissonette
2B—Nap Lajoie
3B—Jim Lefebvre
SS—Lou Boudreau
OF—Frenchy Bordagaray
OF—Bruce Boisclair
OF—Jack Fournier
C—Bruce Bochy
P—Bill Voiselle

For a manager we'll take Leo Durocher. Lajoie and Boudreau are Hall of Famers. Fournier was mostly a first baseman, but we had to get Bissonette's .305 lifetime average into the lineup without losing Fournier's .313. Bochy is the only native-born Frenchman here. Voiselle had a losing record lifetime (74–84) but had one fine year with the Giants, 21–16 in 1944.

—— JEWISH STARS ——

In the beginning there was Lip Pike, the first Jewish major leaguer, who started in the National League in 1876.

1B—Hank Greenberg
2B—Lip Pike
3B—Al Rosen
SS—Buddy Myer
OF—Sid Gordon
OF—Benny Kauff
OF—George Stone
C—Johnny Kling
P—Sandy Koufax

Ken Holtzman would be in the bullpen.

—— NATIVE AMERICANS ——

Baseball may be the American game, but it is not the Native Americans' game.

1B—Willie Stargell
2B—Bob Johnson
3B—Roy Johnson
SS—Mark Christman
OF—Lou Sockalexis
OF—Jim Thorpe
OF—Gene Locklear
C—Chief Meyers
P—Chief Bender

Stargell (half-Indian), Meyers, and Bender were authentic stars. The Johnsons were primarily outfielders who both ended their careers with identical .296 averages. Christman and Locklear were journeymen. Thorpe, the greatest Indian athlete, was less than that. So was Sockalexis, the first Indian in the majors.

—— THE IRISH IRISH ——

That's right. Not an Irish-American team but the real McCoy from the Emerald Isle itself. Most of these players go back to the last century or the early part of this one.

1B—Denny O'Neil
2B—Reddy Mack
3B—Jim Hallinan
SS—Andy Leonard
OF—Jack Doyle
OF—Jimmy Walsh
OF—Patsy Donovan
C—Jimmy Archer
P—Tony Mullane

Although Roger Bresnahan liked to claim that he came from Tralee, he was born in Toledo, Ohio.

—— THE MOTHER COUNTRY ——

Considering the fact that baseball is at least in part derived from the British game of rounders, we might have expected a better team here.

1B—Ed Cogswell (England)
2B—Dick Higham (England)
3B—Jimmy Austin (Wales)
SS—Dave Brain (England)
OF—Hugh Nicol (Scotland)
OF—Bobby Thomson (Scotland)
OF—Tom Brown (England)
C—Al Shaw (England)
P—Parson Lewis (Wales)

Journeymen prevail here. The exceptions are Austin, Brain, Brown, and Thomson.

—— THE CONTINENTALS ——

Very few Europeans have made it to the major leagues.

    1B—Johnny Reder (Poland)
    2B—Joe Strauss (Hungary)
    3B—Reno Bertoia (Italy)
    SS—Willie Kuehne (Germany)
    OF—Elmer Valo (Czechoslovakia)
    OF—Jake Gettman (Russia)
    OF—Olaf Hendriksen (Denmark)
     C—Art Jorgens (Norway)
     P—Bert Blyleven (The Netherlands)

No two players from the same country. And honorable mention to Switzerland's Otto Hess, Greece's Al Campanis, Austria's Kurt Krieger, and Finland's John Michaelson.

—— CANADIAN IMPORTS ——

Baseball spread south across the Caribbean and the Rio Grande and west across the Pacific more readily than north into Canada. The following are the best of those who managed to slip across the world's longest undefended border:

    1B—Bill Phillips
    2B—Sherry Robertson
    3B—Pete Ward
    SS—Blackie O'Rourke
    OF—Tip O'Neill
    OF—George Selkirk
    OF—Terry Puhl
     C—Moon Gibson
     P—Ferguson Jenkins

Jenkins and O'Neill are particularly noteworthy. Phillips was the first Canadian-born major leaguer. And honorable mention to Larry Walker, the first Canadian-born player on a Canadian team.

—— THE PUERTO RICANS ——

The best the Commonwealth has to offer are

1B—Vic Power
2B—Felix Millan
3B—Jose Pagan
SS—Ivan DeJesus
OF—Roberto Clemente
OF—Orlando Cepeda
OF—Jose Cruz
  C—Benito Santiago
  P—Ed Figueroa

The bench would include Ruben Sierra and Sixto Lezcano. Honorable mention to Hi Bithorn (1942 Cubs), the first Puerto Rican in the majors.

—— THE CUBANS ——

Most early Latins in professional baseball were Cubans, and black Cubans were prominent in the Negro leagues. Most of this lineup, however, comes from the post-Castro refugee generation.

1B—Tony Perez
2B—Cookie Rojas
3B—Tito Fuentes
SS—Bert Campaneris
OF—Minnie Minoso
OF—Tony Oliva
OF—Jose Canseco
  C—Mike Gonzalez
  P—Mike Cuellar

The exceptions are Gonzalez, Minoso, and manager Preston Gomez. Honorable mention to the first Cubans, Rafael Almeida and Armando Marsans (both 1911 Reds), and Frank Bancroft, who introduced baseball into Cuba.

—— THE DOMINICANS ——

Ozzie Virgil, Sr., (1956 Giants) was the first. Then came:

    1B—Felipe Alou
    2B—Juan Samuel
    3B—Pedro Guerrero
    SS—Tony Fernandez
    OF—Rico Carty
    OF—Cesar Cedeno
    OF—George Bell
     C—Tony Pena
     P—Juan Marichal

The scouting report: excellent offense, adequate defense, and a pitcher second to none.

—— THE VENEZUELANS ——

Hundreds of Anglo ballplayers flock to Venezuela for the winter leagues. And, starting with Alex Carrasquel (1939 Senators), Venezuela has sent some pretty good players the other way, too.

    1B—Andres Galarraga
    2B—Manny Trillo
    3B—Dave Concepcion
    SS—Luis Aparicio
    OF—Cesar Tovar
    OF—Vic Davalillo
    OF—Tony Armas
     C—Bo Diaz
     P—Luis Leal

Venezuela seems to specialize in shortstops. Aparicio is the best of them. Concepcion can move over to third. But Chico Carrasquel gets squeezed out.

—— SOUTH OF THE BORDER ——

Mexico simply does not send its best players north—probably because the domestic leagues are so good.

    1B—Mel Almada
    2B—Bobby Avila
    3B—Aurelio Rodriguez
    SS—Ruben Amaro
    OF—Jorge Orta
    OF—Manuel Cueto
    OF—Celerino Sanchez
     C—Alex Trevino
     P—Fernando Valenzuela

Almada (1933 Red Sox) was the pioneer.

—— THE PANAMANIANS ——

There are no teams from Honduras, Costa Rica, Nicaragua, Guatemala, or Belize. (In fact, the only major leaguers born between Mexico and Panama are Nicaraguans Dennis Martinez and David Green, and Honduran Gerald Young.)

    1B—Rod Carew
    2B—Rennie Stennett
    3B—Hector Lopez
    SS—Chico Salmon
    OF—Ben Oglivie
    OF—Omar Moreno
    OF—Roberto Kelly
     C—Manny Sanguillen
     P—Hal Haydel

Lopez (1955 Athletics) and Humberto Robinson (1955 Braves) were the first Panamanians.

—— THE ANTILLES ——

Cricket, anyone?

    1B—Jose Morales (The Virgin Islands)
    2B—Horace Clarke (The Virgin Islands)
    3B—Valmy Thomas (The Virgin Islands)
    SS—Andre Rodgers (The Bahamas)
    OF—Ed Armbrister (The Bahamas)
    OF—Tony Curry (The Bahamas)
    OF—Joe Christopher (The Virgin Islands)
     C—Ellie Hendricks (The Virgin Islands)
     P—Wenty Ford (The Bahamas)

An infield that lacks defense, an outfield without offensive punch, and that's Wenty—not Whitey—on the mound. Thomas played one game at the hot corner or this team would have been impossible.

—— PACIFIC ISLANDERS ——

And out there in the Pacific . . .

    1B—Tony Solaita (American Samoa)
    2B—Bobby Fenwick (Okinawa)
    3B—Joe Quinn (Australia)
    SS—Lenn Sakata (Hawaii)
    OF—Mike Lum (Hawaii)
    OF—Prince Oana (Hawaii)
    OF—John Matias (Hawaii)
     C—Tony Rego (Hawaii)
     P—Masanori Murakami (Japan)

Murakami, the only native Japanese to make the jump across the Pacific, pitched well for the Giants in 1964 and 1965 but went back to play in the Land of the Rising Sun for the honor of his family. Bobby Balcena, the only Filipino to play in the major leagues, was born in California and, therefore, doesn't qualify.

15 Folklore

The oral tradition is as much a part of baseball as the record book. This chapter recounts stories both dramatic and zany that make up the game's lore.

— TRIVIA —

These are the answers to some of the most commonly asked trivia questions. What are the questions?

        1B—Babe Dahlgren
        2B—Eddie Miksis
        3B—Harry Steinfeldt
        SS—Frank Duffy
        OF—Willie Mays
        OF—Bobby Bonds
        OF—Jim Delsing
          C—Bill Dickey
          P—Tracy Stallard

Who succeeded Lou Gehrig at first base for the Yankees? Who scored the winning run when Cookie Lavagetto doubled to break up Bill Bevens's near-no hitter in the 1947 World Series? Who was the third baseman in the Cubs' fabled Tinker to Evers to Chance infield? Whom did the Giants get in the trade that sent George Foster to the Cincinnati Reds? Who was on deck when Bobby Thomson hit "the shot heard 'round the world?" Who is the only player to steal 30 bases and hit 30 home runs in five seasons? Who was the pinch runner for Eddie Gaedel after the midget walked? Who broke Carl Hubbell's streak of five consecutive strikeouts in the 1934 All-Star Game? Who served up Roger Maris's 61st home run in 1961?

—— MISCONCEPTIONS ——

Myths, misconceptions, and oversights—baseball history is replete with them. For example:

1B—Marv Throneberry
2B—Eddie Stanky
3B—Buck Weaver
SS—Lou Boudreau
OF—Babe Ruth
OF—Pete Gray
OF—Casey Stengel
 C—Yogi Berra
 P—Monty Stratton

Although he became the symbol of the Mets' buffoonery in their initial years, Throneberry actually played for the New Yorkers in only two seasons and in only one of them regularly. In the year he did play regularly, he had the highest fielding percentage among Mets' regulars.

Despite the backhanded compliment, variously attributed to Leo Durocher and Branch Rickey, that "he couldn't hit, couldn't field, and couldn't throw, all he could do was win," Stanky had batting averages of .320, .285, and .300 in 1948, 1949, and 1950 and led the National League in double plays and putouts several times.

Weaver was thrown out of baseball as one of the infamous Black Sox, but there has never been a shred of evidence linking him to the dishonesty of his seven teammates or to the gamblers of the era.

Boudreau was not the youngest manager ever when he piloted the Indians at the age of 24; that distinction belongs to Roger Peckinpaugh, who was 23 when he took over the Yankees for the last 17 games of the 1914 season.

Yankee Stadium is not known as "The House that Ruth Built" because of all the home runs Babe hit in the Bronx; the epithet actually stems from the fact that the ballpark had to be built because Ruth's homers (and the large number of fans who

came to see them) made the Yankees non grata in the Polo
Grounds, where the landlord New York Giants didn't like being
outdrawn by their tenants.

The one-armed Gray was not a member of the pennant-
winning St. Louis Browns of 1944; his only major league season was the following year, when he hit .218 in 61 games.

Stengel is often credited with dropping a grapefruit out of
an airplane to an unsuspecting Wilbert Robinson, who was
expecting a baseball, but the practical joke was actually the
work of trainer Frank Kelley.

Although he is often thought of as Bill Dickey's immediate
successor as the Yankees catcher, Berra did not take over behind the plate on a regular basis until 1949, six years after
Dickey stopped being a regular; in between there were Mike
Garbark, Aaron Robinson, and Gus Niarhos.

After the 1938 hunting accident that cost him a leg, Stratton did not struggle back to the majors; the furthest he got, and
that only for a brief time, was a low minor league team.

No one any longer believes the myth that baseball was
born in Cooperstown, but that misconception has been replaced
by the belief that the first game was played in Hoboken on
June 19, 1846. Recent research has uncovered another game
played in Hoboken on October 21, 1845. The New York Ball
Club beat a Brooklyn team by a score of 24–4 in this contest.
In a rematch three days later in Brooklyn, New York won again,
37–19.

—— EMBARRASSING MOMENTS ——

Sometimes players wish they were spectators in the bleachers.

> 1B—Fred Merkle (1908 Giants)
> 2B—Chick Fewster (1926 Dodgers)
> 3B—Tommy Glaviano (1950 Cardinals)
> SS—Lyn Lary (1931 Yankees)
> OF—Andy Pafko (1949 Cubs)
> OF—Hack Wilson (1934 Dodgers)
> OF—Gary Geiger (1961 Red Sox)
> C—Tim McCarver (1976 Phillies)
> P—Tommy John (1988 Yankees)

Merkle's infamous boner cost the Giants a pennant. Fewster, the middle runner when Babe Herman "doubled into a double play," was tagged out after wandering off third away from all the confusion. Glaviano botched three consecutive ninth-inning grounders and turned a sure St. Louis win into a loss. Lary cost Lou Gehrig sole possession of a home run title when he assumed one of Gehrig's blasts had been caught and left the basepath. Pafko caught a line drive that the umpire ruled "no catch," ran in from center field to argue, neglected to call time, and allowed two runs to score while the ball was still in his glove. The hungover Wilson chased a line drive and fired a bullet back to the infield—only to discover that the ball had been thrown by pitcher Boom Boom Beck in disgust for having been given the hook. Geiger tripled home the tying run in an extra-inning game, then walked to the dugout thinking he had won the game; he was tagged out, the rains came, and the game was declared a tie. McCarver hit a ninth-inning grand slam on Bicentennial Day in Philadelphia; excited by the fireworks and exploding scoreboard, he passed the runner in front of him and had to settle for a game-winning single. John made three errors on one play: a bobbled grounder, a subsequent errant throw into right field, and a wild throw home on the relay back to the infield.

—— LOUD CLOUTS ——

When these players succeeded, they affected more than their individual statistics.

1B—Frank Chance (1908 Cubs)
2B—Jerry Coleman (1949 Yankees)
3B—Mike Schmidt (1980 Phillies)
SS—Phil Rizzuto (1951 Yankees)
OF—Chet Laabs (1944 Browns)
OF—Hank Greenberg (1945 Tigers)
OF—Dick Sisler (1950 Phillies)
 C—Gabby Hartnett (1938 Cubs)
 P—Floyd Giebell (1940 Tigers)

Chance's double in the third inning of the 1908 makeup game (October 9) necessitated by the Merkle boner drove in two runs and put the Cubs ahead to stay. Coleman's bases-loaded double was the margin of difference as the Yankees defeated the Red Sox on the last day of the season (October 2) to win the pennant. On the final weekend of the season (October 4-5), Schmidt drove in both runs in a 2–1 victory and hit an 11th-inning home run in a 6–4 win that paved the way to a Philadelphia championship. Rizzuto squeezed home Joe DiMaggio with the bases loaded (September 17) to score the winning run and put the Yankees in first place to stay. Laabs hit two home runs and drove in four on the final day of the season (October 1) to clinch the St. Louis miracle. Sisler hit a three-run shot in the top of the 10th (October 1) against the Dodgers to seal the Whiz Kids' pennant. Greenberg's grand slam in the ninth inning of the second-last game (September 30) was the margin of Detroit's pennant. Hartnett's "homer in the gloamin' " in the bottom of the 10th (September 28) assured a Chicago flag. Giebell, whose season record was a mere 2–0, beat Bob Feller with a six-hit shutout by a score of 2–0 to clinch the Detroit pennant on the last weekend (September 27).

—— STREAK BREAKERS ——

The pitchers knew it had to happen eventually. The batters who made it happen were

> 1B—Todd Benzinger (1989 Reds)
> 2B—Eddie Stanky (1947 Dodgers)
> 3B—Debs Garms (1938 Braves)
> SS—Maury Wills (1970 Dodgers)
> OF—Sam Crawford (1904 Tigers)
> OF—Bubba Morton (1962 Tigers)
> OF—Bernie Carbo (1972 Cardinals)
> C—John Stearns (1982 Mets)
> P—Lefty Tyler (1916 Braves)

Benzinger's RBI single in the first inning of Orel Hershiser's first start in 1989 ended the pitcher's 59 consecutive scoreless innings. Stanky singled with one out in the ninth inning to prevent Ewell Blackwell from matching Johnny Vander Meer's back-to-back no hitters. Garms was the batter who finally broke through for a single off Vander Meer after 21 2/3 no-hit innings. Wills managed to put the ball in play against Tom Seaver, ending the Mets pitcher's 10 straight strikeouts. Crawford singled in the sixth inning to end Cy Young's 24 consecutive hitless innings over three games; Young went on to pitch a 1–0 five-hit, 15-inning shutout. Morton drew the first walk off Bill Fischer after the latter's record-setting 84 1/3 innings without yielding a base on balls. Carbo's double off Jim Barr ended the pitcher's streak of retiring 41 straight batters. Stearns touched Greg Minton for the first home run given up by the Giants reliever in 269 1/3 innings. The manager is Al Lopez, whose 1954 Indians and 1959 White Sox prevented the Yankees from claiming a hallucinating 16 consecutive pennants!

—— BIZARRE AT BATS ——

A collection of the weirdest plate appearances:

1B—Stuffy McInnis (1911 Athletics)
2B—George Cutshaw (1916 Dodgers)
3B—George Brett (1983 Royals)
SS—Ray Chapman (1920 Indians)
OF—Jack Tobin (1922 Browns)
OF—George Altman (1960 Cubs)
OF—Dave Augustine (1973 Pirates)
 C—Grover Land (1915 Brooklyn FL)
 P—Rick Camp (1985 Braves)

On June 27 McInnis took advantage of a new—and short-lived—rule prohibiting pitchers to take warm-up pitches between innings and walloped one of Ed Karger's warm-ups for an inside-the-park homer—before the outfielders were on the field.

Cutshaw broke up a tie game in the 11th inning with a shot that struck the right field fence in Ebbets Field, landed in a rain gutter, and spun upward and over the fence for what was in those days a four-bagger.

Brett's home run was disallowed because he had rubbed pine tar too far up the bat, then reallowed by American League President Lee McPhail on the grounds that Brett had never intended to break the rules.

Chapman walked away from the plate with an 0–2 count because, with Walter Johnson pitching, a third strike "wouldn't do me any good."

Tobin grounded out routinely first-to-pitcher to end a 2–1 game in late May, but after the players had dispersed and the crowd had overrun the field, the umpire agreed that Yankee pitcher Sam Jones had bobbled the ball and allowed the tying run to score. The crowd was sent back to the stands, the players returned to the field, and the game continued as the Browns scored five additional runs. (Jones was so shaken he lost his next nine games.)

Altman walked on three balls (on April 24) as a balk was incorrectly counted as a ball.

In the 13th inning of a crucial game (on September 30), Augustine hit a ball onto the top of the wall in Shea Stadium; the ball bounced straight up in the air and into the hands of Mets left fielder Cleon Jones whose throw, relayed by the third baseman, cut down the potential winning run at the plate. (The Mets went on to win both the game and the pennant.)

Umpire Bill Brennan, working alone from behind the pitcher, piled baseballs for future use behind him. Land, with a perfect break-shot line drive, scattered baseballs all over the infield; every infielder had a ball, each of them tagged Land, but Brennan awarded Land a home run.

Camp, a lifetime .074 hitter, turned what was already a marathon into perhaps the most bizarre extra-inning game of all time when in the small hours of July 5 he hit his only major-league home run in the bottom of the 18th inning to tie the score at 11-all against the Mets. The New Yorkers finally won the game after six hours and 10 minutes of play plus a 41-minute rain delay, by scoring five runs in the top of the 19th—but not before the Braves got back two of those runs in the bottom of the 19th and stranded two runners when the final batter—none other than Rick Camp—struck out. It was 3:55 A.M.—the latest completion of a major league game—when the postgame Fourth of July fireworks display finally began.

—— SORRY ABOUT THAT ——

Rules, rule changes, ignorance, and mere spite have contrived to deprive players of opportunities or recognition. How many of the players in this lineup can you identify?

1B—Despite a lifetime .353 average as a regular, he isn't in the Hall of Fame because he played 2 years short of the 10-year minimum.

2B—In 1982 he failed to set the single-season mark for the most consecutive errorless games at 2B because his manager, unaware of the streak, benched him on the last day of the season.

3B—The Hall of Fame stiffened its entrance requirements to make it impossible for him to get in.

SS—He perfected the technique of "fair-foul" singles until a rules committee said balls had to remain fair until reaching first or third; his average plummeted from .429 to the .270s.

OF—He led the AL in most hitting categories in 1922 but was denied the MVP because of rules demanding voters select only one player per team.

OF—His lifetime .349 mark has been ignored by Cooperstown because his 11-year career included 4 as a pitcher.

OF—He was denied the 1938 AL batting title because, although he played in the 100 games required, 39 of them were as a one-time pinch hitter.

C—In 1926, while hitting .326, he was claimed by the Yankees on waivers from the White Sox. When NY refused to pay his original signing bonus money, he was inactivated while lawyers worked out the case; a month later he came back to Chicago but was never the same.

P—He lost the 1981 ERA title because his record was rounded off to the nearest complete inning.

Answers: Dave Orr, Manny Trillo, Pete Rose, Ross Barnes, Ken Williams (the votes went to George Sisler), Lefty O'Doul, Taft Wright, Harry McCurdy, and Sammy Stewart.

—— TOUGHEST RECORDS TO BREAK ——

Play-by-play announcers are always talking about the records that will never be broken. Sometimes they are even right. Some of the following records are relatively unknown, however, and should last into the distant future.

> 1B—Lou Gehrig
> 2B—Rogers Hornsby
> 3B—Piano Legs Hickman
> SS—Bill Dahlen
> OF—Charlie Jamieson
> OF—Joe DiMaggio
> OF—Babe Ruth
>   C—Alex Gardner
>   P—Jack Taylor

You probably guessed Gehrig's 2,130 consecutive games and DiMaggio's 56-game hitting streak. If you are really a trivia expert, you may have gotten Hornsby's .402 average over five years (1921–25 Cardinals) or Ruth's .847 slugging average over two seasons (1920–21 Yankees). But only the assiduous reader of small print knows about Hickman's 91 errors in 118 games for the Giants in 1900, Dahlen's 972 errors in his 21-year career (1891–1911), the two triple plays started by Jamieson while playing for the Indians in 1928, or Gardner's 12 passed balls for Washington (AA) on May 10, 1884. While none of these is in imminent danger of being broken, perhaps the most unbreakable record—especially in this era of specialists—is Taylor's streak of 188 complete games. From June 20, 1901, when he was with the Cubs, to August 9, 1906, when he hurled for the Cardinals, Taylor was never taken out for a relief pitcher. During that stretch he not only pitched 188 complete games but he also finished another 15 as a reliever for a total of 1,727 innings pitched without respite.

—— GEARING UP ——

More than one player has had a hand in encouraging or developing the equipment rules covering baseball.

    1B—Hank Greenberg
    2B—Lena Blackburne
    3B—Heinie Groh
    SS—Phil Rizzuto
    OF—Ralph Kiner
    OF—Pete Browning
    OF—Rusty Staub
     C—Randy Hundley
     P—Bill Doak

Greenberg's request in the 1930s for a first baseman's mitt with extra netting and webbing provoked all kinds of stipulations about glove size that remained in force until the 1980s. Blackburne patented the dirt substance used by umpires to take the sheen off new balls. Groh bred generations of singles hitters with his specially designed bottle bat. Rizzuto was the first to wear a batting helmet in the American League; Kiner the first in the National League. Browning was the first player to have his bats made specifically for him by John Hillerich, who then went on to popularize the arrangement by calling his product a Louisville Slugger. Staub popularized both the ear-flapped helmet and batting gloves. Hundley is considered the pioneer of the hinged flip-over mitt that has given catchers more flexibility behind the plate. Doak was the first to suggest a manufactured pocket in all gloves.

—— THE BAMBINO ——

Some Babe Ruth trivia. See if you can come up with the connection each had with the Babe's career.

    1B—Roger Connor
    2B—Ray Morgan
    3B—Ned Williamson
    SS—Mark Koenig
    OF—Sammy Vick
    OF—Sammy Byrd
    OF—George Selkirk
     C—Joe Glenn
     P—Hub Pruett

Connors' 136 home runs was the career high passed by Ruth on his way to 714. It was Morgan whose lead-off walk against Ruth on June 23, 1917, led to the Babe's ejection from the game and gave Ernie Shore the opportunity to retire 26 consecutive batters in relief after Morgan had been thrown out stealing. Williamson held the season home run record (27 with the 1884 Cubs) until Ruth hit 29 in 1919. Koenig, the Yankees' shortstop in the late 1920s, helped the Cubs win the pennant in 1932. When Koenig was voted only half a World Series share because he had been with the team only half a season, Ruth led the verbal attack on the Cubs for their cheapness. Ruth, legend has it, had his final say by calling his home run in the third game of the Series. Vick was Ruth's predecessor in right field for the Yankees. Byrd was his caddy. Selkirk was his successor. Glenn, the Ralph Houk of his day, was the Yankees third-string catcher in the early 1930s, but he was behind the plate on October 1, 1933, the last time the Babe pitched—a 6–5 complete game against the Red Sox with the winning run provided on a home run by Ruth. Pruett, Ruth's nemesis, struck the slugger out 13 of the first 21 times he faced him.

—— FIELD FOLLIES ——

As Joe Garagiola says, baseball is a funny game.

    1B—Marv Throneberry (1962 Mets)
    2B—Germany Schaefer (1908 Tigers)
    3B—Odell Hale (1935 Indians)
    SS—Ernie Banks (1959 Cubs)
    OF—Jeff Leonard (1979 Astros)
    OF—Johnny Dickshot (1973 Pirates)
    OF—Joe Connolly (1914 Braves)
     C—Morgan Murphy (1898 Phillies)
     P—Jimmy St. Vrain (1902 Cubs)

On June 17 Throneberry tripled but was called out on an appeal for failing to touch second. When Mets manager Casey Stengel complained, the umpire told him not to bother because Marvelous Marv had also missed first.

Schaefer stole second to draw a throw that would allow the runner on third to score. Unsuccessful in this, he stole first, then repeated the theft of second, this time drawing the desired throw that got the run home. Subsequently a rule was passed to prohibit this maneuver.

On September 7, Hale was credited with an assist in baseball's oddest triple play. A line drive off the bat of Joe Cronin hit him in the head and landed in the hands of shortstop Billy Knickerbocker, who tossed to second baseman Roy Hughes for the second out; Hughes then flipped the ball to Hal Trosky at first for the third out.

On June 30 Banks watched helplessly as two baseballs came at him, one thrown by his third baseman and the other by his pitcher. The first originated with the bat boy, who had picked it up after what was either a pitch that hit Stan Musial or a wild pitch ball four; the second originated with the home plate umpire, who had handed a new ball to the catcher, who handed it to the pitcher, who threw it to Banks. Banks tagged Musial with the first ball as Stan rounded second base while the second ball sailed into the outfield. Initially the umpires sent Musial back to first, then they called him out; the ball should have been declared dead when the bat boy touched it.

Leonard routinely flied out to end a 5–0 game on August 21, but Mets' shortstop Frank Taveras had called time before the pitch, so Leonard got a second chance and singled. Mets first baseman Ed Kranepool had, however, left the field after the fly ball, so Leonard had to try a third time and flied out again. When an Astros protest was upheld, play had to be resumed the following day with Leonard on first. The next batter, Jose Cruz, grounded out to second to end the game.

When the wind blew Dickshot's hat off, he allowed two runs to score while he chased the hat instead of the ball. Connolly was knocked out by a line drive that hit him in the head.

Murphy, a third-string catcher, was caught stealing opponents' signals when Reds' third-base coach Tommy Corcoran kicked the dirt in the coach's box and unearthed a wire that led to Murphy sitting in the clubhouse with a buzzer he used to relay the stolen signals to his own third-base coach.

St. Vrain, a weak-hitting, left-handed pitcher who stood at the plate on the right side, almost always without making contact, took his manager's advice and moved to the other side of the plate; from this unfamiliar vantage point he grounded to Honus Wagner at short and promptly ran as fast as he could—to third base.

—— ONE ——

What these players did or what they are associated with comes down to the number 1.

1B—Joe Kuhel (1945 Senators)
2B—Joe Battin (1877 Cardinals)
3B—Bob Maier (1945 Tigers)
SS—Buddy Myer (Career)
OF—Buster Bay (1941 Braves)
OF—Johnny Callison (1959 White Sox)
OF—Jessie Reid (1987 Giants)
 C—Charlie Lindstrom (1958 White Sox)
 P—Pat Jarvis (1966 Braves)

Kuhel hit the only home run at home by the Senators all year, and even that was an inside-the-park job. Battin hit the only homer tagged by his team for the season. Maier played only a single season in the majors, and that as a regular; in addition, he hit safely in his only World Series at bat against the Cubs. Myer played for 17 seasons between 1925 and 1941, hitting .303 and leading the league in batting once and in stolen bases another time. Despite that, Myer has received the same number of votes for the Hall of Fame as such luminaries as Ted Breitenstein and Hal Lanier—1. Buster Bay is one of a small handful of players whose only major league hit (in 11 at bats) was a double. Callison had the only hit (a single) in an 11-run seventh inning against Kansas City that featured three errors, 10 walks, and a hit batsman. Reid is one of three big leaguers whose only major league hit was a home run (the others were Dick Allen's brother Ron and Stan Johnson). The son of Freddie, Lindstrom started and ended his career with a single appearance that produced a triple. Jarvis was strikeout number one for Nolan Ryan.

—— THE LAST TIME—SEASON ——

These are the most recent players to reach specific seasonal goals:

> 1B—Cecil Fielder (1990 Tigers)
> 2B—Juan Samuel (1984 Phillies)
> 3B—George Brett (1979 Royals)
> SS—Alfredo Griffin (1988 Dodgers)
> OF—Ted Williams (1941 Red Sox)
> OF—Jim Rice (1978 Red Sox)
> OF—Kiki Cuyler (1925 Pirates)
> C—Alex Trevino (1990 Astros, Mets, Reds)
> P—Denny McLain (1968 Tigers)

Fielder's 51st home run makes him the most recent of 18 players to hit 50 or more homers in a season. Samuel's 701 at bats was only the second time anyone reached 700. Brett's 42 doubles, 20 triples, and 23 home runs made him only the sixth player to hit 20 or more of each kind of extra base hit. Griffin put his name on the list of seven players to hit bases-loaded triples three times. Williams' .406 put the 13th .400 season of the 20th century into the books. Only 22 times has a batter amassed more than 400 total bases; Rice's 406 was the most recent. Only 19 times has someone hit 25 or more triples; no one has done it since Cuyler's 26. Trevino is the most recent player to wear three different uniforms in a season. McLain won 31 games, the 21st 30-win season in this century. Honorable mention to Stan Musial's 103 extra-base hits for the 1948 Cardinals, the last of nine 100-plus, extra-base-hit seasons. And special mention to Tom Qualters (1954 Phillies), the most recent player to remain on a team's active roster for an entire season without appearing in a game.

—— THE LAST TIME—GAME ——

A lineup of players who most recently matched one-game records:

    1B—Steve Garvey (1977 Dodgers)
    2B—Duane Kuiper (1978 Indians)
    3B—Bill Joyce (1897 Giants)
    SS—Felix Fermin (1989 Indians)
    OF—Luis Olmo (1945 Dodgers)
    OF—Frank Robinson (1970 Orioles)
    OF—George Bell (1990 Blue Jays)
    C—Bob Stinson (1979 Mariners)
    P—Tom Browning (1988 Reds)

Garvey's five extra-base hits (August 28) tied him with six other players. Kuiper was only the sixth player to hit two bases-loaded triples in the same game (July 27). Joyce was the second of two players to leg out four triples in one game (May 18). Fermin's four sacrifices (August 22) made him the sixth player to push that many runners along. Olmo became the eighth player (May 18) to hit a grand slam and a bases-loaded triple in the same game. Robinson is the most recent of seven players to hit two grand slam home runs in the same game and the most recent of three to hit them in consecutive innings (June 26). Bell scored three runners from third with sacrifice fly balls on August 14; only seven others have driven in as many runs without recording an at bat. Incredibly enough, four players have reached base on catcher's interference twice in a game; Stinson (July 24) was the most recent. Browning pitched the last of baseball's perfect games on September 16.

—— COLLISIONS AND CLASHES ——

Fights, feuds, and sometimes just plain accidents can have significant repercussions.

    1B—Steve Garvey (1983 Padres)
    2B—Davey Williams (1955 Giants)
    3B—John McGraw (1902 Orioles)
    SS—Bert Campaneris (1972 Athletics LCS)
    OF—Joe Medwick (1934 Cardinals WS)
    OF—Tommy Tucker (1894 Braves)
    OF—Carl Furillo (1953 Dodgers)
     C—Buck Martinez (1985 Blue Jays)
    DH—Cliff Johnson (1977 Yankees)

Garvey jammed his thumb in the catcher's mask during a collision at the plate; the injury was sufficiently serious to end his consecutive game streak at 1,207 games. Jackie Robinson effectively ended Williams's career when he bunted down the first-base line and ran over Williams, who was covering first on the play. Later in the game, Al Dark retaliated by charging past second on a double, taking out third baseman Robinson, and precipitating a classic Dodgers and Giants melee.

Caught off third on a pickoff play, Detroit outfielder Dick Harley spiked McGraw on the kneecap; the injury virtually ended McGraw's career when he was only 29. After Detroit pitcher Lerrin LaGrow hit Campaneris on the ankle with a pitch during the 1972 American League Championship Series (LCS), the shortstop threw his bat at the pitcher. Campaneris was suspended for the remainder of the LCS plus the first three games of the 1973 season.

Medwick spiked Tiger third baseman Marv Owen in the final, lopsided World Series game in 1934. When Medwick went back to left field, the Tiger fans pelted him with scorecards, food, and everything else they could find until Commissioner Kenesaw Landis ordered him removed from the game. When Tucker hit Baltimore third baseman John McGraw with a hard slide on May 16, McGraw retaliated by kicking Tucker in the face. The ensuing brawl so distracted everyone that a fire in the right-field bleachers went ignored—eventually it burned down Boston's South End Grounds.

When Furillo was hit by a pitch in a September game against the Giants, he challenged not the pitcher but Giant manager Leo Durocher, who had been taunting him all year. Next he attacked the Giants' dugout, punched Monte Irvin, and had his hand broken when Jim Hearn stepped on it. Furillo, who had to sit out the rest of the season, was on the bench when Red Schoendienst and Stan Musial of the Cardinals narrowly missed overtaking his league-leading batting average.

Martinez had his leg broken making a putout at the plate; his throw to third in an effort to nab a second runner went into left field. The broken leg notwithstanding, Martinez took the return throw from the left fielder, endured a second collision, and tagged the second runner out. Martinez was forced to retire soon afterward. Johnson blindsided umpire Lou DeMuro while scoring a run, knocked the man in blue unconscious, and sidelined him for the rest of the season. Honorable mention to Ty Cobb, who went into the stands behind third base on May 15, 1912, and attacked a heckling New York fan, one Mr. Lueker. Cobb's aggression earned him a 10-day suspension and led to a protest strike by the rest of the Tigers.

—— THREE FOR ONE ——

The three players next to each position have something in common with a fourth player identified with that position. The answers range from basic baseball lore to trivia for experts.

1B—Jim Lefebvre, Maury Wills, Jim Gilliam
2B—Rick Sutcliffe, Steve Howe, Fernando Valenzuela
3B—Al Dark, Don Mueller, Whitey Lockman
SS—Woodie Held, Pedro Ramos, Tito Francona
OF—Ted Williams, Roger Maris, Carl Yastrzemski
OF—Bob Feller, Bob Lemon, Satchel Paige
OF—Steve Garvey, Ron Cey, Dusty Baker
C—Joe Bush, Walter Johnson, Howard Ehmke
P—Harry Chiti, Brad Gulden, Willis Hudlin

1B—Wes Parker was the fourth switch-hitting infielder for the Dodgers of the 1960s.

2B—Steve Sax won the fourth consecutive Rookie of the Year award for the Dodgers after these three pitchers.

3B—Bobby Thomson hit his 1951 playoff homer against Brooklyn after these three batters had hit safely.

SS—Larry Brown hit the fourth consecutive home run off Paul Foytack.

OF—Carroll Hardy pinch-hit for each of these stars at one point or another in his career.

OF—Charlie Maxwell's first three homers came off these three Hall of Famers.

O—Reggie Smith and his three teammates on the 1977 Dodgers all hit 30 or more homers.

C—Val Picinich is the only receiver to be behind the plate for no hitters by three different pitchers for three different teams: the 1916 Athletics, the 1920 Senators, and the 1923 Red Sox, respectively.

P—Hoyt Wilhelm was traded for himself as "a player to be named later" just as these three were.

—— TWO FOR ONE ——

The two players listed after each position should tell you the name of a third player, the one who played that position.

    1B—Felix Mantilla and Hank Aaron
    2B—Darrell Evans and Hank Aaron
    3B—Alex Johnson and Kirby Puckett
    SS—Jerry Mumphrey and Gene Richards
    OF—Al Smith and Jim Bagby, Jr.
    OF—Charlie Gehringer and Hank Greenberg
    OF—John Reilly and Bob Meusel
      C—Orlando Cepeda and Ray Sadecki
      P—Babe Ruth and Mickey Mantle

1B—Joe Adcock hit his almost home run to break up Harvey Haddix' perfect game in the 12th inning with Mantilla (a two-base error) and Aaron (an intentional pass) aboard.

2B—Davey Johnson was the third member of the 1973 Braves to hit 40 or more homers.

3B—Carney Lansford has been only the third right-handed batter to lead the American League in hitting in the last quarter-century.

SS—Ozzie Smith was the third player on the 1980 Padres to steal 50 or more bases.

OF—Joe DiMaggio's 56-game hitting streak was ended by these two Cleveland pitchers.

OF—Goose Goslin was the third G-Man on the Tigers in the 1930s.

OF—Babe Herman is the third player to hit for the cycle three times in his career.

C—Joe Torre. In one-for-one deals over a number of years, Cepeda was swapped for Sadecki, Cepeda was traded for Torre, and then, to close the circle, Sadecki was dealt for Torre.

P—Al Benton is the only pitcher who faced both Yankee sluggers.

—— ONE FOR ONE ——

You should be getting the hang of this by now.

    1B—Ron Blomberg
    2B—Eddie O'Brien
    3B—Harvey Haddix
    SS—Hal Breeden
    OF—Gary Roenicke
    OF—Max Flack
    OF—Emmett Mueller
     C—Bubbles Hargrave
     P—Fred Toney

1B—Dan Driessen was the National League's first designated hitter (in the 1976 World Series), something not recalled as readily as the fact that Blomberg was the first DH during the AL 1973 regular season.

2B—Johnny O'Brien was the second-base half of the Pirates' Keystone pair in the early 1950s noted more for the fact that they were twins than for their performance.

3B—Don Hoak made the throwing error that ended Haddix's 12 1/3 inning perfect game.

SS—Joe Cronin is the only player besides Breeden to hit pinch-hit home runs in both ends of a doubleheader.

OF—John Lowenstein was the other half of the Orioles classic platoon in left field.

OF—Like Flack, Cliff Heathcote played in both ends of a Cubs-Cardinals doubleheader in 1938; what makes them unique is that each of them played for both teams since they were traded for each other between games.

OF—Ernie Koy hit a home run in the bottom of the first inning of his first major league game for the Dodgers in 1938; Mueller had hit one in his first major league at bat for the Phillies in the top half of the same inning.

C—Ernie Lombardi and Hargrave are the only catchers ever to lead a league in batting.

P—Hippo Vaughn was the losing pitcher when Toney pitched a no-hitter for 10 innings May 2, 1917; Vaughn also pitched a no-hitter for 9 innings.

16 Other Leagues

The National and American leagues aren't the only circuits that can put together impressive all-star teams. Here are the very best in other loops—major, minor, and miscellaneous.

—— THE NEGRO LEAGUES ——

The old Negro leagues are but a dim memory now, although in the opinion of many people their quality of play was every bit as good as that in the all-white major leagues of the day. Statistics are sketchy and questionable; the abilities of this lineup are not.

1B—Buck Leonard
2B—Bingo DeMoss
3B—Judy Johnson
SS—John Henry Lloyd
OF—Oscar Charleston
OF—Cool Papa Bell
OF—Martin Dihigo
C—Josh Gibson
P—Satchel Paige

Eight Hall of Famers here (all but DeMoss), but only Paige made it to the majors and then only at some advanced—however undeterminable—age. Leonard and Gibson were the Gehrig and Ruth of the Negro leagues; Honus Wagner once said that he was proud to be compared to John Henry Lloyd; Cool Papa Bell was so fast he could go from first to third on a sacrifice; Dihigo was a star at every position.

—— THE AMERICAN ASSOCIATION ——
1882-91

The American Association, the first challenger to the National League's monopoly, was formed because Cincinnati, St. Louis, and Louisville had been dropped from the NL. The association permitted Sunday baseball, sold beer at the parks, and charged only half of the NL's 50-cent admission fee. After one year the two leagues signed a reserve clause agreement that allowed teams to bind players for life. The NL and AA played an interleague championship series from 1884 to 1890. By 1891 weak leadership (as opposed to the early days of such colorful types as Chris Von der Ahe of St. Louis), financial difficulties arising from the Players League war, and arguments over players weakened the association to the point that several of its teams were absorbed into the National League and the rest disbanded.

> 1B—Dave Orr
> 2B—Bid McPhee
> 3B—Denny Lyons
> SS—Bill Gleason
> OF—Pete Browning
> OF—Tip O'Neill
> OF—Harry Stovey
> C—Jack Milligan
> P—Bob Caruthers

The manager is Charlie Comiskey of St. Louis for winning four consecutive pennants and finishing second twice. But the hero of the association was Browning, "The Old Gladiator," who hit like Ted Williams, played like Pepper Martin, and talked like Dizzy Dean. He drank. He boasted. But he hit. And there is no plaque in Cooperstown for him.

—— THE UNION ASSOCIATION ——
1884

Assuming that the American Association's success meant there was room for a third major league, Henry V. Lucas, a St. Louis millionaire, formed the Union Association (UA) to advance the rights of the players. The "Onions" folded after one season when Lucas, who lost a considerable amount of money on the venture, refused to support a second season. The UA produced two oddities: the smallest city ever to hold a major league franchise, Altoona, Pennsylvania, and the briefest franchise, St. Paul, Minnesota, which won only two of its eight games.

1B—Jumbo Schoeneck (Chicago, Pittsburgh, Baltimore)
2B—Fred Dunlap (St. Louis)
3B—Jack Gleason (St. Louis)
SS—Germany Smith (Altoona)
OF—Orator Shaffer (St. Louis)
OF—Henry Moore (Washington)
OF—Emmett Seery (Baltimore, Kansas City)
C—Cannonball Crane (Boston)
P—Billy Taylor (St. Louis)

Dunlap, the star of the league, led in batting and home runs; he also managed St. Louis to the pennant by a wide margin, but by the end of the season, which saw 13 cities get into the act, very few people cared. Taylor won 24 and lost only two. Then he must have figured he had done all he could in the UA, because in midseason he jumped to Philadelphia of the American Association where he compiled an additional 18 wins and 12 losses. The biggest curiosity in this lineup is Moore, who batted over .330 in this his rookie season in the majors—and then never appeared in another game.

—— THE PLAYERS LEAGUE—1890 ——

The Players League arose out of a general labor unrest among the players. The unrest erupted into rebellion when the owners attempted to regulate salaries by imposing a classification system based on performance. Led by pitcher-shortstop-lawyer Monte Ward, scores of players, members of the Players Brotherhood, bolted from the National League and the American Association to form their own league. Everyone ended up losing money, with the National in particular forced to the edge of ruin. The revolt came to an end when the players, unaware of the National League's plight, were outsmarted at a peace conference and agreed to disband.

> 1B—Roger Connor (New York)
> 2B—Lou Bierbauer (Brooklyn)
> 3B—Patsy Tebeau (Cleveland)
> SS—Monte Ward (Brooklyn)
> OF—Pete Browning (Cleveland)
> OF—Hardy Richardson (Boston)
> OF—Jim O'Rourke (New York)
> C—Buck Ewing (New York)
> P—Charlie Radbourn (Boston)

Browning led the league in batting. Connor finished third and led in home runs. But the biggest hero of the insurrection was King Kelly, the Boston player-manager. Widely popular in Boston from his years with the NL franchise there, Kelly brought respectability to the PL franchise, batted over .320 as a part-time shortstop and catcher, and led his charges to a pennant. The National League Boston owners offered him a $10,000 bonus and a blank contract to jump back. Kelly chose to remain with the Brotherhood and refused, although he did end up back with Boston NL the following year after a detour with two AA teams, one of them the Boston entry in that league.

—— THE FEDERAL LEAGUE—1914–15 ——

Unlike the Union Association and the Players League, the Federal League was a capitalist venture. Millionaire James A. Gilmore took over a regional minor league in 1913 and persuaded other like-minded tycoons to challenge the joint monopoly of the American and National leagues. The Feds attracted a number of star players and missed out on many others only because the owners in the two established leagues dramatically increased salaries to dissuade would-be defectors. The Feds seemed to weaken in 1915 but still represented a sufficiently strong threat to force the American and National leagues to sue for peace when the Federals proposed moving their Newark franchise to New York. The terms included the purchase of the Chicago Cubs and St. Louis Browns by Federal owners, long-term buyouts for other owners, and the assumption of $385,000 in player contracts by the older leagues.

1B—Hal Chase (Buffalo)
2B—Duke Kenworthy (Kansas City)
3B—Jimmy Walsh (Baltimore, St. Louis)
SS—Jimmy Esmond (Indianapolis, Newark)
OF—Benny Kauff (Indianapolis, Brooklyn)
OF—Dutch Zwilling (Chicago)
OF—Vin Campbell (Indianapolis, Newark)
C—Ted Easterly (Kansas City)
P—Gene Packard (Kansas City)

Kauff, "the Ty Cobb of the Feds," won the batting championship both years with averages of .366 and .344. Packard was the only pitcher to win 20 games in both seasons. The manager is Joe Tinker for bringing Chicago home second the first year and winning the pennant the next.

—— THE MINORS ——

Once upon a time, there were hundreds of minor league teams. And, players made careers in the minors.

          1B—Joe Hauser
          2B—Eddie Mulligan
          3B—Fritz Maisel
          SS—Joe Boley
          OF—Jigger Statz
          OF—Spencer Harris
          OF—Ike Boone
           C—Ernie Lombardi
           P—Frank Shellenback

Hauser hit 399 minor league home runs; his best years were 63 with Baltimore in 1930 and 69 with Minneapolis in 1933. Mulligan was a mainstay of eight different Pacific Coast League teams from 1919 to 1938. Maisel and Boley were the only ones to play for all seven of Baltimore's International League pennant winners (1919–25). Statz collected 3,356 hits during his 18 years with the PCL Los Angeles Angels; in 1926 he led the PCL with 291 hits. Harris had 3,617 hits in his 26 years in the minors; his lifetime average was .318. Boone won five batting championships in three different leagues; his highest average was .407 with Mission (PCL) in 1929. Lombardi spent only four seasons in the minors but never batted less than .366. Shellenback won 295 and lost 178 for four PCL teams between 1920 and 1938; he also won 20 and lost 14 in the International League. Honorable mention to switch-hitting outfielder-first baseman Buzz Arlett, who spent 13 seasons with the Oakland Oaks of the PCL (1918–30) and hit 251 home runs; and to Hector Espino, who hit 484 home runs, all but three of them for Mexican leagues.

——— MEXICAN JUMPING BEANS ———

The last major defection from the established major leagues occurred in 1946, when 20-odd players were lured by big-money offers to jump to the Mexican League, which was owned in its entirety by Mexican millionaire Jorge Pasquel. Having failed to find paradise, these players drifted back to the states even though they faced five-year suspensions. Among them were

    1B—Nap Reyes
    2B—George Hausmann
    3B—Lou Klein
    SS—Vern Stephens
    OF—Luis Olmo
    OF—Danny Gardella
    OF—Roy Zimmerman
     C—Mickey Owen
     P—Max Lanier

Other jumpers included Roland Gladu and pitchers Sal Maglie, Fred Martin, Alex Carrasquel, Ace Adams, Harry Feldman, and Jean Pierre Roy. The overwhelming majority of the defectors came from the St. Louis Cardinals (Klein, Lanier, and Martin); the Brooklyn Dodgers (Olmo, Owen, Gladu, and Roy); and the New York Giants (Reyes, Hausmann, Gardella, Zimmerman, Maglie, Adams, and Feldman). Stephens belonged to the St. Louis Browns and Carrasquel to the Chicago White Sox. The shortest-lived expatriate was Stephens, who played only two games in Mexico before caving in to threats of being blackballed. The others were, in fact, blackballed until 1949 when a lawsuit brought by Gardella was settled out of court and the door to the major leagues was reopened to those who had not already been reinstated.

── THE JAPANESE LEAGUES ──

Besuboru is no longer an exclusively American sport and no book of this sort would be complete without this Samurai selection. Only native Japanese need apply for this lineup. Excluded are the numerous *Nisei* (American-born) players who have found success in Nippon.

    1B—Sadaharu Oh
    2B—Shigeru Chiba
    3B—Shigeo Nagashima
    SS—Yoshio Yoshida
    OF—Shinichi Eto
    OF—Shigeru Takada
    OF—Isao Harimoto
     C—Katsuya Nomura
     P—Masaichi Kaneda

Oh hit 868 home runs in his long career with the Yomiuri Giants. Chiba covered second for the Giants from 1938 to 1952. Nagashima, also with the Giants (1958–74), was the most popular player in the history of Japanese baseball; he once hit a legendary home run to break up a tie game and allow Emperor Hirohito to avoid a choice between missing the end of the game and missing his train. Yoshida revolutionized infield play during his tenure (1952–69) with the Hanshin Tigers. Eto won three batting crowns, two with the Chunichi Dragons. Takada (Giants) was a .300 hitter and the best defensive outfielder in Japan. Harimoto broke both the career and single season records for highest batting average in a career spent mostly with the Toei Flyers; he is the only Japanese player with 3,000 hits. Nomura played with the Nankai Hawks between 1954 and 1980. Kaneda won 400 games in his 20-year career (mostly with the Yakult Swallows) and struck out 4,490 batters. The manager is Tetsuharu Kawakami, who won 9 consecutive pennants and 11 pennants in 14 years with the Giants.

17 On the Field

This chapter is about the positions major leaguers have played—and how long and how well they played them.

—— POSITION SWITCHERS ——

The names are familiar but not at the positions assigned. Nevertheless, the players in this lineup started off at these positions in the majors.

> 1B—Jackie Robinson (1947 Dodgers)
> 2B—Larry Doby (1947 Indians)
> 3B—Steve Garvey (1970 Dodgers)
> SS—Bobby Murcer (1965 Yankees)
> OF—Honus Wagner (1897 Louisville)
> OF—Graig Nettles (1968 Twins)
> OF—Bill Russell (1969 Dodgers)
> C—Gil Hodges (1947 Dodgers)
> P—Lefty O'Doul (1919 Yankees)

Hodges actually made his debut in 1943 as a third baseman, but only for one game. O'Doul is a major curiosity. He was a less than mediocre pitcher with the Yankees (1919–20, 1922) and the Red Sox (1923), then, after a hiatus of four years spent in the minor leagues, he reemerged as an outfielder. In seven years with the Giants, Phillies, and Dodgers, he compiled a lifetime average of .349, and won batting crowns in 1929 (.398) and 1932 (.368) before returning to the Pacific Coast League. He played and managed in San Francisco for years and parlayed his local popularity into fame and fortune as the West Coast version of restauranteur Toots Shor.

——— VERSATILITY ———

The players on this team appeared in at least 300 games at three different positions. This seems to indicate that versatility is less a matter of knowing how to use your glove at several positions than of swinging a potent bat and forcing the manager to find somewhere to hide you on the field.

        1B—Harmon Killebrew
        2B—Billy Goodman
        3B—Hubie Brooks
        SS—George Davis
        OF—Pete Rose
        OF—Don Buford
        OF—Pedro Guerrero
         C—Joe Torre
         P—Monte Ward

The positions they played and the number of games at each: Killebrew (1B: 969, 3B: 792, OF: 470); Goodman (2B: 624, 1B: 406, 3B: 330); Brooks (3B: 516, OF: 442, SS: 371); Davis (SS: 1378, 3B: 530, OF: 303); Rose, the only one to play 300 or more games at four different positions (OF: 1327, 1B: 939, 3B: 634, 2B: 628); Buford (OF: 555, 2B: 392, 3B: 352); Guerrero (OF: 531, 1B: 433, 3B: 373); Torre (C: 903, 1B: 797, 3B: 515); and Ward (P: 291, SS: 826, 2B: 491). Only Baltimore trivia experts would have remembered that Buford played three positions so frequently. Ward is nine pitching appearances shy of the criterion, but his mobility is sufficiently impressive as it stands. Others who accomplished this are Buck Herzog (2B: 488, 3B: 472, SS: 458); Pete Runnels (1B: 644, 2B: 642, SS: 463); and Derrel Thomas (2B: 608, OF: 542, SS: 339).

—— 900/700 ——

Versatility and longevity is the rare combination displayed by these players who appeared in the most games at two different positions.

1B—Ernie Banks
2B—Rod Carew
3B—Jimmy Dykes
SS—Robin Yount
OF—Stan Musial
OF—Ron Fairly
OF—Pete Rose
 C—Joe Torre
 P—Kid Gleason

Banks (1B: 1,259, SS: 1,125); Carew (1B: 1,184, 2B: 1,130); Musial (OF: 1,896, 1B: 1,016); and Fairly (OF: 1,037, 1B: 1,218) are the only players to appear in more than 1,000 games at two different positions. Rose (OF: 1,327, 1B: 939) just misses, but he also played two other positions more than 600 times each. Torre (C: 903, 1B: 797) doesn't even have a thousand at one position, but he added 515 games at third base. Dykes (3B: 1,253, 2B: 728) and Yount (SS: 1,479, OF: 869) complete the defense. Gleason (P: 251, 2B: 1,574) is the pitcher who combined the most mound appearances with more than 1,000 games at another position. The only other players in the 900/700 club are Tommy Leach (OF: 1,078, 3B: 955); Willie Stargell (OF: 1,293, 1B: 848); Jim Gilliam (2B: 1,046, 3B: 761); Toby Harrah (3B: 1,099, SS: 813); Al Oliver (OF: 1,376, 1B: 733); Tony Perez (1B: 1,778, 3B: 760); and Carl Yastrzemski (OF: 2,076, 1B: 765).

—— TEMPORARY RELIEF ——

Some surprising people took a turn on the mound.

    1B—George Kelly
    2B—Bobby Lowe
    3B—Jimmy Dykes
    SS—Honus Wagner
    OF—Ted Williams
    OF—Tris Speaker
    OF—Stan Musial
      C—Roger Bresnahan
      P—Ron Perranoski

Bresnahan pitched in nine games, Dykes and Wagner in two each, and the rest in just one. Perranoski started in only one of his 737 appearances on the mound.

—— FILLING IN ——

Some pretty good pitchers helped out elsewhere for brief spells.

    1B—Kid Nichols
    2B—Chief Bender
    3B—John Clarkson
    SS—Pud Galvin
    OF—Ed Walsh
    OF—Red Ruffing
    OF—Ted Lyons
      C—George Uhle
    PH—Early Wynn

The number of games they played while helping out: Nichols and Walsh, 6 each; Clarkson, 4; Ruffing, 3; Galvin, 2; and the rest one each. Wynn pinch-hit 90 times in his career but never appeared on the field other than on the mound.

—— FIELDERS' CHOICES ——

The following appeared at every position in one season:

    1B—Gene Paulette (1918 Cardinals)
    2B—Jose Oquendo (1988 Cardinals)
    3B—Jack Rothrock (1928 Red Sox)
    SS—Bert Campaneris (1965 Athletics)
    OF—Cesar Tovar (1968 Twins)
    OF—Sam Mertes (1902 White Sox)
    OF—Jimmy Walsh (1911 Phillies)
     C—Sport McAllister (1899 Cleveland)
     P—Barney Friberg (1898 Cubs and Phillies)

Tovar, Campaneris, and Oquendo played all nine positions in the same game. Rothrock is the only one who also came in as a pinch hitter and a pinch runner. Friberg did not play all three outfield positions. Others who duplicated Friberg's feat are Mike Dorgan (1879), John Grim (1890), Spider Clark (1890), King Kelly (1891), and Charlie Gettig (1898).

—— STAYING PUT ——

This lineup lacks maneuverability. The players in it appeared in the most games at their positions without ever playing anywhere else.

    1B—Jake Daubert (2,001 games)
    2B—Bobby Doerr (1,852 games)
    3B—Frank Baker (1,548 games)
    SS—Luis Aparicio (2,581 games)
    OF—Lou Brock (2,507 games)
    OF—Max Carey (2,422 games)
    OF—Zack Wheat (2,350 games)
     C—Rick Ferrell (1,805 games)
     P—Kent Tekulve (1,050 games)

Tekulve made the most relief appearances for any pitcher who never started a game.

—— PERMANENT FIXTURES ——

Some players seem never to move at all. These entries played the most games at their positions without ever playing another and without ever changing teams—or even cities.

1B—Kent Hrbek (Twins) 1,276
2B—Bobby Doerr (Red Sox) 1,852
3B—Ken Caminiti (Astros) 403
SS—Alan Trammell (Tigers) 1,831
OF—Clyde Milan (Senators) 1,901
OF—Earle Combs (Yankees) 1,386
OF—Dom DiMaggio (Red Sox) 1,373
 C—Bill Dickey (Yankees) 1,712
 P—Red Faber (White Sox) 669

Pinch hitting doesn't interrupt the streak. Neither does serving as the designated hitter, which is not a position by any stretch of the imagination. Can we surmise that third basemen are the players most likely to move—either from the hot corner to another spot on the field or from the franchises where they were rookies to other teams? Faber started 484 games and relieved in another 185. Honorable mention to Carl Furillo, who played 1,789 games in the outfield for the Dodgers without ever playing anywhere else and without playing for anyone else. Unfortunately, the Dodgers moved from Brooklyn to Los Angeles for the last three years of his career, thus keeping him off this team. Yet another sin to be laid on Walter O'Malley.

—— MOST SEASONS ——

Longevity is one hallmark of consistency. These players appeared in the most seasons at each position.

    1B—Willie McCovey (22)
    2B—Eddie Collins (22)
    3B—Brooks Robinson (23)
    SS—Luke Appling (20)
    OF—Ty Cobb (24)
    OF—Hank Aaron (23)
    OF—Willie Mays (22)
      C—Deacon McGuire (25)
      P—Tommy John (26)

Collins played in 25 seasons, but only 22 of them at second. McGuire played in a 26th season in which he did not catch. Al Kaline, Tris Speaker, and Carl Yastrzemski tied Mays, but Mays played in more games.

—— MOST GAMES ——

And these players appeared in the most games at each position.

    1B—Jake Beckley (2,377)
    2B—Eddie Collins (2,650)
    3B—Brooks Robinson (2,870)
    SS—Luis Aparicio (2,581)
    OF—Ty Cobb (2,943)
    OF—Willie Mays (2,843)
    OF—Hank Aaron (2,760)
      C—Bob Boone (2,225)
      P—Hoyt Wilhelm (1,070)

Wilhelm started 52 times; the rest of his games were in relief. The most starts, 818, belong to Cy Young. Although Pete Rose and Carl Yastrzemski played in more games than anyone else—3,562 and 3,308, respectively—neither of them ever played enough games at any one position to qualify here.

—— CONSECUTIVE GAME STREAKS ——

Every fan knows that Lou Gehrig played in 2,130 consecutive games. What a whole lot fewer know is that he did not play all of those games at first base. The members of this team played the most consecutive games at their respective positions.

1B—Lou Gehrig (1925–30) 885
2B—Nellie Fox (1955–60) 798
3B—Eddie Yost (1951–55) 576
SS—Cal Ripken (1982–90) 1,384
OF—Billy Williams (1963–69) 897
OF—Richie Ashburn (1950–54) 694
OF—Walter Brodie (1893–97) 574
 C—Frankie Hayes (1943–46) 312
 P—Mike Marshall (1974) 13

Gehrig's streak of 2,130 games was interrupted several times. He appeared in the outfield twice, once in late 1930 when the streak at first base ended and again in 1931. In 1934, he appeared in the lineup as the shortstop and leadoff hitter—just long enough to single in the top of the first and come out of the game for a pinch-runner. Ripken's 1,384 games at shortstop is the all-time record for most consecutive games at a single position. The runner-up, Everett Scott, doesn't even make this team because his 1,307 consecutive games between 1916 and 1925 were also at shortstop. Steve Garvey appeared in 1,207 consecutive games between 1975 and 1983, but seven of those appearances were as a pinch hitter. Marshall came in to relieve in 13 consecutive games.

—— BATS RIGHT, THROWS LEFT ——

Only about 20 players in the history of the game have possessed this combination.

1B—Hal Chase
2B—Bill Greenwood
3B—Hick Carpenter
SS—Jimmy Macullar
OF—Rickey Henderson
OF—Jimmy Ryan
OF—Rube Bressler
C—Pop Tate
P—Johnny Cooney

Chase and Henderson were stars. Ryan and Bressler both had lifetime averages over .300. Cooney was a fair pitcher for 10 years (1921–30), then became an outfielder—and a pretty good hitter—for 10 more (1935–44). The other four are more obscure, because lefties are seldom asked to catch or play second, third, or short. Tate was behind the plate in 202 games between 1885 and 1890. Greenwood, who was a switch hitter, played second 538 times for five teams in the American Association. Carpenter played 1,059 games at third—mostly for Cincinnati in the American Association between 1879 and 1892. Macullar played short in 325 games in his six-year career in the late 1870s and early 1880s. Carpenter and Macullar were teammates in Cincinnati in 1882 and 1883, and while Macullar did most of his shortstopping later, he played one game there in 1883. Since Carpenter played third 95 times that year, there exists the possibility that for one game the left side of Cincinnati's infield was left-handed.

—— SOUTHPAW ALL THE WAY ——

On the other hand, players who bat left-handed and throw left-handed are quite common except at certain positions.

1B—Lou Gehrig
2B—Lip Pike
3B—Lefty Marr
SS—Bill Hulen
OF—Stan Musial
OF—Tris Speaker
OF—Jesse Burkett
C—Jack Clements
P—Babe Ruth

Ruth, Gehrig, and the outfielders are all in the Hall of Fame; the others are virtually unknown. Even though Pike was primarily an outfielder, he did play second 29 times—22 of which while he was with Cincinnati in 1877. Marr's 129 appearances at third were split about evenly between Columbus of the American Association in 1889 and the Reds in 1890. Hulen played 73 games at short for the Phillies in 1896 and 19 more for Washington in 1899. Clements was the last regular southpaw catcher (1,073 games between 1884 and 1890, mostly with the Phillies). Once having caught back-to-back doubleheaders, he unilaterally canceled a third consecutive twin bill. Mike Squires of the White Sox played 14 games at third in 1984 and 1985 and he also caught twice in 1980, making him the last lefty to play both those positions. The most recent left-handed shortstop was Nino Escalera, who ended up at shortstop—or rather short field—in 1954 in one of the more bizarre defensive alignments designed to stop Stan Musial.

—— CAREER FIELDING AVERAGE ——

With 1,000 or more games played, these players posted the highest fielding averages.

    1B—Steve Garvey (.996)
    2B—Tommy Herr (.989)
    3B—Brooks Robinson (.971)
    SS—Larry Bowa (.980)
    OF—Terry Puhl (.993)
    OF—Pete Rose (.991)
    OF—Amos Otis (.991)
      C—Bill Freehan (.993)
      P—Don Mossi (.990)

The best fielding average for a pitcher is based not on 1,000 games but on 1,500 innings pitched.

—— SEASON FIELDING AVERAGE ——

This team is a pitcher's delight; the players have the highest fielding averages in a season with a minimum of 150 games.

    1B—Steve Garvey (1984 Padres) 1.000
    2B—Jose Oquendo (1990 Cardinals) .996
    3B—Don Money (1974 Brewers) .989
    SS—Cal Ripken (1990 Orioles) .996
    OF—Curt Flood (1966 Cardinals) 1.000
    OF—Terry Puhl (1979 Astros) 1.000
    OF—Brian Downing (1982 Angels) 1.000
      C—Randy Hundley (1967 Cubs) .996
      P—Randy Jones (1976 Padres) 1.000

Many outfielders and pitchers have had perfect fielding marks for an entire season; the four on this team had the most chances accepted in 150 or more games. Flood had 396; Puhl, 359; Downing, 330; and Jones, 112. Garvey's perfect season is unique among first basemen.

—— CONSECUTIVE ERRORLESS —— GAMES

The following players appeared in the most games in a row without making any errors:

1B—Steve Garvey (1983–85) 193
2B—Ryne Sandberg (1989–90) 123
3B—Jim Davenport (1966–68) 97
SS—Cal Ripken (1990) 95
OF—Don Demeter (1962–65) 266
OF—Brian Downing (1982–83) 244
OF—Al Kaline (1970–72) 242
 C—Rick Cerone (1987–89) 159
 P—Paul Lindblad (1966–74) 385

Davenport is the only one in this lineup who played other positions during his streak.

—— CONSECUTIVE ERRORLESS —— CHANCES

Looking at consistent fielding excellence from another angle, we come up with quite a few differences from the preceding team. Included are the seasons covered by the streaks and the number of chances accepted.

1B—Stuffy McInnis (1921–22) 1,700
2B—Manny Trillo (1982) 479
3B—Don Money (1973–74) 261
SS—Cal Ripken (1990) 431
OF—Curt Flood (1965–67) 568
OF—Ken Berry (1971–73) 510
OF—Brian Downing (1982–83) 471
 C—Yogi Berra (1957–59) 950
 P—Claude Passeau (1941–46) 273

Ripken and Downing are the only repeaters from the previous team.

—— MOST CAREER PUTOUTS ——

Casey Stengel once said, "You got to get 27 outs to win."
By that standard this team would have accounted for more
than 2,500 victories.

    1B—Jake Beckley (23,709)
    2B—Bid McPhee (6,545)
    3B—Brooks Robinson (2,697)
    SS—Rabbit Maranville (5,139)
    OF—Willie Mays (7,095)
    OF—Tris Speaker (6,791)
    OF—Max Carey (6,363)
     C—Bob Boone (11,260)
     P—Phil Niekro (386)

Beckley's number is the highest in this book.

—— MOST SEASON PUTOUTS ——

This team would account for almost 180 wins.

    1B—Jiggs Donohue (1907 White Sox) 1,846
    2B—Bid McPhee (1886 Cincinnati AA) 529
    3B—Denny Lyons (1887 Philadelphia AA) 255
    SS—Hugh Jennings (1895 Baltimore) 425
    OF—Taylor Douthit (1928 Cardinals) 547
    OF—Richie Ashburn (1951 Phillies) 538
    OF— Chet Lemon (1977 White Sox) 512
     C—Johnny Edwards (1969 Astros) 1,135
     P—Dave Foutz (1886 St. Louis AA) 57

Donie Bush tied Jennings's record in 1914 but took 157
games to do it; Jennings played in only 131. Ashburn had two
of the four highest season totals, four of the eight 500-plus seasons, and 6 of the 10 highest totals. Edwards is the only catcher
to record 1,000 or more putouts—and he did it twice.

—— MOST CAREER ASSISTS ——

The next time you see an infielder scoop up a ground ball or an outfielder throw out a runner trying to take an extra base, think of these players, who did just that most often.

1B—Keith Hernandez (1,682)
2B—Eddie Collins (7,630)
3B—Brooks Robinson (6,205)
SS—Luis Aparicio (8,016)
OF—Tris Speaker (448)
OF—Ty Cobb (392)
OF—Jimmy Ryan (375)
C—Deacon McGuire (1,859)
P—Cy Young (2,013)

Young must have had a knack for getting batters to hit back to the box.

—— MOST SEASON ASSISTS ——

These players threw out opponents the most times in a single season.

1B—Bill Buckner (1985 Red Sox) 184
2B—Frankie Frisch (1927 Cardinals) 641
3B—Graig Nettles (1971 Indians) 412
SS—Ozzie Smith (1980 Padres) 621
OF—Tom Dolan (1883 St. Louis AA) 62
OF—Orator Shaffer (1879 Cubs) 50
OF—Hugh Nicol (1884 St. Louis AA) 48
C—Bill Rariden (1915 Newark FL) 238
P—Ed Walsh (1907 White Sox) 227

Three of the infielders' marks are relatively recent while the outfielders' marks are ancient. The former probably has something to do with the size of modern gloves, while the latter is probably the result of the dead ball, which allowed outfielders to play shallow.

—— MOST CAREER DOUBLE PLAYS ——

These players turned over the most pitcher's best friends in their careers.

    1B—Mickey Vernon (2,044)
    2B—Bill Mazeroski (1,706)
    3B—Brooks Robinson (618)
    SS—Luis Aparicio (1,553)
    OF—Tris Speaker (139)
    OF—Ty Cobb (107)
    OF—Max Carey (86)
     C—Ray Schalk (221)
     P—Phil Niekro (83)

Obviously, longevity is essential to make this team. In addition to long careers, players needed good range, a strong arm, and better-than-average teammates

—— MOST SEASON DOUBLE PLAYS ——

This team executed double plays most often in one summer.

    1B—Ferris Fain (1949 Athletics) 194
    2B—Bill Mazeroski (1966 Pirates) 161
    3B—Graig Nettles (1971 Indians) 54
    SS—Rick Burleson (1980 Red Sox) 147
    OF—Hap Felsch (1919 White Sox) 15
    OF—Jack Tobin (1919 Browns) 15
    OF—Jimmy Sheckard (1899 Baltimore) 14
     C—Steve O'Neill (1916 Indians) 36
     P—Howie Fox (1948 Reds) 15

Lefty Gomez (1938 Yankees) and Bob Lemon (1953 Indians) also started 15 double plays, but Fox did so in 171 innings pitched. It took Gomez 239 innings and Lemon 286 2/3.

18 In the Clubhouse

Not everything in baseball has happened on the field.

—— SPECIAL ROSTER SPOTS ——

Each of these players held down 1 of 25 spots on various rosters, but not for the usual reasons.

    1B—Steve Bilko (1955 Dodgers, 1961 Angels)
    2B—Steve Macko (1981 Cubs)
    3B—Tommy Carroll (1955–56 Yankees)
    SS—George Davis (1903 Giants)
    OF—Roberto Ortiz (1950 Senators)
    OF—Sherry Robertson (Career)
    OF—Ken Griffey, Sr. (1990 Mariners)
     C—Gus Brittain (1937 Reds)
     P—Charlie Faust (1911 Giants)

Because of Bilko's popularity as a minor league slugger in Los Angeles, both California teams made sure he was a part of their inaugural seasons. The fatally ill Macko was carried as a morale boost for him. Carroll was one of several bonus babies that teams were required to carry for two years in the 1950s. Although filling a roster spot, Davis was kept out of the lineup for all but four games as part of the AL–NL agreement concerning players who had jumped to the new circuit in 1902. Ortiz was kept around as an interpreter for pitcher Connie Marrero. Because he was in the Griffith family, Robertson hung on with the Senators for nine years despite a leaden glove and anemic bat. Griffey was purchased so Seattle could cash in on the novelty of a father and son playing on the same team for the first time. Brittain's job was to act as an enforcer during brawls deliberately instigated by manager Charlie Dressen to make the team more aggressive. Manager John McGraw kept Faust around as something of a good luck charm; his nickname was "Victory."

—— LABOR RELATIONS ——

Curt Flood isn't the only player meriting mention in a labor history of baseball.

1B—Tony Lupien
2B—Nap Lajoie
3B—Jerry Terrell
SS—Monte Ward
OF—Dave Fultz
OF—Herschel Bennett
OF—Ralph Kiner
 C—Ted Simmons
 P—Robin Roberts

Lupien challenged his postwar release by the Phillies on the grounds that it violated laws covering the reintegration of Second World War veterans into their jobs; economic necessity forced him to settle out of court. Lajoie's jump from the Phillies to the Athletics spurred lengthy courtroom maneuvers and an ultimate trade to Cleveland. Terrell cited religious principle in casting the only negative vote against the players strike in 1981. Ward organized the Players Brotherhood that led to the Players League in 1890. Fultz set up the Players Fraternity that established minimum guidelines for farming out players during the First World War. Bennett successfully appealed in the 1930s about having been buried in the minors, but the same commissioner's office ruling implicitly strengthened the validity of a farm club system. Kiner and Allie Reynolds negotiated a pension plan with owners in the early 1950s. Although Simmons played the start of 1972 without a contract to challenge the "option year" basis of the reserve clause, he soon gave in to sign a new pact. Roberts introduced the baseball world to Marvin Miller, the lawyer who led players toward free agency.

—— TEAMMATE TROUBLES ——

These teammates played together but they didn't have to like it.

1B—Hal Chase (Career)
2B—Rob Andrews (1979 Giants)
3B—Dick Allen (1965 Phillies)
SS—Dick Bartell (1941 Tigers)
OF—Ty Cobb (Career)
OF—Alex Johnson (1970–71 Angels)
OF—Reggie Jackson (1977 Yankees)
 C—Moses Walker (1884 Toledo AA)
 P—Fred Klobedanz (1902 Braves)

Chase was so disliked throughout his career that his infielders threw balls in the dirt to make life more difficult for him. Andrews was a member of the God Squad of born-again Christians that created a great deal of divisiveness on San Francisco and caused the firings of two managers. Allen got into such a violent fight with Frank Thomas during batting practice on July 3, 1965, that not even the latter's dramatic ninth-inning homer that night could save him from being released after the game. Bartell's constant hectoring of teammates led to his being traded away. Cobb's legendary troubles included feuds with Sam Crawford and Boss Schmidt. Among the many who went after Johnson were Ken Berry with his fists and Chico Ruiz with a gun. Jackson, the self-proclaimed "straw that stirs the drink," was especially successful in stirring up Thurman Munson. Toledo pitchers made a habit of throwing balls in the dirt to show up the black Walker. Klobedanz was hounded off Boston by teammates for having scabbed during a theatrical union strike in the off-season.

—— MANAGER TROUBLES ——

Members of this team would have preferred somebody else calling the shots.

        1B—Hal Trosky (1940 Indians)
        2B—Gerry Priddy (1947 Senators)
        3B—Lenny Randle (1977 Rangers)
        SS—Garry Templeton (1981 Cardinals)
        OF—Dick Cooley (1897 Phillies)
        OF—Kiki Cuyler (1927 Pirates)
        OF—Reggie Jackson (1978 Yankees)
         C—Glenn Myatt (1935 Indians)
         P—Ken Holtzman (1977 Yankees)

Trosky was a leader of the so-called "crybaby Indians" who eventually succeeded in getting manager Oscar Vitt replaced. Priddy became an unwanted presence when he declined to sign a letter drawn up by manager Ossie Bluege asserting that the team admired its skipper. Randle slugged manager Frank Lucchesi, precipitating his trade to the Mets and a long lawsuit. Templeton was packed off to the Padres shortly after throwing some obscene gestures at St. Louis fans and getting into a dugout melee with manager Whitey Herzog. Cooley was the team spokesman in a successful bid to dump manager George Stallings. Cuyler refused manager Donie Bush's order to bat second in the lineup because he thought it would bring him bad luck; he was suspended and then traded. Jackson's ongoing battles with Billy Martin were pivotal in the latter's first firing. Myatt was sold to the Giants when manager Walter Johnson decided that he was "anti-Johnson." Holtzman, one of the biggest winners in the majors in previous years, was left to seethe and rust in the bullpen because Billy Martin decided that he didn't have the stuff to win; he left New York in 1978.

—— FRONT OFFICE TROUBLES ——

These players either ruffled—or felt ruffled by—team owners or general managers.

    1B—Dick Allen (1974 White Sox)
    2B—Billy Martin (1957 Yankees)
    3B—Sal Bando (1976 Athletics)
    SS—Bobby Meacham (1984 Yankees)
    OF—Dave Winfield (1990 Yankees)
    OF—Elliott Maddox (1980 Mets)
    OF—Ralph Kiner (1953 Pirates)
     C—Bob Boone (1981 Phillies)
     P—Tom Seaver (1977 Mets)

Declaring that the White Sox were a second-class operation, Allen quit the team 16 days before the end of the season (and still won the AL home run title). Martin was dispatched to Kansas City after a Copacabana brawl persuaded the Yankees that he was a bad influence on Mickey Mantle. Ending years of animosity with Charlie Finley, Bando declared that his decision to leave Oakland for free agency was "like leaving the Titanic before it went down." Meacham was shipped to Double A ball after an early season error—a paradigm of owner George Steinbrenner's way of dealing with young players. On the other hand, Winfield fought Steinbrenner for years before finally being shipped to the Angels on the eve of the owner's suspension for being involved with gamblers. Maddox became an embarrassment to the Mets when he decided to pursue a lawsuit against Shea Stadium for an injury; he was released. Kiner's long wars with Branch Rickey ended with the latter's pronouncement that "we can finish last without you" and the outfielder's deal to the Cubs. Boone went to the Angels after being active in the 1981 strike. Seaver's public feud with M. Donald Grant led to his departure to Cincinnati.

—— MEMORABLE QUOTES ——

Who said it?

1B—"Today I can say I consider myself the luckiest man on the face of the earth."

2B—"Some people give their bodies to science, I give mine to baseball."

3B—"If a horse can't eat it, I don't want to play on it."

SS—"The hell it was [a typographical error], it was a clean base hit."

OF—"The only problem I have in playing the outfield is catching the fly balls."

OF—"Hit 'em where they ain't."

OF—"I'm the straw that stirs the drink."

C—"It ain't over till it's over."

P—"Don't look back. Something may be gaining on you."

The answers, of course, are Lou Gehrig during his farewell address at Yankee Stadium. Ron Hunt explaining his ability for getting hit by a pitch. Dick Allen talking about artificial turf. Johnny Logan's response after hearing an explanation about a box score miscue that deprived him of a hit. Carmelo Martinez defending his defensive skills. Willie Keeler explaining his prowess with the bat. Reggie Jackson laying claim to his superiority over teammates such as Thurman Munson and Graig Nettles. Yogi Berra describing his team's dim chances. And Satchel Paige explaining his philosophy of life. The manager would be Leo Durocher for his estimate that Mel Ott's Giants were going nowhere because "nice guys finish last."

—— THE STENGELS ——

During his long baseball life, Casey Stengel had a lot to say about a lot of his players. To whom was he referring when he said:

> 1B—"We was going to get you a birthday cake, but we figured you'd drop it."
>
> 2B—"We traded him while he was hot."
>
> 3B—"He reminds me of a feller who's been hitting for 12 years and fielding 1."
>
> SS—"He looks like the greatest hitter in the world till you play him."
>
> OF—"Son, it ain't the water cooler that's strikin' you out."
>
> OF—"I got a kid, he's 19 years old and in 10 years he's got a chance to be 29."
>
> OF—"I broke in with four hits and the writers said they had seen the new Ty Cobb. It took me only a few days to correct that impression."
>
> C—"You gotta have a catcher. If you don't have a catcher, you'll have all passed balls."
>
> P—"He don't say much, but that don't matter much because when you're out there on the mound, you got nobody to talk to."

Stengel's targets were Marv Throneberry (during a birthday party), and Don Zimmer (who'd been traded to the Reds after getting a double for the Mets that had broken an 0–34 skein). Bobby Brown (future American League president), Jerry Lumpe, Mickey Mantle (after the Hall of Famer had struck out and brought a tantrum back to the bench). Greg Goossen (on the limited prospects of the Mets outfielder), himself, Hobie Landrith (on why the catcher had been the Mets first draft pick), and Johnny Sain.

19 League Championship Series

This chapter contains some teams based on the league championship series (LCS) that have been played since 1969 and on the special playoffs in 1946, 1948, 1951, 1959, 1962, and 1978.

—— BEST CAREER LCS ——

A lineup of players who always showed that little extra effort when they were within reach of the pennant.

    1B—Steve Garvey (1974, 1977–78, 1981 Dodgers, 1984 Padres)
    2B—Steve Sax (1081, 1983, 1985, 1988 Dodgers)
    3B—George Brett (1976–78, 1980, 1984–85 Royals)
    SS—Ozzie Smith (1982, 1985, 1987 Cardinals)
    OF—Reggie Jackson (1971–75 Athletics, 1977–78, 1980–81 Yankees, 1982, 1986 Angels)
    OF—Pete Rose (1970, 1972–73, 1975–76 Reds, 1980, 1983 Phillies)
    OF—Mickey Rivers (1976–78 Yankees)
    C—Thurman Munson (1976–78 Yankees)
    P—Bruce Kison (1971–72, 1974–75 Pirates, 1982 Angels)

Garvey collected eight homers to go with a .356 average. Sax holds a slew of LCS stolen base records to go with his solid batting average of .273 and his perfect fielding average of 1.000. The premier playoff player, Brett has swatted nine homers and four triples to contribute to a batting average of .340 and a slugging mark of .728. Smith batted .351 to lead St. Louis into three World Series. Jackson hit six homers, seven doubles, scored 16, and drove in 20 in his playoff appearances. Rose batted .381—right behind Rivers's .386. Munson compiled a .399 average. Kison went 4–0 with an ERA of 1.21.

—— BEST LCS SERIES ——

Maybe the most surprising thing about this lineup is that not all these players were on winning teams.

    1B—Will Clark (1989 Giants)
    2B—Frank White (1980 Royals)
    3B—Graig Nettles (1981 Yankees)
    SS—Ozzie Smith (1985 Cardinals)
    OF—Fred Lynn (1982 Angels)
    OF—Jeffrey Leonard (1987 Giants)
    OF—Rickey Henderson (1989 Athletics)
     C—Bob Boone (1986 Angels)
     P—Blue Moon Odom (1972 Athletics)

Clark hit an astonishing .650 (13–20), with two homers, three doubles, a triple, eight RBI, and eight runs scored in five games. White went 6–11 (.545) in a three-game sweep of New York. Nettles's contribution to a three-game sweep of Oakland was a .500 average with nine runs batted in. Smith, proving as deft with a bat as with his glove, defeated the Dodgers in one game with his first big league homer from the left side and batted .435 overall. The Angels lost to the Brewers, but not because of Lynn's 11–18 (.611). Leonard's four homers and .417 batting average were good enough to win him the series MVP even though the Giants lost to the Cardinals. Henderson devastated the Blue Jays with a double, a triple, two homers, seven walks, eight runs scored, five RBI, and eight stolen bases. Boone couldn't quite get California past Boston to the World Series, despite going 10–22. Odom started two games, completed one, won both, scattered five hits, and yielded no earned runs. Honorable mentions to Terry Puhl (1980 Astros) for going 10–19, Don Baylor (1982 Angels) for driving in 10 runs, and Mark Grace (1989 Cubs) for going 11–17 (.647) with eight runs batted in.

—— BEST LCS GAME ——

Nobody has hit four home runs or pitched a perfect game in the LCS yet, but in the meantime:

1B—Bob Robertson (1971 Pirates)
2B—Felix Millan (1969 Braves)
3B—George Brett (1978 Royals)
SS—Dave Concepcion (1975 Reds)
OF—Paul Blair (1969 Orioles)
OF—Pete Rose (1973 Reds)
OF—Rickey Henderson (1989 Athletics)
 C—Ray Fosse (1974 Athletics)
 P—Vida Blue (1974 Athletics)

In the second game Robertson went 4–5 with three homers, a double, and five RBI. Millan was on base for all five at bats in the second game with three walks and two hits. Brett hit three homers in game three. Concepcion went 3–4 with a couple of stolen bases and great fielding plays to turn around the second game. Blair banged out five hits and drove home five runs in the third game. Rose's 12th-inning homer in the fourth game not only led the Reds over the Mets but also came the day after Shea Stadium almost rioted because of his rough slide into Bud Harrelson. Henderson set the pattern for Oakland's dumping of Toronto by going 2–2 with two walks, two runs scored, and four steals in game two. Fosse went 3–4 with a double and homer to lead Oakland in the second game. In the third game Blue yielded only two hits, walked none, and struck out nine in a 1–0 victory over the Orioles.

—— WORST CAREER LCS ——

They all had at least 20 swings at it, but none of these players helped his team move on to the World Series.

    1B—Steve Balboni (1984–85 Royals)
    2B—Joe Morgan (1972–73, 1975–76, 1979 Reds, 1980
        Astros, 1983 Phillies)
    3B—Aurelio Rodriguez (1972 Tigers, 1980–81 Yankees,
        1983 White Sox)
    SS—Gene Alley (1970–72 Pirates)
    OF—Billy North (1974–75 Athletics, 1978 Dodgers)
    OF—Cesar Geronimo (1972–73, 1975–76, 1979 Reds)
    OF—John Milner (1973 Mets, 1979 Pirates, 1981 Expos)
     C—Gene Tenace (1971–75 Athletics)
     P—Jerry Reuss (1974–75 Pirates, 1981, 1983, 1985
        Dodgers)

Balboni was a mere 4–35 (.114). Despite his reputation as Mister Clutch, Morgan was only 13–96 (.135). Rodriguez managed only two hits in 22 at bats (.091). Alley's 1–25 (.040) might have stood as the single worst LCS effort if not for North's even worse 1–34 (.029). Geronimo was relatively more reliable with 6–63 (.095). Milner had three hits in 27 plate appearances (.111). Tenace, who is associated with World Series slugging, was the opposite in LCS playoffs—going only 5 for 57 (.087). The southpaw Reuss compiled a record of 0–7 with an ERA of 5.45 in 33 innings. Runnersup include Mookie Wilson (10–58, .172), Dave Parker (11–58, .190), Greg Brock (1–21, .048), and Doyle Alexander (0–4, 8.61 ERA in 23 innings).

—— WORST LCS ——

You should be able to figure out what all the position players in this lineup have in common.

> 1B—Chris Chambliss (1982 Braves)
> 2B—Rich Dauer (1983 Orioles)
> 3B—Aurelio Rodriguez (1972 Tigers)
> SS—Gene Alley (1972 Pirates)
> OF—Chet Lemon (1984 Tigers)
> OF—Willie Stargell (1971 Pirates)
> OF—Rich Coggins (1974 Orioles)
>   C—Bob Didier (1969 Braves)
>   P—Tom Niedenfuer (1985 Dodgers)

That's right, the position players here combined for 105 at bats without a single base hit. Futility frequency: Chambliss, 10; Dauer, 14; Rodriguez and Alley, 16; Lemon, 13; Stargel, 14; Coggins, 11; and Didier, 11. Niedenfuer put together his 0–2, 6.35 ERA record by yielding game-winning, ninth-inning home runs two days in a row, to Ozzie Smith and Jack Clark of the Cardinals. Chambliss could have also made this team for his 1–17 as a New York Yankee in 1977. Among other one-hit wonders have been Tim Laudner (1–14, 1987 Twins), George Hendrick (1 12, 1986 Angels), Freddie Patek (1–13, 1978 Royals), and Gorman Thomas (1–15, 1982 Brewers). Special mention should also be made of Dave Sewart for his record of 0 –2, 40.50 ERA for the 1981 Dodgers in the split-season playoffs.

—— DRAMATIC MOMENTS ——

Bobby Thomson's "shot heard 'round the world" is the most memorable playoff or LCS moment, but not the only one.

> 1B—Chris Chambliss (1976 Yankees)
> 2B—Willie Randolph (1980 Yankees)
> 3B—Bobby Thomson (1951 Giants)
> SS—Bucky Dent (1978 Yankees)
> OF—Jack Clark (1985 Cardinals)
> OF—Dave Henderson (1986 Red Sox)
> OF—Billy Hatcher (1986 Astros)
> C—Mike Scioscia (1988 Dodgers)
> P—Jesse Orosco (1986 Mets)

Chambliss's ninth-inning homer gave New York the pennant over Kansas City. When Randolph was thrown out at home trying to score on a Bob Watson double in the second game, the Yankees lost the game, George Steinbrenner lost his head, and third base coach Mike Ferraro was headed toward the loss of his job. Thomson's shot off Ralph Branca and Bucky Dent's off Mike Torrez of the Red Sox are part of the traumatic history of Brooklyn and Boston, respectively. Clark's ninth-inning homer off Tom Niedenfuer gave St. Louis the pennant because Tom Lasorda declined to walk him in favor of pitching to Andy Van Slyke. Henderson's ninth-inning homer and extra-inning sacrifice fly in the fifth game yanked the pennant out of California's hands. Hatcher's extra-inning homer tied up the exhausting sixth game against the Mets that finally ended in the 16th inning when Orosco struck out Kevin Bass with the tying and winning runs on base. Scioscia's two-out, 9th-inning homer off Doc Gooden in game four headed off an almost certain Mets pennant by tying the game and giving Kirk Gibson a shot at heroics in the 12th inning.

—— MOMENTS IN THE SUN ——

A few of these men had steady careers, most of them less than that; all of them had sparkling moments during the LCS or postseason playoffs.

> 1B—Jim Lindeman (1987 Cardinals)
> 2B—Rob Wilfong (1986 Angels)
> 3B—Wayne Garrett (1969 Mets)
> SS—Mark Belanger (1971 Orioles)
> OF—Charlie Moore (1982 Brewers)
> OF—Tito Landrum (1983 Orioles)
> OF—Pat Sheridan (1987 Tigers)
> C—Jim Sundberg (1985 Royals)
> P—Gene Bearden (1948 Indians)

Lindeman's homer and three RBI led St. Louis over the Giants in the third LCS game. Wilfong reknotted the fifth game in the bottom of the ninth with a single after Dave Henderson's astonishing homer in the top of the inning. Garrett, who had not homered since May 9, chose the third game against Atlanta to hit one and assure the Mets the pennant. Belanger, the epitome of the weak-hitting fielder, drove in the winning run against Vida Blue with a single in the first game against Oakland. Moore's disputed pop behind the mound in the fifth game, ruled a hit by Don Denkinger, opened the gates to the rally that gave Milwaukee the pennant over the Angels. Landrum's homer in the top of the 10th inning of the fourth game against Chicago broke a scoreless tie and gave the Orioles the pennant. Sheridan's eighth-inning homer in game three brought Detroit back against the Twins. Sundberg's triple and four RBI in the last game eliminated Toronto. Bearden pitched a complete-game victory in a one-game playoff against Boston; without counting his 1948 record of 20–7, his career mark would have been 25–31.

—— OVERSHADOWED FEATS ——

This lineup features the critical supporting players in divisional and predivisional playoff games.

    1B—Whitey Lockman (1951 Giants)
    2B—Bobby Grich (1986 Angels)
    3B—George Brett (1976 Royals)
    SS—Bill Russell (1978 Dodgers)
    OF—Norm Larker (1959 Dodgers)
    OF—Mike Marshall (1985 Dodgers)
    OF—Jose Oquendo (1987 Cardinals)
     C—Alan Ashby (1986 Astros)
     P—Fernando Valenzuela (1981 Dodgers)

Lockman doubled to set the table for Bobby Thomson's playoff homer against Brooklyn. It was Grich who hit the shot that Dave Henderson swatted over the fence with his glove to give California a lead that it would lose traumatically to the same Henderson in the fifth game of the series against Boston. Brett's three-run shot was a prelude to the Chris Chambliss pennant winner. Garry Maddox's error in game four set up the LA win over Philadelphia, although Russell had to single it in. Larker singled in two runs in the bottom of the ninth in the playoffs against Milwaukee to set up the later blows that tied and won the game. Marshall had homered to break a tie before Tom Niedenfuer's gopher ball to Jack Clark. Oquendo's three-run homer was all Danny Cox needed to blank the Giants for the pennant. Mike Scott's mastery over the Mets in the 1986 LCS was partly because of Ashby's catching and partly because of the homer he hit to win game four for the right-hander. Valenzuela scattered three hits for eight and two-thirds innings until Rick Monday's homer gave the Dodgers the pennant over Montreal.

—— LCS SPECTATORS ——

All of these players entered the majors after the start of LCS play in 1969, all played for at least 10 years, but none of them appeared in a playoff game. The number of career years follows each name.

1B—Andre Thornton (14)
2B—Bill Almon (14)
3B—Buddy Bell (18)
SS—Toby Harrah (17)
OF—Jerry Morales (15)
OF—Joel Youngblood (14)
OF—Willie Montanez (13)
 C—Butch Wynegar (12)
 P—Greg Minton (16)

Honorable mentions to Danny Darwin (14 years) and Alex Trevino (12 years).

—— LCS REGULARS ——

Through the 1990 season, Don Baylor (5) and Danny Heep (4) have worn the greatest number of uniforms in LCS competition. Their teammates are

    1B—John Milner (Mets, Pirates, Expos)
    2B—Joe Morgan (Reds, Astros, Phillies)
    3B—Graig Nettles (Twins, Yankees, Padres)
    SS—Phil Garner (Athletics, Pirates, Astros)
    OF—Don Baylor (Orioles, Angels, Red Sox, Twins,
           Athletics)
    OF—Danny Heep (Astros, Mets, Dodgers, Red Sox)
    OF—Reggie Jackson (Athletics, Yankees, Angels)
     C—Cliff Johnson (Yankees, Athletics, Blue Jays)
     P—Tommy John (Dodgers, Yankees, Angels)

Garner is the only infielder with three teams who played some shortstop in the LCS. Other three-team players include Merv Rettenmund, Enos Cabell, Richie Hebner, Davey Lopes, George Hendrick, Dave Parker, Nolan Ryan, Doyle Alexander, and Bill Madlock.

20 World Series

This chapter contains the bests, worsts, and oddities for the World Series.

—— BEST CAREER WORLD SERIES ——

Reggie Jackson hasn't been the only Mister October.

1B—Lou Gehrig (1926–28, 1932, 1936–38 Yankees)
2B—Billy Martin (1951–53, 1955–56 Yankees)
3B—Pepper Martin (1928, 1931, 1934 Cardinals)
SS—Pee Wee Reese (1941, 1947, 1949, 1952–53, 1955–56 Dodgers)
OF—Babe Ruth (1915–16, 1918 Red Sox, 1921–23, 1926–28, 1932 Yankees)
OF—Reggie Jackson (1973–74 Athletics, 1977–78, 1981 Yankees)
OF—Mickey Mantle (1951–53, 1955–58, 1960–64 Yankees)
C—Yogi Berra (1947, 1949–53, 1955–58, 1960–63 Yankees)
P—Bob Gibson (1964, 1967–68 Cardinals)

In seven World Series, Gehrig swatted 10 homers. In four series, Martin went 33–99 (.333) with five homers and 19 RBI. Martin of St. Louis went 23–55 (.418) in two fall classics. Reese compiled 46 hits and a .272 mark in seven series. Ruth hit at least .300 6 out of 10 times and belted the ball out of the park on 15 occasions. In five fall appearances, Jackson hit 10 homers and accumulated a .755 slugging average. Mantle hit 18 homers (the record) in 12 series, while Berra's .274 mark in 14 series includes 12 round-trippers. Gibson put together a record of seven wins and two losses in three series. Honorable mentions to Lou Brock of the Cardinals for the highest WS batting average (.391 for 3 series) and to Duke Snider of the Dodgers for 11 homers in six series.

—— BEST WORLD SERIES ——

The players in this lineup turned in individual performances worth remembering.

> 1B—Lou Gehrig (1928 Yankees)
> 2B—Bobby Richardson (1960 Yankees)
> 3B—Brooks Robinson (1970 Orioles)
> SS—Mark Koenig (1927 Yankees)
> OF—Babe Ruth (1928 Yankees)
> OF—Reggie Jackson (1977 Yankees)
> OF—Billy Hatcher (1990 Reds)
>   C—Gene Tenace (1972 Athletics)
>   P—Christy Mathewson (1905 Giants)

Gehrig hit four home runs and had a slugging average of 1.727. Richardson went 11–30 with 12 runs batted in. Robinson not only turned singles into outs and doubles into double plays with his glove but also ended up with 17 total bases in five games. The Yankees swept the Pirates in part thanks to Koenig's nine safeties in 18 at bats. In the following year's four-game sweep of the Cardinals, Ruth banged out four singles, three doubles, and three homers in 16 at bats for a .625 average. Jackson's five homers helped him to a slugging average of 1.250. Hatcher broke most existing offensive records for a four-game series when he led Cincinnati over Oakland with four singles, four doubles, and a triple in 12 official at bats, plus two walks and a hit-by-pitch. Tenace went 8–23 with four homers and nine RBI in Oakland's seven-game win over Cincinnati. Mathewson threw three shutouts in a five-game series against the Athletics.

—— BEST WORLD SERIES GAME ——

Or, rising to the heights atop the heights:

1B—Vic Wertz (1954 Indians)
2B—Bobby Richardson (1960 Yankees)
3B—Paul Molitor (1982 Brewers)
SS—Honus Wagner (1909 Pirates)
OF—Babe Ruth (1926 and 1928 Yankees)
OF—Reggie Jackson (1977 Yankees)
OF—Billy Hatcher (1990 Reds)
 C—Johnny Bench (1976 Reds)
 P—Don Larsen (1956 Yankees)

Everyone remembers Willie Mays's great catch against Wertz in the opening game; what many may not recall is that the drive was the first baseman's bid for a *fifth* hit in the opener. In the third game, Richardson knocked in six runs. In the opening game, Molitor became the first player to get five hits in a WS contest. In game three, Wagner had three hits, three runs batted in, and three stolen bases to turn the WS tide against the Tigers. In the fourth game of both series, Ruth hit three homers. Jackson waited for game six to clinch the championship against the Dodgers by clouting three shots. Hatcher picked up four hits in the second game to extend his consecutive WS hit mark to seven and to send the Reds rushing toward their sweep of the Athletics. Bench completed a four-game sweep of the Yankees with two homers and five runs driven in. Larsen's game five performance against the Dodgers has never been equaled in postseason play.

—— WORST CAREER WORLD SERIES ——

The players on this team each had at least 50 World Series at bats and yet failed to reach the .200 mark.

1B—Orlando Cepeda (1962 Giants, 1967–68 Cardinals)
2B—Frank White (1980, 1985 Royals)
3B—Travis Jackson (1922–23, 1933, 1936 Giants)
SS—Dal Maxvill (1964, 1967–68 Cardinals, 1974 Athletics)
OF—Taylor Douthit (1926, 1928, 1930 Cardinals)
OF—Mule Haas (1929–31 Athletics)
OF—Willie Davis (1963, 1965–66 Dodgers)
C—John Roseboro (1959, 1963, 1965–66 Dodgers)
P—Don Newcombe (1949, 1955–56 Dodgers)

Cepeda was only 13–76 (.171) with two homers and nine RBI. White was 9–53 (.170) with a homer and six RBI. Hall of Famer Jackson, who played more third base than his regular shortstop in the series, was a mere 10–67 (.149) with four RBI. Maxvill, a candidate for baseball's worst hitter of all time, remained true to form with his 7–61 (.115) and two RBI. The outfielders: Douthit, 7–50 (.140), a home run and three RBI; Haas, 10–62 (.161), two homers and nine RBI; and Davis, 9–54 (.167) with 3 RBI. Roseboro could do no better than 11–70 (.157) with a homer and seven RBI. Although several pitchers lost more WS games than Newcombe, they also won more and had significantly lower ERAs; Newcombe's numbers were 0–4, 8.59 ERA. Among other anemic WS hitters are Dave Bancroft (16–93, .172), Max Bishop (12–66, .182), Frankie Crosetti (20–115, .174), and Jimmy Sheckard (14–77, .182).

—— WORST WORLD SERIES ——

Sometimes even the most dependable hitters can't do anything right in the fall.

> 1B—Gil Hodges (1952 Dodgers)
> 2B—Davey Lopes (1981 Dodgers)
> 3B—Gene Freese (1961 Reds)
> SS—Roger Peckinpaugh (1925 Senators)
> OF—Jack Murray (1911 Giants)
> OF—Willie Davis (1966 Dodgers)
> OF—Willie Wilson (1980 Royals)
> C—Johnny Bench (1972 Reds)
> P—George Frazier (1981 Yankees)

Hodges was hitless in 21 at bats. Lopes made six errors officially and could have been charged with more. Freese managed only one hit in Cincinnati's four out of five game loss to the Yankees. Peckinpaugh, the AL MVP in 1925, belied his reputation as a defensive whiz by committing eight errors in 40 chances. Murray, New York's cleanup hitter, went 0 for 21. Davis went 1 for 16 and made three errors. After a regular season of .326 and 79 stolen bases, Wilson batted only .154 (4–26) and stole merely two bases; he also struck out 11 times. Bench was not only limited to a single run batted in but he also managed to strike out on an intentional pass (against Oakland's Rollie Fingers). Frazier suffered three of the four New York losses against Los Angeles and had an ERA of more than 17. Dishonorable mention to Don Newcombe of the 1956 Dodgers, who yielded 11 runs and 11 hits in less than five innings against the Yankees for an ERA of 21.21.

—— MOMENTS IN THE SUN ——

The World Series brings out the best in some players—and not just in the best players.

1B—Fred Luderus (1915 Phillies)
2B—Al Weis (1969 Mets)
3B—Buck Herzog (1912 Giants)
SS—Buddy Biancalana (1985 Royals)
OF—Al Gionfriddo (1947 Dodgers)
OF—Dave Robertson (1917 Giants)
OF—Dusty Rhodes (1954 Giants)
C—Hank Gowdy (1914 Braves)
P—Jim Beattie (1978 Yankees)

Luderus, a career .277 hitter, batted .438 and 12 RBI in his only series. Weis, .219 lifetime, hit .455 and clouted a key homer in the final series game. Herzog went 12–30 to belie his .259 career record. Biancalana became a national TV hero for putting his lifetime .205 average behind him to lead Kansas City to a title with a .278 average and a steady glove. Gionfriddo's steal of second prior to the breakup of Bill Bevens's no-hitter and his circus catch of a Joe DiMaggio drive have become part of WS lore. Robertson wiped out a regular season mark of .259 with an 11–22 spree. Rhodes hit a pinch homer to beat Cleveland in the first game, then hit another in the second game, and batted .667 during New York's four-game sweep of the Indians. Beattie, a career 52–87 pitcher and an object of public scorn from New York owner George Steinbrenner, turned in a complete game victory against the Dodgers in the fifth game to break a series tie and direct the Yankees toward a world championship.

—— PERFECT SERIES ——

Even though most of these players didn't have distinguished careers, they retired with 1.000 career averages for World Series play.

    1B—Chico Salmon (1970 Orioles)
    2B—Jerry Buchek (1964 Cardinals)
    3B—Rip Russell (1946 Red Sox)
    SS—Jim Mason (1976 Yankees)
    OF—Ed King (1922 Giants)
    OF—Bob Maier (1945 Tigers)
    OF—Al Ferrara (1966 Dodgers)
     C—Clay Dalrymple (1969 Orioles)
     P—Lefty Gomez (1932, 1936–38 Yankees)

Russell and Dalrymple were 2–2, the others got a hit in their only official at bat. Mason is the only player to have homered. Gomez won six games without losing. Jack Coombs and Herb Pennock each won five.

—— PERFECTLY AWFUL SERIES ——

Although some players failed more often in the World Series, the following always failed:

    1B—Barbaro Garbey (1984 Tigers)
    2B—Lonny Frey (1939–40 Reds, 1947 Yankees)
    3B—Flea Clifton (1935 Tigers)
    SS—Bill Dahlen (1905 Giants)
    OF—Wally Berger (1937 Giants, 1939 Reds)
    OF—Carl Reynolds (1938 Cubs)
    OF—Jim Rivera (1950 White Sox)
     C—Billy Sullivan (1906 White Sox)
     P—Rip Collins (1921 Yankees)

Hitless at bats: Garbey, 12; Frey, 20; Clifton, 16; Dahlen, 15; Berger, 18; Reynolds, 12; Rivera, 11; and Sullivan, 21. Collins made the least of his only WS appearance—compiling a record 54.00 ERA.

—— FIELDING GEMS ——

Willie Mays's astonishing catch of Vic Wertz's drive in the opening game of the 1954 series was one dazzler. Can you remember the others?

> 1B—Pete Rose (1980 Phillies)
> 2B—Bill Wambsganss (1920 Indians)
> 3B—Graig Nettles (1978 Yankees)
> SS—Pee Wee Reese (1955 Dodgers)
> OF—Sandy Amoros (1955 Dodgers)
> OF—Willie Mays (1954 Giants)
> OF—Tommie Agee (1969 Mets)
> C—Jim Hegan (1948 Indians)
> P—Bob Gibson (1964 Cardinals)

With the Royals having bases loaded and one out in the ninth inning of game six, Rose was alert enough to nab a foul ball that popped out of catcher Bob Boone's mitt. In game five, Wambsganss snatched a liner off the bat of Clarence Mitchell and turned it into an unassisted triple play. In the third game, Nettles's acrobatic stops defused Los Angeles rallies and pointed the Yankees toward their championship. Amoros's running one-handed catch of a slicing drive by Yogi Berra in the seventh game killed a New York rally. Reese then completed the play by doubling Gil McDougald off first with a long relay throw and sealed Brooklyn's only WS win. Mays's back-to-the-plate catch of Wertz's drive took the stuffing out of an Indians' rally. Agee's diving catches on Elrod Hendricks and Paul Blair in the third game symbolized the WS win by the Miracle Mets. Hegan snared a would-be bunt off the bat of Sibby Sisti in the ninth inning of the final game and fired to first to double off the potential winning run; Cleveland won the series in the bottom of the ninth. In the ninth inning of game five, Gibson took a liner in the hip, chased it down, turned 180 degrees in the air, and nipped batter Joe Pepitone at first with a jump shot.

—— MISPLAYS ——

These players' errors were so costly to their teams that their names became synonymous with disaster in some cities.

1B—Bill Buckner (1986 Red Sox)
2B—Mike Andrews (1973 Athletics)
3B—Heinie Zimmerman (1917 Giants)
SS—Buddy Myers (1939 Reds)
OF—Fred Snodgrass (1912 Giants)
OF—Max Flack (1918 Cubs)
OF—Hack Wilson (1929 Cubs)
C—Hank Gowdy (1924 Giants)
P—Hugh Casey (1941 Dodgers)

Buckner missed the Mookie Wilson grounder that climaxed the Mets' astounding two out, 10th-inning comeback in the sixth game. Andrews's two errors in the 12th inning of the second game permitted the Mets to score three runs. In the sixth game, Zimmerman made a two-base error and then chased the winning run across home plate. Myers bobbled a potential double play grounder in the ninth inning of the fourth game and opened the door to a Yankees win. Snodgrass dropped a fly in the 10th inning of the fifth game to set up a two-run inning that gave Boston the championship. Flack's error against the Red Sox in the final game permitted the two runs that were the margin of Chicago's defeat. Wilson misjudged a fly into a 3-run inside-the-park homer in the fourth game, setting in motion a 10-run inning that overcame a 8–0 Chicago lead. Gowdy dropped a foul ball when he tripped over his mask; given another chance, Muddy Ruel doubled and scored the winning run to give the Senators the championship. Many observers still think that Mickey Owen's infamous passed ball in game four was actually a Casey wild pitch.

— CONTROVERSIAL CALLS —

Were the umpires right or wrong?

    1B—Gil Hodges (1952 Dodgers: 5th Game)
    2B—Larry Doyle (1911 Giants: 5th Game)
    3B—Jackie Robinson (1955 Dodgers: 1st Game)
    SS—Lou Boudreau (1948 Indians: 1st Game)
    OF—Cleon Jones (1969 Mets: 5th Game)
    OF—Bernie Carbo (1970 Reds: 1st Game)
    OF—Reggie Jackson (1978 Yankees: 4th Game)
     C—Carlton Fisk (1975 Red Sox: 3d Game)
     P—Todd Worrell (1985 Cardinals: 6th Game)

Hodges got a call on a grounder from umpire Art Passarella despite photos that showed runner Johnny Sain well past the bag. Doyle scored the winning run on a sacrifice fly; Bill Klem admitted later that he never touched home. Ed Summers called Robinson safe on a steal of home; Yogi Berra said later that Robinson never touched home and he never tagged Robinson. To everyone but ump Bill Stewart, Boudreau seemed to have called a successful pickoff of Phil Masi; Masi later scored the only run of the game. Lou DeMuro bought manager Gil Hodges's argument that Jones had been hit on the foot with a pitched ball (the old shoe polish trick) and helped set up Donn Clendenon's subsequent homer. The Reds lost by a run when Ken Burkhart, his back to the play, called Carbo out at home on a sweeping tag by Elrod Hendricks; Hendricks made the tag with the wrong hand. Jackson's hip movement on the bases to break up a double play was missed by three umpires and set up a game-winning rally. Larry Barnett also missed an interference call on Ed Armbrister against Fisk, prompting a wild throw and a Cincinnati win. Don Denkinger said Worrell's foot wasn't on first in a play against Jorge Orta, thereby giving Kansas City another out that was to decide the World Series in favor of the Royals.

—— THE LAST BATTER ——

Some seasons have gone right down to the last batter in the last inning of the last World Series game.

    1B—Willie McCovey (1962 Giants)
    2B—Bill Mazeroski (1960 Pirates)
    3B—Larry Gardner (1912 Red Sox)
    SS—Johnny Pesky (1946 Red Sox)
    OF—Earl McNeely (1924 Senators)
    OF—Bing Miller (1929 Athletics)
    OF—Goose Goslin (1935 Tigers)
     C—Bob O'Farrell (1926 Cardinals)
     P—John Miljus (1927 Pirates)

McCovey's wicked liner to Bobby Richardson with two on gave the Yankees a 1–0 victory. Mazeroski's home run defeated the Yankees. Gardner's 10th-inning sacrifice fly climaxed a Boston comeback made possible by the legendary error of Giants outfielder Fred Snodgrass. Pesky hesitated on an outfield relay, allowing Enos Slaughter of the Cardinals to roar from first to home with the championship run. McNeely's bad hop past Freddie Lindstrom at third made the Giants losers. The Cubs saw their WS victory disappear on a homer by Mule Haas and doubles by Al Simmons and Miller in the bottom of the ninth. Goslin singled home Mickey Cochrane in the ninth to send the Cubs packing. With Bob Meusel at the plate for the Yankees in the ninth inning with St. Louis ahead 3–2, Babe Ruth tried to get the tying run to second by stealing, but O'Farrell ended the series by throwing him out. Miljus was so rattled by Earle Combs's dancing lead off third base that he uncorked a wild pitch to give the Yankees the WS title.

—— DRAMATIC MOMENTS ——

Not all World Series dramatic moments have been put off until the last batter in the last game.

    1B—Tommie Henrich (1949 Yankees)
    2B—Billy Martin (1952 Yankees)
    3B—Ray Knight (1986 Mets)
    SS—Phil Rizzuto (1951 Yankees)
    OF—Babe Ruth (1932 Yankees)
    OF—Reggie Jackson (1977 Yankees)
    OF—Kirk Gibson (1988 Dodgers)
     C—Carlton Fisk (1975 Red Sox)
     P—Bill Bevens (1947 Yankees)

Henrich's home run in the ninth inning of the opening game settled a scoreless duel between Allie Reynolds and Don Newcombe of the Dodgers. Martin's catch of Jackie Robinson's twisting pop with the bases loaded in the seventh inning of the seventh game effectively made the Yankees champions. Knight's home run in the seventh inning of the seventh game put the comeback Mets ahead to stay. Rizzuto ended up holding a lot of air when Eddie Stanky kicked the ball out of his hand and went on to score the winning run in the fifth inning of the third game. Did Ruth or didn't Ruth call his home run against Charlie Root in the fifth inning of the third game? Reggie's third home run of the sixth game against Charlie Hough sealed the New York victory over the Dodgers. The seriously injured Gibson's pinch homer off Dennis Eckersley of Oakland on a 3–2 count with two out in the ninth inning of the first game set the Dodgers on the path to an unlikely championship. Fisk's 12th-inning homer off Pat Darcy in the sixth game ended what many considered the greatest single WS game. Bevens was only one Brooklyn batter (Cookie Lavagetto) away from a no-hitter in the fourth game; one double later, he was the losing pitcher.

—— OVERSHADOWED FEATS ——

The World Series players in this lineup performed critical supporting roles that made possible well-known achievements.

1B—Gil Hodges (1955 Dodgers)
2B—Bucky Harris (1924 Senators)
3B—Ray Knight (1986 Mets)
SS—Glenn Wright (1925 Pirates)
OF—Carl Furillo (1953 Dodgers)
OF—Lou Johnson (1965 Dodgers)
OF—Bernie Carbo (1975 Red Sox)
 C—Hal Smith (1960 Pirates)
 P—Bob Kuzava (1952 Yankees)

Hodges drove in the two runs that gave Johnny Podres his 2–0 win over the Yankees and Brooklyn's only championship. Harris hit a bad hop single over Freddie Lindstrom's head to tie the score in the eighth inning of the last game against New York and set up the second bad hop hit by Earl McNeely. Knight's single was the glue in the sixth game dramatics that ended with Bill Buckner's error. Wright, who hit only 93 homers in 11 years, set up Kiki Cuyler's game-winning blast in the second game with a round-tripper. Furillo homered with two out in the ninth of the last game, tying the score and precipitating Billy Martin's 12th (and game-winning) hit in the bottom of the inning. Sandy Koufax overwhelmed the Twins in game seven but needed Johnson's two-run homer to win. Carbo's three-run pinch homer in game six set up Carlton Fisk's dramatic blast. Smith hit a three-run homer in the eighth inning of the last game that the Yankees had to offset before losing on Bill Mazeroski's blast. Billy Martin made a great catch on Jackie Robinson to clinch the 1952 WS, but it was Kuzava who fed the popup and retired the last eight Brooklyn batters.

—— MINOR CONTRIBUTORS ——

A lineup of players who usually had key roles in the pennant fortunes of their clubs but who, for one season anyway, were carried into the World Series by their teammates.

    1B—Pete Rose (1983 Phillies)
    2B—Tony Lazzeri (1938 Cubs)
    3B—Jackie Robinson (1955 Dodgers)
    SS—Dave Concepcion (1972 Reds)
    OF—Sherry Magee (1919 Reds)
    OF—Harry Walker (1946 Cardinals)
    OF—Gus Bell (1961 Reds)
     C—Yogi Berra (1962 Yankees)
     P—Larry French (1938 Cubs)

For the most part reflecting their advancing years: Rose hit only .245 with a mere 14 doubles. Lazzeri hit only five homers with 23 runs batted in. Robinson was down to .256 with eight homers. Concepcion, still on the threshold of his offensive career, batted only .209. Magee bade farewell to the majors in the 1919 Series after contributing a season of .215 with 21 RBI and four stolen bases. A year before he won the batting crown, Walker hit only .237 for the pennant-winning Cardinals. Bell, a mainstay of Cincinnati's power-hitting teams in the 1950s, was down to three homers and 33 runs batted in when the Reds finally got into the World Series. Berra had only 10 homers and 35 runs batted in to go with his .224 average. French is the only pitcher to have lost as many as 19 games for a pennant-winning team.

—— UNKIND CUTS ——

After they played vital roles in getting their teams to the World Series, last-minute injuries prevented these players from taking the field for most or all of the fall games.

    1B—Hank Greenberg (1935 Tigers)
    2B—Willie Randolph (1978 Yankees)
    3B—Red Smith (1914 Braves)
    SS—George Davis (1906 White Sox)
    OF—Reggie Jackson (1972 Athletics)
    OF—Jim Rice (1975 Red Sox)
    OF—Vince Coleman (1985 Cardinals)
     C—Chief Meyers (1913 Giants)
     P—Rube Waddell (1905 Athletics)

Greenberg broke a wrist in the second game of the series against the Cubs. Randolph's injury in the LCS created the opportunity for replacement Brian Doyle to become a hero. Smith broke a leg and missed Boston's sweep of the Athletics. Davis's preseries injury forced third baseman Lee Tannehill to move to short and utility man George Rohe into the lineup at third; when Rohe batted .333, Tannehill lost his job with the unexpected return of Davis for the final game. Jackson pulled a hamstring during the LCS; Rice missed both the LCS and series because of a broken wrist. Meyers broke a finger in the first game of the series and was replaced by Larry McLean, who went on to bat .500. Waddell's sore arm saved him from inevitable matchups with Christy Mathewson, who pitched three shutouts in the series.

—— THREE IS A CHARM ——

Each of these players appeared in the World Series for three different teams. Remember the teams?

    1B—Fred Merkle
    2B—Eddie Stanky
    3B—Heinie Groh
    SS—Mark Koenig
    OF—Andy Pafko
    OF—Mike McCormick
    OF—Don Baylor
     C—Wally Schang
     P—Burleigh Grimes

Merkle was with the 1911–13 Giants, 1916 Dodgers, and 1918 Cubs. Stanky was with the 1947 Dodgers, 1948 Braves, and 1951 Giants. Groh played for the 1912, 1922–24 Giants; 1919 Reds; and 1927 Pirates. Koenig was with the 1926–28 Yankees, 1932 Cubs, and 1936 Giants. Pafko performed for the 1945 Cubs, 1952 Dodgers, and 1957–58 Braves. McCormick was with the 1940 Reds, 1948 Braves, and 1949 Dodgers. Baylor played with the 1986 Red Sox, 1987 Twins, and 1988 Athletics. Schang was with the 1913–14, 1930 Athletics; 1918 Red Sox; and 1921–23 Yankees. Grimes performed for the 1920 Dodgers, 1930–31 Cardinals, and 1932 Cubs. Other three-timers include Stuffy McInnis, Lonnie Smith, Earl Smith, Joe Bush, Paul Derringer, Dutch Reuther, Grant Jackson, and Vic Davalillo. Bill McKechnie (1925 Pirates, 1928 Cardinals, 1939–40 Reds) and Dick Williams (1967 Red Sox, 1972–73 Athletics, 1984 Padres) are the only managers to lead three different teams into the series.

—— WS SPECTATORS ——

The position players all appeared in at least 2,000 games, but never once in a World Series contest. The number of career games follow each name.

   1B—Rod Carew (2,469)
   2B—Nap Lajoie (2,475)
   3B—Ron Santo (2,243)
   SS—Ernie Banks (2,528)
   OF—Billy Williams (2,488)
   OF—Andre Dawson (2,018)
   OF—Cy Williams (2,002)
    C—Joe Torre (2,209)
    P—Gaylord Perry (22 Years)

In terms of years, Bobby Wallace with 25 seasons has had the longest career without playing in the fall. Wallace and five members of this lineup—Carew, Lajoie, Banks, Williams, and Perry—are members of the Hall of Fame. Other Cooperstown residents who have never played for a WS championship are George Sisler, George Kell, Elmer Flick, Ted Lyons, Ralph Kiner, and Ferguson Jenkins. The manager is Gene Mauch, who skippered for 26 years without winning a pennant.

21 Three Last Things

—— FOR FANATICS ONLY ——

Some of these players appeared in the major leagues, but that isn't why they made this lineup. The fact that some of them didn't exist didn't prevent them from getting into box scores. A couple of others were told that they shouldn't exist.

    1B—Ivan Bigler
    2B—Charlie Grant
    3B—Levi Meyerle
    SS—Fred Pfeffer
    OF—Al Reach
    OF—Lou Proctor
    OF—Albert Olsen
     C—Bert Blue
     P—Jackie Mitchell

Bigler was a typographically erroneous rendering of George Sisler's name listed in the *Baseball Encyclopedia* as a member of the 1917 Browns. Grant was the black player that John McGraw tried to pass off as a Native American for the 1901 Orioles; the deception didn't work. Meyerle was the star of stars for the National Association that preceded the National League; his 1871 average of .492 is the highest ever recorded on any level in baseball. Second baseman-shortstop Pfeffer was a leader in the aborted attempt to form another rival American Association in 1894. Al Reach, whose career ended with the National Association Athletics in 1875, is thought to be the first player paid openly for his services. Lou Proctor was a Western Union man who periodically slipped his name into box scores he was transmitting and so also ended up in official documents. Albert Olsen was an AL rendering of either Leon Culberson or Joe Dobson's name for a May 1943 game. Blue was one of the more visible players in the 1912 and 1913 attempts to float a United States League. Jackie Mitchell, the first woman to play baseball professionally, struck out Babe Ruth and Lou Gehrig in a 1931 exhibition game.

—— THE ALL-TIME ALL-STAR ——
EVERYTHINGS

By way of summation, these players' names appear most often in the lineups in this book.

    1B—Lou Gehrig (23)
    2B—Rogers Hornsby (18)
    3B—Brooks Robinson (14)
    SS—Ernie Banks (19)
        Honus Wagner (19)
    OF—Babe Ruth (34)
    OF—Ty Cobb (30)
    OF—Ted Williams (24)
     C—Yogi Berra (16)
     P—Nolan Ryan (9)

Shortstop is a tie. Banks and Wagner are each named on 19 teams as the shortstop and once each at another position: first base for Banks and the outfield for Wagner. Ruth has an additional place as the pitcher for an overall total of 35. Berra is on one team as an outfielder to bring his grand total to 17. Other than shortstop, the closest race was at third base, where Pete Rose made 13 teams; in addition, Rose appears seven times in the outfield, twice at first base, and once at second base. Other runners-up: Cap Anson and Stan Musial at first with 7 (although the latter appears on 12 additional teams in the outfield); Eddie Collins at second (13 plus a single shortstop entry); Hank Aaron (17), Willie Mays (15), and Reggie Jackson (15) in the outfield; Johnny Bench (11) behind the plate; and Walter Johnson (7) on the mound.

—— LEFT OUT ——

When all is said and done, after 327 teams and more than 1,600 players, these are the best at each position who failed to make any other team in this book.

1B—Lee May
2B—Del Pratt
3B—Bill Madlock
SS—Red Kress
OF—Earl Averill, Sr.
OF—Bug Holliday
OF—Vada Pinson
 C—Smokey Burgess
 P—Mickey Welch

May, whose 354 home runs is the most by anyone who appears on no other team, played from 1965 to 1982 with the Reds, Astros, Orioles, and Royals. Pratt hit .292 and stole 246 bases in a 13-year career (1912–24) with the Browns, Yankees, Red Sox, and Tigers. Madlock won four National League batting championships and hit .305 in 15 years (1973–87) with the Rangers, Cubs, Giants, Pirates, Dodgers, and Tigers. Kress was a lifetime .286 hitter with the Browns, White Sox, Senators, and Tigers (1927–40) and a brief stint with the Giants in 1946. Averill has the highest batting average (.318) by any player on no previous team; he also hit 238 home runs in his 13 years (1929–41) with the Indians, Tigers, and Red Sox. Holliday is right behind him with a .316 average compiled with Cincinnati in both the American Association and the National League between 1889 and 1898. Pinson has more hits (2,757) than anyone else not on another lineup; he batted .286 with 256 homers in his 18 years (1958–75) with the Reds, Cardinals, Indians, Angels, and Royals. Burgess hit .295 with five teams (the Cubs, Phillies, Reds, Pirates, and White Sox) over 18 years (1949, 1951–67). Welch won 311 games and lost only 207 in his 13 years (1880–92) with Troy and the Giants.